Mobilizing Resources for District-Wide Middle-Grades Reform

**National Middle School Association** is dedicated to improving the educational experiences of young adolescents by providing vision, knowledge, and resources to all who serve them in order to develop healthy, productive, and ethical citizens.

# Mobilizing Resources for District-Wide Middle-Grades Reform

*by*

Holly Hatch
and
Kathy Hytten

National Middle School Association
Columbus, Ohio

National Middle School Association
2600 Corporate Exchange Drive, Suite 370
Columbus, Ohio 43231
Telephone (800) 528-NMSA

Copyright© 1997 by National Middle School Association.

All rights reserved. No part of this publication may be reproduced or transmitted in any form or by any means, electronic or mechanical, without permission in writing from the publisher except in the case of brief quotations embodied in reviews or articles.

The materials presented herein are the expressions of the authors and do not necessarily represent the policies of NMSA.

NMSA is a registered servicemark of National Middle School Association.

Printed in the United States of America

Sue Swaim, Executive Director
Jeff Ward, Director of Business Services
John Lounsbury, Editor
Mary Mitchell, Copy Editor/Designer
Marcia Meade, Publications Sales

ISBN: 1-56090-118-7     NMSA Stock Number: 1247

**Library of Congress Cataloging-in-Publication Data**
Hatch, Holly, date
      Mobilizing resources for district-wide middle-grades reform/by
   Holly Hatch and Kathy Hytten.
         p.  cm.
      Includes bibliographical references.
      ISBN 1-56090-118-7 (pbk.)
      1.  Middle schools--United States--Case studies.  2.  School
   management and organization--United States--Case studies.  3.  School
   improvement programs--United States--Case studies.  4.  Educational
   change--United States--Case studies.   I.  Hytten, Kathryn Ann.
   II. Title.
   LB1623.5.H38    1997
   373.236'0973--dc21                                         97-36916
                                                                  CIP

# Contents

**Foreword** *by Hayes Mizell* — vii

**Acknowledgements** — ix

**Part I**    **Rationale and Recommendations** — 1

     1. The District Role in Middle-Grades Reform — 3

     2. Standards for District-Wide Middle-Grades Reform — 17

     3. Findings from Planning and Conducting Audits — 43

     4. Mobilizing Resource: Lessons Learned — 51

**Part II**    **Resources and Tools for Change** — 71

**Part III**    **Case Studies** — 171

     5. Corpus Christi Independent School District: Small Town Culture and Urban Challenges — 173

     6. Minneapolis: Balancing School Choice and Systemic Accountability — 185

     7. San Diego City Schools: Middle Schools for a Changing America — 197

     8. Atlanta Public Schools: Reaching for Student Achievement in a Center City School System — 205

**About the Authors** — 218

**Project Advisory Panel** — 219

# Foreword

There is an internal contradiction in the current movement for school reform. If schools should have greater opportunity and authority to chart their own destiny, what happens if those with many low-performing students choose not to improve? On the other hand, if central offices should focus more on supporting and coordinating schools than on regulating them, how do they make sure that schools do improve? Can school districts find a creative role that bridges the chasm between central offices controlling schools and schools controlling central offices?

In most communities, citizens are unaware of these dilemmas or how the resulting uncertainties and tensions paralyze school system staff and inhibit school reform. Educators, however, are all too familiar with this phenomenon. Some superintendents are slow to take action against persistently low-performing schools for fear that doing so will not be consistent with their commitment to school-based decision making. Some schools may demand less interference, or simply less interaction with the central office but then complain when standards for what students should learn differ from classroom to classroom, or when curriculum becomes stagnant or there is no support to improve instruction. The problem of how a central office can exercise leadership and accountability for reform while providing schools with the freedom and support they need to make reform happen is an operational problem, not just a philosophical one.

> Can school districts find a creative role that bridges the chasm between central offices controlling schools and schools controlling central offices?

For the past several years, a small team of experienced middle level educators and consultants has wrestled with this dilemma. Members have not only studied it, but they have become intimately familiar with school systems and schools where this issue is embedded in the fabric of daily assumptions and practices. Holly Hatch and her colleagues have drawn on their experiences in assisting these school systems to develop and test an "audit" of how school districts organize themselves to reform middle grades education. This book describes the rationale and research that underlies this effort and supports the audit process. The lessons learned from its administration and use in several school systems are presented. It shows school systems how they can take the first steps around the either-or snares of central office control and building-level independence.

The strength of the audit process is that it is comprehensive. It honors the reality that if schools are going to improve, they require leadership and collaboration among many decision makers – students, families, teachers, principals, central office staff and superintendents, and school board members. The audit recognizes that the roles, actions, and the perceptions of each of these groups is critical to systemic reform, and it provides a means to understand systematically how they do and do not interact to improve schools. Consequently, a school system can use the audit to gain the information and insights it needs to forge a new role, one that respects both the integrity of individual schools and the legal responsibilities school districts have to provide all students a quality education.

The audit process can also help school systems gain a coherent understanding of many different initiatives and projects that have sprung up and evolved over time. In nearly all cases, school systems and schools launched these to benefit students, but it may no longer be apparent whether or how they contribute to improving students' academic achievement and healthy development. District-wide reform may be complex, but it should not be confusing, and the audit can assist school systems in gaining a clearer view of whether separate initiatives are in conflict or alignment to bring reform to fruition.

For all of the audit's strengths, it lacks one essential component – a self-starter. There is no mechanism that will cause school systems to use the audit process, or to learn from and apply its results. Of course, it is not possible for the audit to include such a device. In the final analysis it is the will of school boards and superintendent to reform that must trigger the administration of the audit and the use of its results. There is no guarantee that the audit will produce the comforting news that so many decision makers seek. Indeed, it is almost certain to generate unsettling information that will explicitly or implicitly suggest the need for tough decisions and concrete actions. Understandably, school system leaders often shrink from the chore of cutting through one more set of knotty problems, but that is what is necessary if they are going to produce the higher levels of student performance they say they want. The price of school boards and superintendents gaining the respect of building-level educators is to have a tough-minded vision for improving education and the determination to implement a workable plan for achieving it. This volume shows these leaders how to open the door to systemic, middle-level reform, but it is up to school boards and superintendents to step through it, hand-in-hand with teachers, administrators, students, and families.

— M. Hayes Mizell
Director, Program for Student Achievement
The Edna McConnell Clark Foundation

# Acknowledgements

A great many people contributed to this work. First, a very special thanks goes to Hayes Mizell of the Edna McConnell Clark Foundation, without whose financial and conceptual support this book would not be possible. His vision and high expectations serve as a model for leaders of middle-grades education reform. Then I would like to acknowledge the hundreds of interviewees and participants in the audit who shared of their time and insights. The colleagues who helped to refine and field test the audit instruments and to review and present the findings at each district are really co-creators. My gratitude goes to Carlos Espinoza, former project associate, Charles Palmer of the California League of Middle Schools, and Carlene Murphy of Augusta, Georgia, for their skills, knowledge, and team work. In addition, I wish to thank those who participated as part of an audit team: Howard Hardin of Louisville, Kentucky; Alice Haskins of Howard County Public Schools; Aretha Marshall of Detroit City Schools; Barbara Dale of Atlanta's Council of Intown Neighborhoods; Joana Fox and Donna Whiting of the Center for Education in Science, Math, and Computing; Miriam James, parent advocate; John Norton of the Focused Reporting Project; and Lucretia Peebles, Assistant Professor of Education at Spelman College. Innumerable colleagues in each district shared their suggestions. It is impossible to name them all, but we especially want to thank the site coordinators and contacts: Cat Xandor in San Diego; Kathy Anauf in Milwaukee; Howard Hardin and Sandra Ledford in Louisville; Roseana Garza in Corpus Christi; Anika Jones and Marcia Klenbort of the Southern Regional Council in Atlanta; and Gloria Patterson of Atlanta Public Schools. The forty-five members of the project's Advisory Committee deserve recognition for their ideas, critical questions, and encouragement in developing the audit and planning process. Their input was invaluable and some of their work is reflected in the resource sections. Their names are listed on pp. 219-221. David Dodson of MDC and Leon Finkelstein of LBF Associates attended meetings with other audit team members to conceptualize the initial framework. Anne Wheelock provided generous review of the first draft of the documents.

My former colleagues at the Center for Early Adolescence provided support, encouragement, and input into this project. I especially want to thank Nancy Cox, Deborah Evans, Dr. Frank Loda, Robin Pulver, Suzanne Rucker, Peter Scales, and Karen Thompson.

I express appreciation to John Lounsbury of the National Middle School Association for his support, patience, and encouragement as the project expanded and went way beyond original deadlines. His editorial assistance improved the book greatly. I also thank Mary Mitchell of NMSA publications who provided layout, design, and advice on the content and organization of the book.

— Holly Hatch
Director, Middle-Grades Reform Project

# I.
## Rationale and Recommendations

A major question confronts public education reform in the 1990s – how can the successes achieved in individual exemplary schools be translated to the whole school system? Those seeking to improve achievement, equity, and to create effective school learning communities for all students have learned a great deal about the kinds of changes that must be made to reach these goals as they have worked with a targeted school. However, the gap between individual effective schools and whole systems of effective schools remains, particularly in large systems serving great numbers of children in poverty.

This volume addresses this question. The book represents seven years of experience in urban district-wide reform aimed at improving achievement for middle-grades students. The three sections of the volume range from the theory and research related to district-wide middle-grades reform, to cases illustrating the specific experiences and changes initiated in four diverse school districts. It also provides extensive resources and suggested activities so district leaders can engage diverse groups in the planning and implementation of middle grades education reform.

Section I describes the theory, research, and framework for district middle-grades reform that underlie the audit and planning process described in the following sections. Chapter 1 examines the role of the district and particularly central office staff in reform, including the need to redefine district leadership to include all the key implementers of intended policy changes. It also describes the procedures of the Middle-Grades Reform Audit, a district assessment, planning, and consensus-building process that sets the stage for implementation of specific changes to improve middle-grades education across the district.

Chapter 2 outlines three main components of the infrastructure of district-wide middle-grades reform: leadership, support, and accountability. The chapter then presents and details eighteen standards for reform that cover the three components. Supporting research and examples of how each standard is implemented in a district are also included.

Chapter 3 describes the audit and planning process carried out in four diverse urban districts. Findings include recommendations from our experience that will be useful to those using the audit as well as other assessment and planning tools.

Chapter 4 addresses common themes and concerns found in the districts working to establish effective systems to increase middle-grades student achievement across a whole district. Recommendations and examples of how to address the concerns come from the four districts in the case studies as well as other districts throughout the country engaged in systemic reform.

# 1.
## The District Role in Middle-Grades Reform

The past two decades of education reform have centered on schools as the locus of change. Diverse sources such as Ted Sizer of the Coalition of Essential Schools (1984, 1992) and the Carnegie Council on Adolescent Development (1989) call for school decisions to be made as close to the students as possible in order to free schools from bureaucratic policies that would interfere with innovation. In order to improve achievement, school reform advocates uniformly call for greater involvement of parents, teachers, and students in school improvement efforts. This wide involvement is particularly important in urban schools where the teachers and school administrators often do not live in the school neighborhood and thus require the perspective of parents and community members to help them understand their students' backgrounds and needs.

The advocacy of change, one school at a time, has frequently been supported by national projects of like-minded schools such as Accelerated Schools, Coalition of Essential Schools, and the Paideia Project, each with its own strengths and weaknesses. A school reform model and network can give support and guidance to the individual school's faculty. The outside network also can provide leverage with the district to free a school from policies that may hamper the staff's ability to make changes based on the school's unique needs and student population. One assumption behind this decentralized approach to school restructuring, one school at a time, is that as individual exemplary restructured schools are created, others will be inspired by these examples to implement similar changes. In some cases this does occur, as the numbers of schools belonging to one or more reform networks increase rapidly.

More often however, particularly in large urban districts, while individual schools have improved, they have not had the ripple effect on other schools envisioned by reform leaders. Individual school changes have not led to broader systemic effects for several reasons.

First, demonstration or lighthouse schools often have outside funding and technical assistance available that support changes in ways that are not possible at schools that are not part of funded projects. These model schools are able to draw staff from around the district who are committed to change efforts, and as a result these teachers and staff often leave the schools most in need. This may exacerbate quality differences between schools in an urban district.

Second, the more innovative schools often draw the most knowledgeable parents who can demand higher standards in these schools. With little central accountability or few standards to direct school improvement, the district often ends up creating a two-tiered system with the children from families in poverty attending schools with the worst facilities, least prepared teachers, and the fewest resources for school improvement; while the more affluent schools acquire more than their fair share.

Third, few plans for information coordination exist for district-wide school improvement, leaving the district with no effective lines of communication established for sharing the successes of exemplary schools. Currently, few, if any, mechanisms exist to usefully codify and disseminate the lessons learned from school restructuring efforts within a district (Olsen, Chang, De La Rosa Salazar, Leong, McCall Perez, McLain, & Raffel, 1994).

### Public calls for systemic accountability

With the growing public demand for higher student achievement, school district personnel feel increased pressure for more systemic school improvement efforts. This pressure is compounded by state and national initiatives that call for increased accountability for student performance based on standards and new forms of assessment. However, while the successes of individual schools are often well documented in the literature on educational reform, much less attention has been given to the changing role of the central office. In an era of school decentralization, a proactive and positive role for district staff in leading and supporting reform can be the key to forging links between state and national policies, emerging content and performance standards, and to making effective changes at the school site. Involving teachers, principals, parents, and community members in this effort can build a district collaborative that will help education reform move beyond individual exemplary schools.

While a few districts have been successful in supporting multi-school change efforts, little attention has been paid to ways that districts can achieve reform on a systemic level. Olsen and associates (1994), in discussing the restructuring of entire public school systems, suggest that the renegotiation of roles causes significant confusion and tension that reflect an overall "policy cloud about the vision of a central administration, about the role of district-wide planning, and about where power should reside" (p. 258). This points to the importance of paying more sustained attention to the role of the district in moving restructuring efforts beyond the creation of exemplary individual schools, as well as instigating creative thinking about the role that district personnel can and should play in improvement efforts. Since, as Olsen and associates suggest, "there is little overall vision, leadership or policy guiding this renegotiation process" (p. 259), clarifying the role of the school district in school improvement is becoming increasingly urgent.

> ...clarifying the role of the school district in school improvement is becoming increasingly urgent.

### The changing role of the central office

The new job of a central office leader is to balance seemingly contradictory functions: setting direction and accountability measures on the one hand and providing services and support to empowered school staff on the other. The shifting role of the central office from being a director and regulator to a supporter and facilitator is the predominant theme that runs through current writings on the district's role in school reform. In an era characterized by the call for increased school-based autonomy, roles of superintendents and central office staff have to change. No longer are district office personnel called on to mandate; instead, they must act as coordinators, enablers, service providers, and support centers. David (1989) argues that effective school reform involves a shift "from a system characterized by controlling and directing what goes on at the next lower level to guiding and facilitating professionals in their quest for more productive learning opportunities for students" (p. 28). This shift is supported in research studies. Holcomb and McCue (1991) suggest the district's orientation should be away from monitoring and reporting towards facilitation, service provision, and technical assistance. Asayesh (1994) argues districts should work with individual schools to help each find the right kind of improvements it needs and act as a broker of services to assist schools in getting the external support needed. Glickman (1993) characterizes the new role of the district as moving away from the anachronistic mentality of standardizing and controlling schools to a 21st century mentality of principled response and assistance. Fullan and Stiegelbauer (1991) add that an integral district role is to help schools decide upon and carry out the right choices.

In describing the new roles that restructuring schools and school systems require of central office leaders, Murphy (1990) suggests that they can be grouped into five categories: (1) visioning, (2) developing themselves and others, (3) creating an environment where change can happen, (4) establishing a facilitative working style, and (5) flattening organizational relationships. Each of these categories leads to specific responsibilities for central office leaders. Visioning requires leaders to create, articulate and communicate school improvement visions and support the transformation of goals and visions into practice. Central office leaders must be active in staff development efforts, remain abreast of current literature, model continuous learning, develop clear decision allocation, and sharpen their leadership skills. Creating an environment in which change can happen necessitates abandoning outdated practices, focusing on service provision, building new coalitions, providing conditions for collegial interaction, and creating an atmosphere in which experimentation and risk taking are encouraged. The working style of leaders should be one of guidance and facilitation. Lastly, organizational structures need to become "flatter" as leaders become more generalists and layered administrative relationships become less hierarchical.

As the role of the district in school improvement effort evolves, varied views on how much control the central office should maintain over improvement efforts have become evident. On one end of the continuum is complete decentralization, with all decisions made at the school building level, while on the other end is a maintenance of top-down control, with all improvement efforts mandated from the district or above (i.e. state or federal entities). Most plans, however, fall somewhere in the middle, with the value of site-based management for schools becoming widely accepted. Much of the research, in fact, begins with the premise that school-based management will improve student achievement as site-based control puts decisions closer to children. However, recent research (Odden & Wohlsetter, 1995; David, 1996) shows that site-based decision making alone does not lead to improved achievement. The how, what, and why of decentralization proved key factors. How site-based decision making was structured – including the power of governance teams to make key decisions related to curriculum and instruction; what the team focused on in their meetings – whether matters leading to classroom change or more peripheral issues; why school governance – whether it was seen as a means or an end in itself; all contributed to its success or failure in leading to improved student performance. However, few argue against some site-level control of planning and decision making as a key means to education reform

Among the more decentralized visions is that of the Cross City Campaign for Urban School Reform (1994). Framers of this campaign argue that the role of the district should be limited to three main functions: equity assurance, district-wide data maintenance, and intervention in failing schools. In terms of the traditional functions of the central office, they propose dismantling centralized bureaucracy with individual schools taking on the functions often associated with the central office. Thus, they suggest school-based decision making and authority for: curriculum and instruction, all substantive personnel decisions, the budget and the contracting of services, and school governance. They add that the school should also be the primary site of accountability. In its scaled down view of the central office, this group envisions eight small central office units with specific and limited responsibilities: equity assurance, intervention (in failing schools), budget and treasury (including emergency funding), information management (mainframe computer), data collection and analysis, legal/labor, personnel (to perform background checks), and entrepreneurial service departments (transportation, payroll, food services).

> ...along with developing and communicating district-wide strategic goals and plans, districts should set decision-making parameters and help monitor school progress.

While much of the research supports more school-based management, few visions give as much power and responsibility to the schools as does the Cross City Campaign. Typically more of a balance between school-based efforts and district level initiatives are advocated, with superintendents and central office staff providing what Payzant and Gardner (1994) call "leadership from the middle," entailing mediation between top-down and bottom-up pressures. Similarly, Levine (1991) characterizes the role of the district as one of "directed autonomy," that is, giving schools freedom within certain parameters while also providing guidance for implementing wise choices. Louis (1989) also argues for a "middle way" involving co-management of the improvement process by district and school personnel. Describing this need for balance, Holcomb and McCue (1991) claim "the school district must take responsibility for those activities that are needed to support all schools, and which can apply to all schools....All other decision making and activities should be reserved for the collaborative involvement of stakeholders at the individual sites" (p. 3). In supporting all schools, they argue that the central office should provide a district-wide mission statement, draft broad policy guidelines for school improvement processes, and be involved in the determination of general student outcome goals. Asayesh (1994), David (1989), and Glickman (1993) all suggest that along with developing and communicating district-wide strategic goals and plans, districts should set decision-making parameters and help monitor school progress.

### Role in staff development

As part of a new vision for the central office in an era of restructuring, district personnel take on new roles and responsibilities particularly in the area of staff development. Payzant and Gardner (1994) argue that "systematic training must be provided for principals and staff members to help them understand the change process and how to make shared decision making work" (p. 12). For central office staff, skills needed to help manage change include: knowing how to ask useful and appropriate questions, helping to foresee problems and manage conflicts, and assisting in the development of group consensus. The district is also being called upon to stay abreast of new ideas and research findings and become professionally well informed. Often, districts in conjunction with individual schools will decide upon a specific change model which then necessitates a comprehensive staff development agenda so that the model can be successfully implemented (see Castner, Costella, & Hess, 1993; Johnson, 1994; and Middleton, Smith & Williams, 1994).

### Support for school improvement

Along with staff development, recent literature details many other ways in which central office staff can support school improvement plans. One common way is for districts to act as both data management and resource centers. In terms of manipulating data, districts can help in the collection, coordination, monitoring, and analysis of the information needed to gauge school progress. As resource centers, districts would aim to keep up on new ideas and innovations, feed information back to the schools, and network with others involved in educational improvement efforts. Glickman (1993) suggests districts should "coordinate and implement active assistance to the schools," by which he means linking them to information for school renewal, providing "venture capital" for improvement efforts, and formally connecting schools with resources through such things as newsletters, E-mail messages, site visits, and identification of experts in the field. In this role, districts can help schools to consider various options for school improvement and help them to decide which is best for their particular circumstances. While working with individual schools, the district is also being called upon to be a liaison with the public, communicating ideas and the rationale behind improvement efforts.

### Creating an environment for sustained improvement

Strategies to manage the changing role of the district in school improvement efforts are also detailed in various studies. Fundamentally, district staff need to exhibit attitudes that create an environment conducive to bringing about substantial and sustained improvement. The district administrator is the single most important individual for setting the expectations and tone of the pattern of change within the local district. While the amount of top-down control that the central office should assume is debatable, research supports a significant leadership role for all personnel in the central office, whether this means leading by example, leading by supporting, or leading by influence rather than authority. Cited ways in which the central office can exhibit leadership include: replacing controlling, competing, and blocking behaviors with collaborating, enabling and facilitating behaviors (Payzant & Gardner, 1994); convening reform panels to review school improvement efforts and provide waivers from school board policy (Middleton, Smith & Williams, 1994); providing a stable policy environment in which meaningful change can occur (Louis, 1989); seeking out materials and strategies that have been successful in other districts as tools for guidance and change (Levine, 1991; Asayesh, 1994); developing the management capacities of school-based administrators to lead change (Fullan and Stiegelbauer, 1991); encouraging experimentation and demonstrating shared decision making (David, 1989); giving school staffs the authority, flexibility, and resources needed to solve problems particular to their schools (Hord & Smith, 1993); providing money, technical services, and human consultation (Glickman, 1993); setting up district level advisory boards for information dissemination and participation in school level training sessions and on school improvement teams (Asayesh, 1994); and maintaining a long-term perspective and commitment (Holcomb & McCue, 1991).

> ...while central office staff has an integral role in school improvement efforts, effective change cannot be mandated from above.

Overall, the main theme in current research studies is that while central office staff has an integral role in school improvement efforts, effective change cannot be mandated from above. The shifting image of the district is away from monitoring, controlling, and dictating and towards supporting, encouraging, and facilitating school-based efforts. There are still many roles the district can play in implementing system-wide improvement efforts, and the call for eliminating district offices completely is very rare. The challenge for district leaders involves creating a proper balance between district level and school-based initiatives and providing district level leadership that is systemic, sets high standards for quality, equity, and student achievement, while at the same time being supportive and enabling. Ultimately, a meaningful role for the district in school improvement efforts is essential if restructuring is to go beyond the individual exemplary school.

**Standards for a district infrastructure to support middle-grades student achievment.**

Since 1988, the District Middle-Grades Reform Project[1] (DMGRP), funded by the Edna McConnell Clark Foundation, has assisted urban school districts to plan, implement, and evaluate strategies to improve the achievement of middle-grades students. DMGRP staff initially provided consultation and information for two or three pilot schools in a district and helped central office staff determine mechanisms to support school-based planning for improved teaching and learning. Over the past three years, this technical assistance function shifted to assisting district leaders in developing and implementing strategies to transform middle-grades education in *all* schools within a district. The program's initial pilot school reforms, while intended to be applied throughout the district, included limited plans for how to move reform beyond these schools. The project staff realized there was a lack of clarity about the role of the central office in reform efforts. The rhetoric of change came easily enough. Espousing the benefits of facilitative versus directive leadership was no problem; however, actually making specific changes in behavior and practices proved much more difficult.

Drawing on the literature on middle schools and on systemic education in general, and from our own experience, DMGRP staff discovered that while a great deal is known about the theory and practice of school level improvement, and some broad guidelines for new district staff roles exist, districts as a whole had little to guide them on how to plan, implement, and assess systemic middle-grades reform that would improve student achievement. Despite a wealth of information available on practices and organizational structures that lead to increased student achievement in middle-grades schools, even when staff know about them, few implement these practices. When a school adopts reform efforts that result in higher student achievement, it often remains an isolated case. Rarely does that school become part of a district's systemic plan to move other schools forward. Given the absence of specific and detailed information on how districts can best support middle schools and create a system of high-achieving schools, over the past three years DMGRP staff have been creating resources and materials to provide guidance in conducting standards-based district middle-grades reform.

**Systemic culture of continuous improvement**

The cornerstone of the District Middle-Grades Reform Project is a set of eighteen standards for district-wide middle-grades reform. These standards,

---

[1] The District Middle-Grades Reform Project began as the Urban Youth Initiative at the Center for Early Adolescence in UNC-Chapel Hill's School of Medicine. When the Center closed in 1995 the project relocated to the School of Education and was renamed the District Middle-Grades Reform Project. Other publications and projects of the Center for Early Adolescence moved to Search Institute, a non-profit youth development organization located in Minneapolis.

presented in Chapter 2, grew out of research on best practices, consultation with a 45 member advisory board of middle-grades experts, and years of working with districts and assessing their most pressing needs. Concurrently, staff developed and piloted an audit based on this framework to help districts gather data for their strategic plan for middle-grades reform based on these standards. The audit and planning processes were developed to address four specific needs that arose in the districts. These needs are: (1) clarifying the role of central office in an era of decentralization; (2) moving beyond rhetoric to actions and structures that contribute to systemic change; (3) informing and involving all key stakeholders in the reform process; and (4) ensuring that plans lead to visible action and ongoing coordination.

Three key components comprise the standards for district-wide middle-grades reform: *leadership*, *support*, and *accountability*. While these general areas may be common to all systemic change efforts, in the middle-grades reform standards they refer to the specific structures necessary for effective middle-grades schooling. Each contributes to a systemic culture of continuous improvement for all middle schools in a district. Specific attention to district reform standards at the middle-grades is important since this is often a neglected area in district planning. Different grade configurations and philosophies may exist in different schools in the system: the configuration and philosophy driven by facilities' demands and individual principals' expertise, rather than a proactive view of the education best suited to young adolescents. As students move to and from the middle school, student achievement often drops. In 1989, the Carnegie Council on Adolescent Development argued that schools serving young adolescents "have the potential to make a tremendous impact on the development of their students – for better or for worse – yet they have been largely ignored in the recent surge of educational reform" (*Turning Points*, p. 12-13). While individual school transformation for young adolescents accelerated since the 1989 *Turning Points* report, only recently has attention turned to the district role in middle-grades reform.

> For reform to reach where it counts – the classroom – significant leadership roles must also be played by teachers, families, community members, and students.

### Leadership

District leadership is usually thought of as consisting of the school board, superintendent, and central office staff. Principals are sometimes viewed as part of the leadership team. The district middle-grades reform standards define leadership more broadly. A particular central office staff person to spearhead the middle school reform effort and the strong support of the board and superintendent is crucial. For reform to reach where it counts – the classroom – significant leadership roles must also be played by teachers, families, community members, and students. A district steering committee that includes representatives of all the stakeholders should guide the reform process. The standards delineate the particular role of the central office in coordinating reform efforts. Equally important, they outline the ways in which all the stakeholders can be involved in decision making and implementation of the middle-grades reform effort.

Foremost, the district must provide leadership in setting the tone for improvement efforts and in articulating the vision for middle-grades education in the district. Key district leaders will:
- Establish and model a shared district middle-grades vision based on goals for what students should know and be able to do;
- Ensure that policy and practice decisions are based on research, knowledge, core values, and beliefs about early adolescence;
- Develop academic content and performance standards for what students should know and be able to do in conjunction with school and community involvement;
- Maintain policies that are proven to contribute to student learning and growth, and which support the district middle-grades vision, plans, and standards;
- Develop, with school and community involvement, a district strategic plan with outcomes and timelines to improve middle-grades learning;
- Engage parents, community members, teachers, and school personnel in improving education at the middle-grades; and
- Model new leadership roles, undergirded by a service orientation and the belief that all stakeholders provide leadership.

**Support**

Each of these district leadership functions needs to be coupled with mechanisms that support its realization. This support develops the individual and organizational capacities necessary for the new roles, responsibilities, and skills required of all stakeholders. A collaborative culture dedicated to continuous improvement in the district and at schools must be modeled. To sufficiently support implementation, district leadership will:
- Provide resources, including financial, human, and time necessary to the change process;
- Develop mechanisms and structures for the coordination and communication of information and skill development across schools, grade levels, and departments, and to broad external constituencies;
- Ensure that schools and all constituencies have access to current information on content standards and teaching and learning practices that contribute to the academic and social development of young adolescents;
- Model and sustain a district culture of continuous improvement;
- Provide assistance to schools in assessing their current state and developing and implementing school improvement plans;
- Maintain supportive staff development activities that are based on the district strategic plan, school plans, and on successful change models for individual and organizational development;
- Lead the development of curriculum that provides core content standards; and
- Offer support and plans for addressing individual student needs based on current research and practices in adolescent development, second language learning, special education, and gifted and talented education, while ensuring equity for all groups.

### Accountability

The third key component for district-wide middle-grades reform is accountability. In order to ensure that the leadership and support functions of the district are working, and more importantly, that they lead to gains in student achievement, frequent assessment and revision of plans are essential. District leadership and support are thus undergirded by the development of new conceptions of accountability. At heart, accountability involves holding individuals, schools, and the central office itself responsible for instructional processes and outcomes and explaining the research-based evidence for making professional decisions about organization and practice. It involves taking shared responsibility for the academic success of every child. There are three important areas in which accountability is paramount: student assessment, program assessment, and systems assessment. Districts hold schools and themselves accountable by assuring that:

- Student performance is assessed by multiple sources and compared to benchmark goals for what students should know and be able to do;
- Schools and districts together gather and analyze data and use it to continuously evaluate programs and school environments for purposes of continuous improvement; and
- District policies and practices are reviewed and aligned when necessary with visions, plans, accountability mechanisms, and with school and community needs.

### The audit: using the standards to guide a district self-assessment and planning process

To assess the level at which a district meets these research-based standards for middle level reform, DMGRP staff developed an audit to examine the current state of middle-grades education in a district. While many school assessments exist, few processes examine the entire district plan for middle-grades reform and its implementation across schools. Our goal in developing the audit was to provide broad exemplars of research-based effective district functions. Rather than a checklist of "essential elements," the standards provide a baseline for a cross-role group to create its own vision and plan for improving middle-grades education. The district middle-grades audit and planning process includes:

- Development of a purpose and specific focus areas for the middle-grades audit by a local steering committee representing all district stakeholders;
- Assessment of the current state of district implementation of middle-grades education reform based on review of preexisting data and documents, and a site visit (which may be conducted by external colleagues, a team from the district trained in the use of the assessment tool, or a combination of both);
- A report of audit team findings, including recommendations; and
- A process to facilitate broad consensus on the priority recommendations and to develop and monitor a focused plan for improvement.

The audit reviews the current state of the district in middle-grades education and its infrastructure for systemic change in the broad functions identified in the district reform standards: leadership, support, and accountability. Under leadership, the audit team looks for evidence of middle-grades vision, content standards, supporting policies, and strategic plans in both documentation and in action. The goal is to see whether policies and plans exist and how they are implemented and understood in practice. In relation to support, the audit team looks at mechanisms, resources, and consultation to support the middle-grades education plan in the areas of curriculum and instruction, academic outcomes, middle level practices, student services, and policy alignment. Through observations and interviews, the audit team seeks to uncover both the stated and actual practice and belief systems in the district in relationship to support. The staff development plan and other structures for improving practice are reviewed, along with the roles and responsibilities of the central office and schools. Finally, the audit looks at mechanisms for accountability and assessment of the plan, including tracking student outcomes. Interviews with evaluation and research departments, school improvement teams, staff development personnel, families, and school board members highlight available resources and gaps. An examination of assessment and reporting mechanisms used, and an appraisal of stakeholder awareness of district functions point to the meaning and importance of these assessments.

The audit process has several steps:

1. When a district decides to examine its current state, the first step is to convene an audit steering committee and gather data for review by the audit team. This includes:

    Policy and belief statements;

    Committee reports;

    Vision and strategic plans for middle-grades education;

    Staff development plans;

    District and state content;

    Performance and delivery standards;

    Middle school reform initiatives; and

    Demographic and performance information on all schools in the district that serve sixth, seventh and eighth graders.

This steering committee may also decide on areas of specific concern that they want the audit team to address more directly, such as staff development, multicultural or inclusion issues, or site level strategic planning. At this point the steering committee decides whether to conduct the audit with a local or external team or with a combination team.

2. Following team acceptance the four to five-member audit team reviews the district documents and data and any questions raised by the steering committee. At this time, the audit team, in conjunction with the steering committee, sets the date and agenda for the site visit, to include visits at select middle schools and interviews with: all superintendents or program supervisors, principals, representatives from each of the district offices, teachers, students, school staffs, parents, com-

munity members, board members, and union representatives. The team also tailors the base interview guides to match the district demographics and organizational structure, to address any issues that arise from the initial review of district-provided data, and to attend to particular areas of concern detailed by the steering committee.

3. The audit team spends four to five days on site, conducting interviews with various stakeholders, visiting as many middle schools as possible to observe and interview, analyzing data collected on site, summarizing information gathered in each interview, and providing preliminary feedback to the steering committee and/or school board.

4. Team members compile notes from their interviews and complete a series of summarizing sheets. The data gathered in the audit are compared to the district context standards for middle-grades reform. The data are summarized according to each of the eighteen standards and for each constituency group, seeking items of consensus as well as divergent findings. Team members' summaries are combined to present a comprehensive picture of the current status of middle-grades education across the district. One member of the team, usually the chairperson, prepares a report of findings based on the summarizing sheets and interview and observation information from each team member. All members read and review drafts of this report and make suggestions and amendments before the final report is sent to the district.

5. Within three to six weeks of the site visit, the team submits the final written report to the district for dissemination to all stakeholders. An executive summary of the report should include the district's strengths and challenge areas and a summary listing of recommendations for next steps in district-wide middle-grades reform. The body of the report includes information, understandings, concerns, and comments reported by each constituency; and a detailed list of recommendations and resources promotes the implementation of middle-grades reform. These recommendations are organized by each of the eighteen standards under the areas of leadership, support and accountability.

6. Then, the audit report data are used by the steering committee with various constituencies to build consensus on the current state of middle-grades education, determine the priority recommendations and the next steps to take in middle-grades reform.

# References

Asayesh, G. (1994). The changing role of the central office and its implications for staff development. *Journal of Staff Development 15* (3). 2-5.

Castner, K., Costella, L., & Hess, S. (1993). Moving from seat time to mastery: One district's system. *Educational Leadership 51* (1), 45-50.

Carnegie Council on Adolescent Development (1989). *Turning points: Preparing America's youth for the 21st century*. New York: Carnegie Corporation of New York.

Cross City Campaign for Urban School Reform (1995, June). *Reinventing central office: Toward a system of successful urban schools*. Chicago, IL: Author.

David, J. (1989). *Restructuring in progress: Lessons from pioneering districts*. Washington, DC: Center for Policy Research, National Governors' Association.

David, J. (1996). The who, what, and why of site-based management. *Educational Leadership, 53* (4), 4-10.

Fullan, M., with Suzanne Stiegelbauer (1991). *The new meaning of educational change*. New York: Teachers College Press.

Glickman, C. (1993). *Renewing America's schools: A guide for school-based action*. San Francisco: Jossey-Bass.

Holcomb, E., & McCue, L. (Eds.) (1991). The district role in support of school improvement. In *A handbook for implementing school improvement*. Madison, WI: National Center for Effective Schools Research and Development.

Hord, S., & Smith, A. (1993). Will our phones go dead? The changing role of the central office. *Issues...about Change 2* (4).

Johnson, F. (1994). Transforming District Nine. *Educational Leadership 51* (8), 68-71.

Levine, D. (1991). Creating effective schools: Findings and implications from research and practice. *Phi Delta Kappan 72* (5), 389-392.

Louis, K. (1989). The role of the school district in school improvement. In M. Holmes, K. Leithwood, & D. Musella (Eds.), *Educational policy for effective schools*. Toronto, Ontario: OISE Press.

Middleton, J., Smith, A., & Williams, D. (1994). From directing to supporting school initiatives: One district's efforts. *Journal of Staff Development 15* (3), 6-9.

Murphy, C.(1990, October 16). *The role of the central office staff in restructuring*. Luncheon Address, International Society for Educational Planning Annual Conference, Atlanta, Georgia.

Murphy, J. (1991). *Restructuring schools: Capturing and assessing the phenomena*. New York: Teachers College Press.

Odden, E.R., & Wohlsetter, P. (1995). Making school-based management work. *Educational Leadership, 52* (2), 32-36.

Olsen, L., Chang, H., De La Rosa Salazar, D., Leong, C., McCall Perez, Z., McLain, G., & Raffel, L. (1994). Towards restructuring an entire public school system. In *The unfinished journey: Restructuring schools in a diverse society*. San Francisco: Tomorrow.

Payzant, T., & Gardner, M. (1994). Changing roles and responsibilities in a restructuring school district. *NASSP Bulletin 78* (560), 8-17.

Sizer, T.R. (1984). *Horace's compromise: The dilemma of the American high school.* Boston: Houghton Mifflin Company.

Sizer, T.R. (1992). *Horace's high school: Redesigning the American high school.* Boston: Houghton Mifflin Company.

# 2.
# Standards for District-Wide Middle-Grades Reform

Leadership, support, and accountability are three interrelated components of a district culture that seeks to improve student achievement. Each is integral in assuring that sufficient attention is paid to the unique place of middle-grades schools in the district and that district staff and all stakeholders play meaningful roles in the continuous improvement of them. This chapter details these three main components along with the standards for practice that support each component. In each section an overview of the key component is presented, followed by a number of standards related to its practice. The total of eighteen standards presented in the three components were ones that emerged from a review of the literature on school improvement, from conversations with practitioners and district personnel, and from our work with school districts. In our discussions of each of these, a rationale for why each is important is offered along with ways in which the district can approach the standard in practice.

The three components and their supporting standards comprise the framework used in the audit for examining districts. During each audit, we gather information on the status of leadership, support, and accountability in the district and assess the current status of the district in relationship to the standards in each area. In most cases, districts have several particular areas of concern relative to these standards, and we cater the audit to examining those areas in the most detail. In our report to the district, we provide narrative information about salient concerns and issues as well as recommendations for next steps which directly link to each of the standards. In this chapter, we offer background information on leadership, support, accountability, and each of the standards. Our aim is to show why these areas are so important in district-wide school improvement efforts and to provide a greater familiarity with the types of district and school issues examined by the audit. In the case studies of the four districts (Part III), we clarify the direct links between the standards and the audit in practice.

# LEADERSHIP

Quality leadership is integral to the success of schools and school districts. This is especially true for districts that set out to implement recent findings about the changing nature of leadership in high-achieving schools. Traditional notions of leadership which usually involve commanding, dictating, and controlling have given way to more emergent views of collaborative, team-oriented, developmental leadership. Patterson (1993) defines leading as "the process of influencing others to achieve mutually agreed upon purposes for the organization" (p. 3). The emphasis on leadership as a strategic process as opposed to a quality inherent in an individual or in a position is significant. Describing the type of strategic leadership needed for today's schools, Mauriel (1989) suggests that it "demands an ability to manage and direct a process that ensures that the organization is working toward the achievement of a set of key goals that move it in a direction consistent with its mission, purpose and strategy" (p. 3). Leadership in toto is a matter of providing the vision, beliefs, policies, and plans that move schools and districts in mutually agreed upon directions.

A growing body of literature identifies the qualities, behaviors, and values necessary for leaders in reforming or restructuring schools. Based on a survey of leaders in successfully restructured school districts, Reavis and Griffith (1992) identify a number of these important leadership behaviors and values. First and foremost, leaders must have a working knowledge of the change process, including preparation for change, holistic change planning, and the stages of the change process. To involve all significant stakeholders in this process, they must exhibit a collaborative leadership style and build coalitions or teams who share a common sense of purpose and are committed to implementing the necessary changes.

Leaders in restructuring schools must also have a high moral purpose, a sound, well-reasoned philosophy and vision, extensive knowledge of curriculum and instruction issues, and intense commitment to providing the best education for all students. In contrast to more traditional views of leadership – mandating, pushing, and controlling – restructuring school leadership can be better described with terms such as: *collaborative, open, developmental, reflective, diverse, values-driven, team oriented*, and *focussed on instruction*.

The new roles required of leaders in continuously improving school districts suggest that it is better to think in terms of **leaders** than expect leadership to come from a single individual. Authority and power become diffused in restructuring schools and districts as leadership is shifted from control in the hands of the few to shared authority and responsibility which multiplies, according to Mojkowski (1991), "the power of the organization to decide upon and achieve its goals" (p. 32). Developing and empowering others, along with this shared decision making and responsibility become important leadership qualities. Mojkowski believes that such leaders: create dissonance, prepare for and create opportunities, forge connections and create interdependencies, encourage risk taking, follow as well as lead, use information, foster the long view, acquire resources, negotiate for win-win outcomes, employ change strategies, provide stability in change, and change people while getting the work accomplished (p. 28-31).

The concept of shared leadership is particularly important at the middle level where interdisciplinary teaming is emphasized. There teachers, students, and sometimes others are involved in leadership roles. In addition, it is essential that leadership at the middle level reflect an in-depth understanding of the nature and needs of early adolescents. George and Alexander (1993) suggest that middle school leadership is comprised of three key sets of behaviors. First, "a clear understanding of the characteristics and needs of young adolescents" is necessary and should be translated into "a vision of an appropriately organized and effective middle level school." Second, school programs, implementation strategies, and evaluation techniques should be planned "in such a way as to create a unique and effective learning environment based on the characteristics of young adolescents." Third, and perhaps most important when it comes to middle level leadership, it is essential that all stakeholders are engaged "in a process of shared decision making which has, as its aim, the continued long-term maintenance and improvement of the school(s)" (p. 497).

> The concept of shared leadership is particularly important at the middle level where teaming holds sway.

Several important standards for district-wide middle level leadership emerge from the literature on the role of leaders in improving school districts and from a review of how school districts can best support middle level schools. Districts must foster the articulation of a shared vision of the middle level that is based on core values and beliefs about early adolescent learning, shared by parents and the community, and supported by clear standards for what students should know and be able to do by the time they complete middle school. This vision is critical because it determines the direction the district will take. According to Keefe, Valentine, Clark, and Irvin (1994), "when shared by administrators, teachers, staff members, students, parents, and community, a vision becomes a powerful tool for building consensus, establishing direction, and facilitating cooperative decision making" (p. 33). Further, for the vision to be actualized, policies and strategic improvement plans must be aligned with it, and leadership must be marked by more supportive and facilitative roles. For district-wide middle-grades reform efforts to be successful, the district must exhibit leadership in a number of important areas, including: middle-grades vision, beliefs, content standards, policies, strategic plan, family and community involvement, and new leadership roles.

## LEADERSHIP STANDARD

# 1. Middle grades vision

**Establish and model a shared district vision based on goals for what students should know and be able to do.**

The existence of a clear vision for middle-grades education in a district is essential to assure that the unique developmental and educational needs of early adolescents are addressed. Essentially, a vision is a projection of ideals, of how schools and the school district could be. Deal and Peterson (1990) believe that "a vision is a mental image of a better and more hopeful future. Visions engage people's hearts as well as their heads – especially when widely shared" (p. 101). A vision sets the tone for improvement efforts and engages all stakeholders in commitment to change efforts. Mizell, in a talk, "New Wagons for a Rugged Trail" (October, 1992), minced no words in making the case for a real vision

> *A school system's vision for middle school reform should both point the way and serve as a rallying call for action. The lack of such vision is one reason middle schools in so many urban areas are in such trouble, adrift and without focus. They cling to remnants of middle school philosophy and structure with little understanding or conviction about why middle schools exist or what goals they are seeking to achieve. This is unacceptable. If school boards and superintendents want young adolescents to perform better, they have to develop a vision that challenges, unifies, and mobilizes middle schools.*

The role that vision plays in the school is comparable to the role it can play in a more general level at the central office. Districts need to establish a clear middle-grades vision to guide decision making at that level and set expectations for district-wide middle grades practices. All stakeholders should be involved in developing the vision so that the middle-grades are viewed as a critical educational juncture in their own right and not as an afterthought to accommodate the elementary and high school programs and structures or facilities needed. ❑

## LEADERSHIP STANDARD

# 2. Beliefs

**Define core values and beliefs about student learning based on knowledge of the age group.**

Leadership for district-wide middle-grades reform should reflect research-based knowledge about early adolescence. In the past two decades, there has been a significant amount of research on this life stage. The advancement of the middle school movement in the 1960s and 1970s focussed attention on this often misunderstood and neglected age group of 10-15 year olds. Since the 60s, many schools have adopted the middle school model and shifted away from junior high school organization. Between 1980 and 1984, the Center for Early Adolescence created and field tested its Middle-Grades Assessment Program. This program has been a valuable resource in helping schools assess the quality of their programs. Building on the momentum of the middle school movement, in 1989 the Carnegie Council on Adolescent Development offered a series of recommendations for middle-grades schools that reflected knowledge of the age group, core values, and beliefs about student learning. The recommendations include: "creating small communities of learners which ensure more stable relationships, teaching a core academic program geared for middle-grades students, maintaining high expectations for all students by eliminating tracking and promoting cooperative learning and flexible use of time, and staffing middle-grades schools with teachers who are expert at teaching young adolescents" (p. 9). In order for districts to effectively serve their students, the growing body of research on middle level practices needs to be understood, shared, and systematically incorporated into the plans and decisions that affect those involved with middle schools in the district.

Research-identified best middle-grades characteristics should be in place throughout the district, including: teaming, which attends to the importance of small learning communities; curriculum integration, which reduces fragmentation; advisory programs, which provide time for teachers and students to interact on a personal level; flexible scheduling, which allows for varied use of time; heterogeneous grouping, which supports high expectations for all students; exploratory programs, which allow students to pursue interests and identify aptitudes; and a core curriculum, which ensures rich and rigorous content for all. It is particularly important that these practices be viewed as means to reach the goal of high achievement for all students, rather than as ends in themselves. In addition, practices should be thoroughly implemented if they are to meet goals. Too often teams are organized administratively but do not function as teams. Without careful attention to how various practices relate to local student needs, changes may become divorced from their purpose of improving student learning. ❏

## LEADERSHIP STANDARD

## 3. Academic standards

**Develop with school and community involvement academic and performance standards for what students should know and be able to do by the end of eighth grade.**

Leadership for district-wide middle-grades reform should be directed by academic content standards that establish what students should know and be able to do at the end of middle school. According to the U.S. Department of Education (1994), "they describe the knowledge, skills, and understanding that students should have in order to attain high levels of competency in challenging subject matter" (p. 2). Standards focus curriculum and instruction decisions on what students should learn and thus allow students and teachers to strive for clearly articulated and meaningful goals. Standards are also important because they ensure access to valued knowledge for all students, not just those in higher level classes. Without clear goals and expectations, curricular decisions can become haphazard and the achievement of high core content expectations for all students can be compromised.

Standards for what students should know, created with school, community, district, and professional input are essential tools in school restructuring. Standards cannot be effectively mandated from a national, state, or even district level without the involvement of teachers, families, and students. Districts play an important role in ensuring that these standards are based on discussions of student work and desired outcomes and focus on high core content for all students rather than lowering expectations and content for special needs students. ❏

**LEADERSHIP STANDARD**

## 4. Policies

**Base policies on research-based practices that support student learning and growth and align with the district middle-grades vision, plans, and academic standards.**

Leadership for district-wide middle-grades reform shapes research-based policies that reflect what is best for students. In order to realize the district's middle grades vision, it is essential that district policies be aligned with this vision and supportive of the school level strategic plans for improvement.

The Education Commission of the States (1991) identifies five key roles for policymakers in supporting schools' efforts to bring about higher learning for all students. First, a vision must be established that clarifies what students should know and be able to do and how the education system should work. Second, existing policies need to be reviewed in order to determine if they hinder or promote restructuring the education system for higher learning for all students. Third, options for policy changes need to be explored and debated by all stakeholders. Fourth, policy adjustments that stimulate desired change, deeper understandings, and sharing of insight need to be made. Finally, the impact of policy changes on student learning needs to be monitored and evaluated, thus guarding against undesired consequences. (p. ii) Ultimately, it is important for districts to ensure that key stakeholders, including students in some cases, are involved in the development of policies, and that all policies are based upon research findings of what is best for students and what achieves desired outcomes ❏

**LEADERSHIP STANDARD**

# 5. Strategic plan

**Develop a plan to improve student learning that includes goals and timelines and involves schools and community fully.**

Leadership for district-wide middle-grades reform employs strategic planning to set specific plans and guidelines for improvement. Kaufman and Herman (1991) offer that "strategic planning is a dynamic, active process. It scans current realities and opportunities in order to yield useful strategies and tactics for arriving at a better tomorrow" (p. xvii). Strategic planning is, then, a process in which the current state of affairs is examined, strengths and weaknesses are assessed, specific and detailed plans for improvement are determined, and provisions for continuously updating and assessing progress are included.

If districts are to actualize envisioned improvements, strategic planning that provides the framework, direction, possibilities, and guidelines for reform efforts is essential. Kaufman and Herman (1991) argue that strategic planning for educational reform entails three key stages: "rethinking what education should deliver, restructuring the educational enterprise in order to deliver the required results, and revitalizing the students and the system to make extraordinary change in and for society" (p. xv). Strategic planning is particularly valuable because it is an organizational change process in which long-range, systematic plans guide decisions and actions rather than relying on haphazard, piecemeal, and reactionary reform responses. It is important to emphasize that strategic planning is also a flexible process. While initial plans provide a starting point for change efforts, these are continuously modified in practice, thereby ensuring that they are linked to evaluation techniques and to what is actually implemented in practice. To adequately support middle schools district-wide, strategic planning must involve school and community personnel and include long-range plans for K-12 alignment and articulation, while still focusing on the unique place of middle schools within the district. ❑

**LEADERSHIP STANDARD**

## 6. Family/community involvement

**Engage families and community members in all efforts to improve education at the middle grades.**

Leadership for district-wide middle-grades reform engages all interested school and community stakeholders in improvement efforts. The importance of connecting home, school, and community has been a central theme of the middle school movement over the past decade. The Carnegie Council on Adolescent Development (1989) includes parent and community involvement in two of its eight recommendations for middle schools of the future. First, the Council's report calls for middle-grade schools that "reengage families in the education of young adolescents by giving families meaningful roles in school governance, communicating with families about the school program and student's progress, and offering families opportunities to support the learning process at home and at the school" (p. 9). This is a key step to ensure the varied developmental needs of the whole child will be addressed, and such involvement is integral to positive student achievement. Writing about the importance of parent involvement at middle level schools, Kochan (1992) argues that the focus of support for students should "encompass the needs of the young adolescent within the context of the culture in which he or she exists and in which he or she must function in the future" (p. 63). This context includes the home, the community, and eventually the workplace. Another Carnegie Council recommendation follows from this theme of addressing the spectrum of early adolescents' needs. It calls for middle schools that "connect schools with communities, which together share responsibility for each middle-grade student's success through identifying service opportunities in the community, establishing partnerships and collaborations to ensure students' access to health and social services, and using community resources to enrich the instructional program and opportunities for after-school activities" (p. 9-10).

The district plays an important role in forging these connections between parents and the community by involving families and community representatives in meaningful roles and positions, by coordinating services with community agencies and business partners, and by upholding the philosophy of parents as partners and the community as a classroom. Ultimately, the district sets the tone for how open and inviting schools are to families, community members, and business organizations. ❑

**LEADERSHIP STANDARD**

## 7. New leadership roles

**Develop a central office climate that engages staff in the schools and encourages leadership from all stakeholders.**

Leadership for district-wide middle-grades reform is sustained by the presence of a service orientation in the central office. A major theme in the school reform movement of the 1980s and 1990s is the call for more school level control and decision making. Traditionally, the district office has played a top-down, directive role in school reform mandating compliance, controlling decisions, regulating programs, and delivering and monitoring policy implementation. Decentralizing reform and restructuring require a new understanding of how district staff can most usefully be involved in schools and support reform efforts, as the image of the district as controller is no longer adequate. Hord and Smith (1993) captured a vision of this new district role concisely: "…in the decentralized district, the central office takes on the role of service provider or support agency. Central staff are no longer the sole authority figures, distributing directives and monitoring compliance. Instead they become active resources for, and facilitators of, school-level efforts for change" (p. 1).

To provide the support and leadership needed in successful reform efforts, the district can no longer focus upon mandating and controlling, but rather needs to act as coordinator, enabler, facilitator, coach, service provider, and technical assistant to schools. In this more diffuse view of leadership, all stakeholders can provide leadership. Essential elements of these new leadership roles required of a service-oriented central office include: a focus on vision and outcomes; shared decision making; consistent attention to what is best for students; district staff involvement at school sites; parents, teachers and students as leaders and change agents; site level autonomy and flexibility; emphasis on initiative; and district staff modeling of desired values. ❑

# SUPPORT

The best-articulated vision for middle-grades education will mean little unless it is implemented. To be significant, the vision must guide educators' work to improve student learning in classrooms and schools. The past 20 years of educational reform highlight the difficulty of implementing and sustaining deep changes to the system. Successful change efforts require support for the new roles, responsibilities, and skills required of all stakeholders. As Michael Fullan and Matthew Miles (1992) state:

> *Change is learning, loaded with uncertainty....Even well-developed innovations represent new meaning and new learning for those who encounter them initially and require time to assimilate them....Assistance may include training, consulting, coaching, co-ordination, and capacity-building. Many studies have suggested that good assistance to schools is strong, sustained over years, closely responsive to local needs, and focused on building local capacity. Louis and Miles found that at least 30 days a year of external assistance - with more than that provided internally – was essential for success.* —p. 749-750

Studies of successful implementation of school and classroom change emphasize the need for ongoing and sustained internal and external support as well as the coordination and problem-solving mechanisms to assist in the implementation of innovations. This support role relies on facilitative rather than directive leadership, to allow time for stakeholders to reach their own conclusions by networking with those at other schools, learning and practicing new skills, and monitoring and assessing their results.

Successful change is both top-down and bottom-up. District-wide support mechanisms for middle-grades reform can move the change process past isolated pockets of excellence, and bring together expertise from across the system. For the purpose of developing a district-wide plan and implementation of reform, district support must not come solely from district staff but must be driven by a steering committee or representative group that will bring teacher, principal, family member, student, and community perspectives to the table. The central office staff, however, through its vantage point in the district is in a unique position to provide overall guidance to a steering group. To be successfully implemented where it counts with students, the group's vision and plan will require the buy-in of a much broader group.

Based on the literature dealing with ways that districts can work with and help schools, several important standards for district-wide middle level support are apparent. Primarily, districts must provide the resources necessary to sustain improvement efforts. They must also coordinate improvement efforts across schools and programs so that successes are shared and schools are linked more efficiently with resources and information for renewal. Furthermore, districts support schools by sustaining a district culture in which continuous improvement is the norm, by offering a wide variety of staff development linked to student learning, through assisting schools in using data to develop site-specific improvement plans, and by maintaining core curriculum frameworks and guidelines. Finally, districts coordinate and monitor student support services.

**SUPPORT STANDARD**

# 8. Resources

**Provide financial and human resources necessary for the change process.**

Effective support entails providing adequate resources so schools can sustain and be successful in their change efforts. When the district takes on its new role as coordinator and facilitator, several aspects of this new role come into play. In addition to helping the district define its core beliefs and objectives, central office staff need to provide the resources necessary to achieve success. They also need to link schools to specific resources for renewal. Strategies for linking schools to renewal resources may include newsletters, teacher study groups, site visits, staff development, and identification of experts or model programs around the country.

Resources must be focused where they are most needed and allocated in light of specific school needs and improvement plans. Resources such as time, space, and scheduling are also critical. Involvement in reform requires additional resources, especially time, to learn and reflect on new skills and practices with other colleagues. The National Education Commission on Time and Learning (1994) found a need to fundamentally redefine the professional use of teachers' time in order to meet the reform goals of enabling students to meet high standards. "We recommend that teachers be provided with the professional time and opportunities they need to do their jobs" (p. 36)....To lock teachers into the existing system which defines a teacher's professional activity almost solely as the time spent in front of students in classrooms, is to guarantee failure" (p. 39), argued the report.

Further, schools must have significant decision-making powers and control over their budgets and over personnel configuration and hiring. This is particularly important at the middle level, as most middle school teachers were not specifically trained for this level. It has often been the placement of last choice. ❏

## SUPPORT STANDARD

## 9. Coordination/ communication

Provide mechanisms for coordination and communication among schools, grade levels, departments, and external constituencies.

Effective support ensures that effective lines of communication exist between and across schools, grade levels, teams and/or departments and entails coordinating improvement efforts. Typically teachers are isolated from one another most of the day. Rarely do they have the time or encouragement to visit each others' classes or to even talk about teaching and instruction with others. Principals also remain isolated, both from teachers and from other administrators in the district. Yet coordination, cooperation, and communication are keys to the success of schools and school districts. In her study of teaching cultures, Judith Warren Little (1993) found the development of a collegial culture to be a cornerstone of successful school-wide change to improve teaching and learning. Teachers look to colleagues for a variety of reasons. Johnson (1990) suggests that colleagues help teachers meet "their *personal needs* for social interaction, reassurance, and psychological support; their *instructional needs* for pedagogical advice and subject matter expertise; and their *organizational needs* for coordinating students' learning, socializing new staff, setting and upholding standards, and initiating and sustaining change" (p. 156).

Central office staff can play an important role in fostering collegiality, as they occupy a key vantage point for developing and facilitating structures for communication and strategic planning. They can provide this support by organizing study groups and networks for professional discussion and dialogue, ensuring that multi-role teams are involved in planning and developing clusters and plans for K-12 articulation. ❏

**SUPPORT STANDARD**

## 10. Information/research

Provide schools with current research on content and performance standards, teaching strategies, and practices that contribute to the academic and social development of young adolescents.

Effective support requires knowledge of current thinking and research on best practices. In the past two decades, a significant amount of research has been done on the educational and developmental needs of young adolescents. Educators now recognize early adolescence as a unique stage as youngsters make the transition from childhood into adolescence. Ten to fifteen-year-olds have particular developmental, social, emotional, and physical needs different from those of elementary and secondary students. The middle school movement grew out of a recognition of these needs. In the 1980s the burgeoning middle school movement received impetus from a variety of foundations who earmarked money for research on early adolescence. One prime example culminated with the publication of *Turning Points: Preparing American Youth for the 21st Century* (1989), the seminal middle school resource. According to Holmes (1994) "*Turning Points* was and is regarded as a compelling call for the focusing of national attention on middle-grades education as well as a blueprint for structure and policy of middle-grades schools and their communities, emphasizing the unique needs of the young adolescent learner" (p. 3). Several conditions important to middle schools were identified in *Turning Points*, including teams of teachers and students, advisory periods, core middle-grades academic content, interdisciplinary curriculum and instruction, and flexible grouping and scheduling. While these are not new ideas, each has its own body of research and information on how it can most effectively be implemented in practice.

To support middle schools adequately, the district must provide schools with access to this growing body of knowledge. This is particularly important at the middle level, where there is a growing, but too often neglected, research base undergirding the middle school concept and detailing practices that best meet the varied needs of early adolescents. Districts can assist schools by helping them use the knowledge base to guide all decision making by engaging faculty in action research projects, and by linking research at the district level to state and national projects and networks. ❑

## SUPPORT STANDARD

## 11. Culture

**Model and sustain a culture of continuous improvement.**

Effective support entails building a culture in which improvement is the norm. The culture of a school or school district refers to the collective character or dynamics of the people involved, as well as the beliefs, values, traditions, and practices accepted by group members. It is reflected in the way things are done and defines what is possible. Deal and Peterson (1990) define culture as an "invisible, taken-for-granted flow of beliefs and assumptions that give meaning to what people say and do...(and) consists of the stable, underlying social meanings that shape beliefs and behavior over time" (p. 7). As the underlying school and district culture is a strong determinant of the beliefs and practices of the individuals involved, it also serves to shape how these individuals will respond to new initiatives and change efforts. Rossman, Corbett and Firestone (1988) argue "that the acceptance of improvement projects at the building level and the 'effectiveness' of that school depend in profound ways on the existing school culture" (p. 1). This is true too at the district level, where district staff set the tone for how school-based efforts will be received and for modeling and supporting continuous improvement throughout the district.

It is thus essential that the district establish a pervasive district culture that makes continuous improvement the norm and fosters this type of culture in several key ways. First, it can reward responsible risk taking, rather than compliance to stagnant norms. Second, it can encourage collegial sharing among faculties and school staffs both within and across schools. Third, it can create opportunities for faculty and staff renewal by encouraging leadership, initiative, research, and exploration. Fourth, it can model desired behaviors as lifelong learners. And finally, it can encourage cross-role sharing, which allows people to get a better understanding of how things are done throughout the district and can be fostered. ❑

## SUPPORT STANDARD

# 12. Staff development

**Provide staff development based on the district plan, school plans, and proven models for individual and organizational change.**

Effective support calls for sustained staff development for all stakeholders involved in improvement efforts. In the past, educators viewed staff development in a very piecemeal way, with passive, one-shot workshops with limited follow-up being the typical pattern for staff development. However, staff renewal as a tool for ongoing and systematic learning for all those involved with students, not just teachers, and aligned with specific school needs and improvement plans has become more and more the ideal. Much has been done in recent years about the role that staff development plays in the continuous improvement of schools and districts. In 1994, the National Staff Development Council offered a series of standards for staff development at the middle level organized into three different categories: context, process, and content. Context standards address the type of climate and culture necessary for continuous improvement. They are based on the assumption that "some contexts are more supportive to improvement than others." Process standards highlight the "how-to," or the means for acquiring new knowledge, involving "group development, follow-up and support, and evaluation." Content standards are the "actual skill and knowledge effective middle-level educators need to possess or acquire through staff development" (p. 1).

This organization reflects an understanding of staff development as ongoing, featuring intensive follow-up and requiring adequate support. Epstein, Lockard, and Dauber (1991) believe that middle-grades staff development should: improve middle schools by fostering the creation of a positive school culture which supports the staff working together as a group and relating better with community; assist middle-grades teachers by "increasing their knowledge (content), skills (pedagogy), and understanding of early adolescence" and of school structures which best support middle-graders; and promote the success of early adolescents by "increasing student learning and development through more effective teaching and more responsive school organization" (p. 40).

The district plays an important role in staff development by making it a district priority, allocating time and resources, offering several different types and models of staff development, ensuring appropriate follow up and implementation, and making sure that school level development and improvement plans are aligned with broad district goals for the middle level. ❑

**SUPPORT STANDARD**

## 13. School improvement planning

Provide schools with data and assistance to assess their current state, and develop and implement improvement plans.

Effective support attends to the need for schools to develop site-specific improvement plans. School improvement planning involves developing a process by which school staffs evaluate their programs, determine where changes could be made to increase student performance, implement carefully thought out strategies for reform, and systematically review and update these plans. In a study of school improvement efforts, David and Peterson (1984) found that schools are able to establish a viable improvement process if they focus on instructional content and are provided support for change (p. 81). They identify three conditions that greatly increase the likelihood improvement planning will result in positive changes: a climate which supports change efforts, instructional leadership in the planning and review process, and support from the outside, particularly the district. They suggest that active support from the district "includes incentives for improvement, relief from rules and demands that severely constrain what the school can do, and allowance for success and failure on several dimensions. Instructional improvement is not fostered by asking schools to plan their own reforms while simultaneously requiring them to administer frequent district and state tests which are tied to a particular curriculum" (p. 83).

Support from the district is essential to ensure that schools have the knowledge and resources needed to assess their current state and develop and implement site-specific improvement plans. The district also plays a supportive role by helping schools collect and analyze data, targeting low performing schools for additional assistance, and by freeing up district staff to act as facilitators of the improvement process and to work with all stakeholders in developing improvement plans. ❑

**SUPPORT STANDARD**

## 14. Core curriculum & instruction

**Establish core middle-grades curriculum that enables students to meet the content standards for eighth grade.**

Effective support involves guidelines for creating core curriculum and instruction to ensure all students can meet content standards. Beane (1993) addresses the basic question of what a middle school curriculum should look like and offers a number of thoughts on how to respond to the diverse needs of early adolescents. He says first, the curriculum must relate to "the characteristics of early adolescents, their relation to the world around them, and their prospects in it" (p. 85). Second, it should be developed collaboratively, with middle school students actively involved in planning. Third, grouping should be heterogeneous as "such labels as 'gifted' or 'learning disabled' would have no meaning since they are products of the subject curriculum and adult value systems" (p. 92) and do not emerge from the characteristics and needs of early adolescents. And fourth, "the middle school ought to be a general education school with a coherent, unified, and complete curriculum" (p. 71). These ideals highlight the importance of providing developmentally appropriate materials for middle school students, offering diverse instructional materials that address the needs of students of all ability levels and cultures, and of creating integrated curriculums that are carefully developed and evaluated.

The district plays an important role here by providing support and resource personnel to schools and by helping to establish frameworks for what students should know and be able to do by the time they complete eighth grade. These content frameworks give guidance and direction to curriculum decision making. The district also provides professional materials and offers guidance in curriculum development, implementation, and assessment. ❑

**SUPPORT STANDARD**

## 15. Student services

**Develop plans to address individual student needs that recognize student diversity and are based on current research and practices.**

Leadership for district-wide middle-grades reform recognizes the diversity of student needs and provides student services accordingly. Diversity in the student population is becoming more and more apparent in schools throughout the country. Today's classrooms contain a mix of students from different ethnic groups, races, cultures, economic classes, and religions, as well as many students whose first language is not English. This diversity has made planning for curriculum and instruction much more difficult.

To respond effectively to this diversity and assure success for all, districts and schools need to make sure that all teachers understand diverse student needs and then sufficiently support these teachers in their efforts to provide meaningful learning opportunities for all. Carbo (1995) argues that "the influx into mainstream America of large numbers of students from a variety of cultures calls for *schools* to adapt to their new clientele, not for students to adapt to schools" (p. 6). This adaptation requires that exceptional education services be integrated into the mainstream curriculum, that developmentally appropriate materials be provided in all subject areas, and that a diversity of curriculum resources be available to match the strengths and experiences of all young adolescents. Carbo adds that a new paradigm of schooling "would recognize students for their abilities in their primary language; would identify and accommodate students' learning style strengths; would encourage students and teacher to learn from each other; would set consistently high expectations for success; and would allow students, teachers, parents, and the entire community to act as mutual resources for learning" (p. 6-7). Ultimately, what is necessary is a broader view of how student needs are planned for, one based on the fundamental belief that all students can achieve at high levels and that services need to be individualized to meet each student's particular needs. ❑

## ACCOUNTABILITY

District leadership in system-wide school reform is undergirded by mechanisms that support schools. At heart, the related accountability involves holding the district and schools responsible for instructional processes, professional and research-based practices, and outcomes. Districts play a significant role in ensuring accountability, particularly through the comprehensive, system-wide collection and monitoring of varied sources of student performance data. Mauriel (1989) usefully defines accountability as:

> ...the responsibility and obligation that the superintendent and the school system have to multiple stakeholder groups, including the obligation to use resources entrusted to them in a manner prescribed by law and regulation, to pursue the goals and mission and purposes of the school system and its stakeholders as approved by the school board, and to report in a clear, concise and comprehensive manner at regular intervals to different stakeholder groups on the state of and strategic plans for the school system. — p. 288

This definition underscores the importance of schools and districts making goals and expectations explicit so that school staff and district personnel can explain their practices and results can be measured against them. Additionally, Darling-Hammond (1992) offers that creating successful accountability systems requires districts to correct practices that are not in the best interest of students. She claims,

> Accountability is achieved when a school's, school system's, and state's policies and operating practices work both to provide good education and to correct problems as they occur. There must also be methods for changing school practices – even totally rethinking certain aspects of schooling – if they are not working well on behalf of students. — p.11

In an era characterized by increased calls for school reform along with shifting roles and responsibilities, stakeholders at all levels want and need to know how schools are doing, how are they meeting their goals, and what changes need to be made.

A variety of ways are available for districts to structure meaningful accountability systems. While in the past standardized tests scores were the predominant means of determining accountability, new forms of assessment and more school-based decision making necessitate that new ways be employed to show how schools and districts are meeting their goals. Both qualitative and quantitative measures, reports on site visits, personal inspections of teaching practices and instructional goals, and demonstration of results are highlighted. Darling-Hammond (1992) adds that an expanded notion of accountability is sustained by a "duty of care" owed to parents and students by schools and districts. This is a "duty to treat students well and responsibly, to provide them equal access to educational opportunities, to adhere to professional standards of practice, and to use the best available knowledge in developing appropriate strategies for teaching each child" (p. 5).

While individual schools must be held responsible for student achievement, it is equally important that they are supported in their efforts. District-wide leadership in achieving greater accountability is thus critical. Districts can help provide accountability by:
- Articulating system-wide goals, expectations, and intent to use outcome data;
- Following up on the implementation and success of improvement plans;
- Ensuring that performance data are used systematically to evaluate programs for the purposes of continuous improvement;
- Maintaining flexibility and adapting to the changing needs of individual schools;
- Enabling greater school-level involvement in monitoring processes;
- Intervening in failing schools; and
- Providing both material and personnel support in the review and assessment of goals and performance data from system schools.

In discussing the need for new forms of accountability in the *California Tomorrow* publication, Olsen and associates (1994) highlight the integral role districts play in supporting schools' efforts and in providing for system-wide accountability. They suggest that "as the restructuring movement progresses...it is only through strong data systems, reflective processes and external accountability that reform efforts will hold themselves to delivering schools that work for all children" (p. 290). The district's efforts are critical in providing for these accountability systems that support school-based efforts. Additionally, Wheelock (1995) argues that "accountability policies should be part of a broader school reform strategy that strives to ensure that all students, regardless of where they live, which school they attend, or the social circumstances in which they find themselves, receive a high quality education" (p. 3).

To create effective district-wide accountability systems, the following three standards are important.

**ACCOUNTABILITY STANDARD**

# 16. Student assessment

**Assess student performance using multiple sources and compare to benchmarks for what students should know and be able to do.**

Meeting the standards of best practices necessitates systematic, multi-sourced student assessment. All school and district improvement efforts are directed toward improving student achievement. In order to determine how students are performing, if they are achieving benchmark standards, and if improvement is occurring, regular assessment is essential. Over the past several years the many weaknesses of traditional means of assessing have become apparent. Short-answer tests do not gauge true understanding and instead focus upon lower-order thinking skills. Alternative assessment philosophies have taken center stage. Two concepts emerge from the writings: student performance needs to be measured in multiple ways and formats, and the benchmarks, rubrics, or standards that clarify expectations and performance criteria need to be developed.

The district can support schools in implementing these varied methods of assessing student progress in several ways. First, it can work with schools, families, and community members in order to set standards for performance that are specific to the middle-grades, attend to content deemed important, and take into account an in-depth understanding of early adolescent development. Second, the district can give schools the latitude to experiment with different forms of assessment and the time to truly measure their effectiveness. And third, the district can help schools to better understand alternative forms of assessment by providing in a resource center a wide variety of assessment materials for different subjects and grade levels, examples of design criteria; case studies of experimentation with alternative assessment from both the district and beyond; and information about staff development activities related to assessment, study groups, and resource teachers. ❑

## ACCOUNTABILITY STANDARD

## 17. Program assessment

**Gather and analyze data with input from central office staff and stakeholders for use in evaluating and planning school improvement programs and environments.**

Accountability entails routine program assessment to determine the effectiveness of school programs and the success of improvement efforts. In their discussion of assessment of middle level programs and practices, Clark and Clark (1994) argue that evaluation and assessment of middle level programs provide four key pieces of information: (1) insights into the dynamics of how programs are operating, (2) data on the extent to which they are serving various constituencies, (3) information which helps to identify strengths and weaknesses, and (4) material on cost effectiveness of programs. Further, evaluation serves to assist in decision making, setting priorities, and determining both the effectiveness and satisfaction level of innovations aimed at student improvement.

A number of important criteria for quality program assessment exist. First, there has to be ample time for faculty and staff evaluation and reflection. Second, the district needs to work with schools to establish assessments that are viable, and to help gather and interpret data. Third, program assessment needs to have a meaningful rationale and should be primarily based on results for students and staff. Fourth, comparable to student assessment, it is important that program assessment be multi-sourced, and that both qualitative and quantitative measures are used. Finally, it is essential that criteria be based on an understanding of early adolescent development and best middle-grades practices. Ultimately, regular and systematic program assessment assures that data on effectiveness are gathered and used for the purposes of continuous improvement. ❑

**ACCOUNTABILITY STANDARD**

## 18. Systems assessment

Review and align district practices with the articulated vision, reform plans, accountability mechanisms, and school and community needs.

Accountability involves routinely examining the workings of the whole district, including the central office, to ensure that the system operates in the best interest of students. Just as student and program assessment are essential for measuring gains in student achievement and program effectiveness, systems assessment is integral to ensuring that the district as a whole is functioning adequately, that district plans are systematically reviewed and updated, and that district policies and practices consistently serve to support schools. In describing evaluative criteria for the central office, the National Study of School Evaluation (1994) suggests that "an educational unit like a central office, should be judged in terms of what it is striving to achieve (its philosophy, mission and goals) within a particular situation (context) of the school and community that it serves" (p. 2).

In her discussion of systems evaluation, Jenks (1994) maintains that "the evaluation focus must be expanded to the entire educational system – as a system – rather than being limited to what is more traditionally done – evaluating programs or components of the system for their worth" (p. 36). Systems assessment recognizes the interdependency and interrelatedness of programs and practices throughout the district and attends to the fact that piecemeal assessment of parts of the system must be linked to an overall assessment of the vision, policies, plans, and practices of the district as a whole. Only then can the district be held accountable to these plans, to stakeholders, and to student and program achievement standards and expectations. ❑

# References

Beane, J. A. (1993). *A middle school curriculum: From Rhetoric to reality* (Second Edition). Columbus, OH: National Middle School Association.

Carbo, M. (1995). Educating everybody's children. In Robert W. Cole (Ed.), *Education everybody's children: Diverse teaching strategies for diverse learners*. Alexandria, VA: Association for Supervision and Curriculum Development.

Carnegie Council on Adolescent Development (1989). *Turning points: Preparing American youth for the 21st century.* New York: Carnegie Corporation.

Clark, S. N., & Clark, D. C. (1994). Evaluating middle level programs and practices. In *Restructuring the middle level school: Implications for school leaders* (pp. 268-288). Albany, NY: State University of New York Press.

Darling-Hammond, L. (1992). *Standards of practice for learner-centered schools.* New York: NCREST.

David, J. L., & Peterson, S. M. (1984). *Can schools improve themselves? A study of school-based improvement programs.* Palo Alto, CA: Bay Area Research Group.

Deal, T. E., & Peterson, K. D. (1990). *The principal's role in shaping school culture.* Washington, DC: The U.S. Department of Education.

Deal, T. E., & Peterson, K. D. (1994). *The leadership paradox: Balancing logic and artistry in schools.* San Francisco: Jossey-Bass.

Education Commission of the States (1991). *Exploring policy options to restructure education.* Denver, CO: Author.

Epstein, J. L., Lockard, B. L., & Dauber, S. L. (1991). Staff development for middle school education. *Journal of Staff Development, 12* (1), 36-41.

Fullan, M. G., & Miles, Matthew B. (1992). Getting reform right: What works and what doesn't. *Phi Delta Kappan, 73* (10), 745-752.

George, P. S., & Alexander, William M. (1993). *The exemplary middle school* (Second Edition). Fort Worth, TX: Harcourt Brace College Publishers.

Holmes, P. (1994). *Critical issues in middle school reform: Structuring school for the young adolescent learner.* Philadelphia: PATHS/PRISM: The Philadelphia Partnership for Education.

Hord, S.M., & Smith, A. (1993). Will our phones go dead? The changing role of the central office. *Issues ... about Change, 2* (4).

Jenks, L.C. (1994). Evaluating an educational system systematically. In C. M. Reigeluth & R.J. Garfinkle (Eds.), *Systemic change in education.* Englewood Cliffs, NJ: Educational Technology Publications.

Johnson, S.M. (1990). *Teachers at work: Achieving success in our schools.* New York: Basic Books, Inc.

Kaufman, R., & Herman, J. (1991). *Strategic planning in education: Rethinking, restructuring, revitalizing.* Lancaster, PA: Technomic Publishing Co.

Keefe, J.W., Valentine, J., Clark, D.C., & Irvin, J.L. (1994). *Leadership in middle level education, Volume II: Leadership in successfully restructuring middle level schools.* Reston, VA: National Association of Secondary School Principals.

Kochan, F.K. (1992). A new paradigm of schooling: Connecting school, home, and community. In J.L. Irvin (Ed.), *Transforming middle level education: Perspectives and possibilities.* Boston: Allyn and Bacon.

Little, J.W. (1993). *Teachers' professional development in a climate of educational reform.* (Reprint Series). Columbia University. New York: Teachers College. National Center for Restructuring Education, Schools and Teaching.

Mauriel, J.J. (1989). *Strategic leadership for schools: Creating and sustaining productive change.* San Francisco: Jossey-Bass Publishers.

Mizell, H. (1992, October). *New wagons for a rugged trail.* Talk presented at Conference for Program for Disadvantaged Youth Grantees, Milwaukee, Wisconsin.

Mojkowski, C. (1991). *Developing leaders for restructuring schools: New habits of mind and heart.* Washington, DC: U.S. Department of Education.

National Education Commission on Time and Learning. (1994). *Prisoners of time research: What we know and what we need to know.* Washington, DC: U.S. Government Printing Office.

National Staff Development Council. (1994). *National Staff Development Council's standards for staff development: Middle level edition.* Oxford, OH: Author.

National Study of School Evaluation. (1991). *Central office evaluative criteria (Revised).* Falls Church, VA: Author.

Olsen, L., Chang, H., De La Rosa Salazar, D., Leong, C., McCall Perez, Z., McLain, G., & Raffel, L. (1994). *The unfinished journey: Restructuring schools in a diverse society.* San Francisco: California Tomorrow.

Patterson, J. L. (1993). *Leadership for tomorrow's schools.* Alexandria, VA: Association for Supervision and Curriculum Development.

Reavis, C., & Griffith, H. (1992). *Restructuring schools: Theory and practice.* Lancaster, PA: Technomic Publishing Co., Inc.

Rossman, G.B., Corbett, H.D., & Firestone, W.A. (1988). *Change and effectiveness in schools: A cultural perspective.* Albany, NY: State University of New York Press.

U.S. Department of Education. (1994, June). *High standards for all students.* Washington, DC: Author.

Wheelock, A. (1995, May 30). *School rewards, school accountability, and school reform.* Essay prepared for the Carnegie Task Force on Learning in the Primary Grades.

# 3.
## Findings from Planning and Conducting Audits

From 1994-1996, the District Middle-Grades Reform Project staff piloted the audit with five diverse urban districts: Minneapolis, Minnesota; Jefferson County, Kentucky; San Diego, California; Corpus Christi, Texas; and Atlanta, Georgia. After each audit, materials and procedures were updated and refined, and the process systematized. Chapters 5-8 are case studies of four of the five systems. They describe in ample detail the experiences in those cities. In this chapter the key lessons learned from these urban school audits are presented.

District middle-grades education reform is complex and requires balancing seemingly contradictory principles of systemic change. Eleven key themes emerged related to the leadership, support, and accountability for a system of high-performing schools. These themes, along with recommendations and specific examples from each of the districts are summarized in Chapter 4. The overarching finding from the entire project is a lesson that must be taken to heart by educators. Stated simply it is that ***reforming middle-grades education to improve student achievement means changing the whole system, not just schools.*** Central office staff and leaders from every constituency group can best facilitate reform by modeling themselves the beliefs, practices, and shared power relationships that we want to see in high-performing schools and by creating environments and networks that foster the growth of a community of learners and leaders across the system.

The practice and use of the audit and planning tools did not always go as planned. In three of the districts described the audit was conducted by an external team. For the most part they planned the agenda, site visits, and questions with a local steering committee already engaged in planning for an implementation proposal related to standards-based reform. The steering committees varied in their use of the final report. Most did not disseminate the results and recommendations widely, nor formally use the data for study in the proposal planning process. This may be partly due to our assumption that the steering committee or convenor would consult with our staff on how to utilize the audit report in its planning. Thus, we did not outline a specific method to share the data or a timeline on when this should be done. We relied on personal communication with a main audit convenor. We did conduct phone consultation with the central office audit convenor and proposed ways that the report could be disseminated and used to guide public discussion. These failings may be due to the timing of the assessments, which came late in the planning year when local leaders were preoccupied with developing their proposals, and were overwhelmed with other responsibilties. In addition, our staff was focused on the development and revision of the actual assessment tool and summarizing process, including a useful report format.

In Atlanta, our staff was contracted to train a local audit team, co-lead the audit, and assist in utilizing the data with the planning group. We knew from the beginning that we would come back to help lead the planning process. This work was co-facilitated by an Executive Director for Middle Schools, and a staff person from the Southern Regional Council. In addition, the local volunteer audit team and members of the Middle School Advisory Council provided external impetus for the audit results to be broadly released and acted upon. This process was conducted in a way very similar to our original vision for the audit tool.

> District assessment can be a powerful tool to unite diverse constituencies on a common understanding of middle-grades reform.

District assessment can be a powerful tool to unite diverse constituencies on a common understanding of middle-grades reform and to agree on a common reform agenda. It provides a vehicle for common work, builds a team, and leads to improved student learning. However, it should be conducted in an inclusive fashion that includes perspective of all stakeholders and external colleagues if followed by action on specific recommendations.

In our assessment and study of district middle-grades reform we learned a great deal about the district infrastructure necessary to lead, support, and be accountable for a system of high-performing middle-grades schools. We also learned a great deal about how to best use the audit tool and planning process so that it enhances that district infrastructure. These lessons are products of what didn't go as planned, as well as what went well. While the lessons came about from our specific experience developing and piloting the Middle-Grades Reform Audit, they are applicable to the use of other assessment and planning tools for the whole district. The data for these findings come from our own experience and field notes, from post interviews and surveys with the fifteen people who conducted the pilots, interviews with the district leaders and participants in the audit, and from feedback on the use of district assessments (of any kind) with middle-grades reform leaders from 17 urban districts across the country. Atlanta was the only district in which we were directly involved and helped lead the use of the audit data to create a plan, thus it is the only district in which we have first-hand evidence on the use of the data. The recipients of the reports felt that the report captured the district's strengths and challenges related to district reform and provided a wealth of concrete recommendations.

What we learned from planning and conducting audits can be summarized in eight major findings. These are identified and elaborated on in the pages following.

**1. The use of a participatory assessment and planning process contributes to developing a district culture for student achievement.**

Beyond the specific data gathered and the plan developed, the audit and planning processes create a district infrastructure for middle-grades reform by:

*A. Developing a common vision, language, and knowledge base of the process and content of middle-grades reform to increase student achievement.*

Educational terms can devolve quickly into jargon, leading to confusion about the rationale, content, and application of reform efforts. Reading and engaging in discussion of the research-supported district reform standards helped members of the assessment team and Advisory Council develop a common language and the context needed to support middle school improvement. As team members visited schools together, their informal conversation between interviews and observations deepened their own understanding of the effective components of a middle-grades systemic reform initiative. In addition, those being interviewed often commented that the questions the team asked caused them to step back and think about their goals and "the bigger picture of middle-grades education."

"You think you are all alone at your school with your problems and day-to-day concerns. Then I heard the audit findings and I realized we have so much in common with other schools. We really need to pull together," stated one teacher who participated in a community meeting in Atlanta. Developing criteria for an assessment makes an abstract concept, such as vision, become tangible, and vague reform ideas become more manageable.

*B. Developing consensus about the current state of the district that includes diverse perspectives.*

As Fullan and Miles (1992) explain, "Change goes best when it is carried out by a cross-role group...In such a group different worlds collide, more learning occurs, and change is realistically managed" (p. 751). Conducting a district assessment which involves prioritizing the results with all stakeholder groups models respect for the input of all groups and surfaces traditionally locked-out perspectives. Assessment team members often were surprised by the clarity of student views on the school and system. Their views rarely are heard or given weight at this level. Cross-role groups break down the traditional isolation fostered by large bureaucratic school systems. Members of all groups are at the table to share their views on issues. Through this dialogue, common understandings and goals begin to emerge.

*C. Learning to use varied assessment techniques, analyze data, and base action plans on key findings.*

Data-based decision making is the key to effective change. The Atlanta audit team members each brought varied experience in conducting qualitative evaluations. The one-day training and ongoing discussions following each interview allowed the audit team members to practice and improve their interview and observation techniques. Learning varied assessment techniques and carrying out a district audit increase the skills of staff to conduct assessments at their own schools. Team members especially, but also those who helped prioritize the recommendations or facilitated a community meeting, voiced the benefits of seeing the big picture of middle-grades education in the district. They also learned how to conduct a self-assessment and develop a three-year plan with the involvement of a broad range of interest groups.

### D. Building a culture based on open discussion of strengths and challenges.

Inviting an external team, as well as diverse local stakeholders, to review the whole system may seem politically risky, however it is one way to create the open atmosphere crucial to successful change efforts. In a study of urban schools' styles of coping with problems, Louis and Miles (1990) found that successful schools did not have fewer problems than other schools – they just coped with them better. When the district leadership models openness and problem solving, a culture of continuous improvement is demonstrated through actions, not exhortations. Individual school leaders and teachers may then be more willing to take risks as well.

| | |
|---|---|
| **2. The audit standards provide a valid framework to assess the district infrastructure to lead, support, and be accountable for middle-grades reform.** | The fifteen diverse team members who piloted and/or were trained to conduct the audit found the 18 standards and summaries a useful framework to guide their assessment of the district. The standards provided enough separate categories to look at each aspect of the system while the three overriding themes of leadership, support, and accountability also helped to organize broad categories of similar functions and recommendations. In one district, the team felt that four large themes (which were also subsumed under the 18 standards) emerged so strongly that they needed to be expressed in the overall executive summary in addition to their appearance as parts of the 18 standards and the constituency summaries and recommendations. (These are discussed in the Atlanta study chapter.) They also felt that the standards were broad enough to allow us to tailor the assessment to capture specific questions that a district might have about its reform goals. |
| **3. The audit tools proved reliable when used by diverse audit team members.** | The first two district audit pilots were conducted by five diverse educators who had worked with our project over the previous three years. They included a former middle-grades principal and central office staff leader, a staff developer and former central office leader, a middle-grades community social service partner, a former middle school science and bilingual teacher and leader of middle school integration and at-risk programs, and a qualitative researcher. Three of the team members developed the audit tools and process, and the other two had reviewed the materials and made suggestions prior to the site visits. They independently found similar results using the interview protocols and the summarizing sheets. The methods of summarizing the data were refined and streamlined after each pilot. We |

expected this type of reliability in a group that had worked together for some time and had quite a bit of agreement on the goals and practice of middle-grades reform at the district level. In the third and fourth audits we added three team members, each of whom was a central office staff member guiding middle grades education reform. They also used the interview protocols and data summarizing forms very similarly. At the fifth audit we trained a local team to conduct the audit under the leadership of three of the original team, the developers, and a long-time consultant with the project. This group in Atlanta represented very diverse constituencies. They conducted the audit on the first day led by one of the original team members. After that the group split up into pairs that rotated for the rest of the audit. Each team member's individual summaries had great overlap and coincidence in findings, with the exception of a few recommendations, which will vary based on the audit member's expertise and point of view. Based on this experience the audit instrument is quite reliable when the training and leadership are provided by a member of the staff of the District Middle Grades Reform Project and an experienced team leader summarizes the data in the report.

**4. Utilize both internal and external assessment processes to provide outside perspective and inside buy-in.**

An external assessment of the district provides the advantages of credibility, objectivity, rapid results, and avoidance of political issues that may skew the findings and recommendations. Its disadvantages are that the assessment criteria and values may not dovetail with those of the district, that the report often becomes an artifact rather than a data source for local use, the costs may be high, and there is less buy-in to the report by implementers when the assessment is conducted completely by outsiders. A totally internal assessment provides the advantage of extensive ownership, the process becomes a form of professional development, and the assessment can be tailored to the district's specific needs and concerns. The disadvantages are the lack of external perspective and information, the extensive time it takes to conduct the assessment internally, and the suspicion that the data may not be objective if gathered internally. Thus, we recommend a combination of external and internal assessment. The external aspect signals the importance of the task, provides guidance and specific expertise to jump start the process. The internal aspect will help to build a common understanding of the current state and provide buy-in to taking action by those who actively participate in conducting the audit as well as by district and school leaders. These can be combined to include external audit team leaders and trainers from outside the district; a local audit team of those involved in, but not employed by, the school system; and a planning process led by all stakeholder groups, but that engages teachers and principals particularly in prioritizing recommendations and implementing the plan for improvement. This process was described in detail in Atlanta's case study (Chapter 5).

| | |
|---|---|
| **5. Use the assessment to guide action** | School systems often contract for external audits. These audit reports, nicely bound, grace bookshelves throughout the district. Such reports may not be widely distributed and usually are not discussed sufficiently to gain consensus on the report's findings and recommendations. They may lead to administrative action, but are often not formally studied with varied stakeholders. In the worst case scenario, the report is not used at all to inform practice. Assessments that do not lead to action waste precious energy and resources. They fuel cynicism and mistruct of the system. The inclusion of diverse constituency representatives on the assessment team or planning group provides safeguards to ensure that the plans will lead to action. For example, in one case, the results of a school's self-assessment were carefully protected by the teachers on the assessment team, even though the principal did not act on the recommendations. They continued to present the recommendations for action. Ultimately they waited three years for a new principal who was more amenable to change to openly revise the assessment results.<br><br>Self-assessments provide greater ownership yet require tremendous time to complete effectively. Balance the planning and assessment with visible actions so the group doesn't run out of steam before reaching the implementation phase. Timing the assessment so that some initial changes can be made before the end of the school year will help maintain momentum. |
| **6. Adapt and adopt premade tools and processes.** | The development of a reliable assessment tool is resource-intensive. Many good tools exist and are easily obtainable. Our project staff located over ten middle school assessment tools. Fewer district assessments exist, but some processes are available. (Some school assessment tools are indicated in Part II.) Make sure that the assessment's criteria, philosophy, and process fit with your district's goals or the data gathered will not be helpful to you. |
| **7. Include district, school, and student assessments in planning for systemic reform.** | A whole district assessment such as the Middle-Grades Reform Audit does not substitute for individual school assessments. It will not lead to individual school improvement plans, except in the major priority areas that will be implemented district-wide. All of these assessments should align with each other and provide additional, not redundant, data collection and analysis. |
| **8. Keep widening the circle.** | A district assessment and planning process can involve large numbers of people in significant, but manageable, roles. By the end of the Atlanta audit and planning process, over 1000 people were involved in one or more phases of the work. In addition, broad dissemination of the plan, findings, and actions throughout the community allows increasing numbers to learn about the initiative's results. |

## References

Fullan, M.G., & Miles, M.B. (1992). Getting reform right: What works and what doesn't. *Phi Delta Kappan, 73* (10), 744-752.

Louis, S.L., & Miles, M.B. (1990). *Improving the urban high school: What works and why*. New York: Teachers College Press.

# 4.
## Mobilizing Resources: Lessons Learned

The four district cases described in Chapters 5-8 represent systems across the country engaged in standards-based reform. They are striving for new, more effective ways to scale up reform for middle-grades student achievement, going beyond pilots and individual schools of excellence. None has effectively addressed all of the challenges. They are still grappling with the difficulties of educational reform. Their experiences indicate that effective change projects demand leaders who can maintain a delicate balance between seemingly contradictory processes. Effective reforms are both bottom-up and top-down, require both pressure and support for implementation, and must begin with small, concrete steps towards a large, systemic vision. The process is multi-dimensional and slow to complete.

### Complexity of systemic change

The cases illustrate the complex nature of systemic middle-grades reform. Supportive national, state, and local education policy contexts rarely align with a district culture and structures to effectively lead, support, and be accountable for student performance, individual school transformation, and systemic change. State-wide efforts to align policies and practice in curriculum, instruction, assessment, school organization, and staffing – such as those in California in the early 1990s – often are casualties of today's volatile political climate surrounding education. Thus, different parts of the system unintentionally work at cross-purposes. Leadership, particularly in urban districts, changes frequently, leading to the rapid shifting and abandonment of initiatives. Leadership personnel are reassigned with little regard for the long-term needs of systemic change. It is no surprise, then, that many principals, teachers, and families view large-scale reform with a skeptical eye. Principals seek to protect their schools, and teachers their classrooms, from the volatile and often unexpected consequences of systemic reform. Thus, educators' resistance to jump on board new reform bandwagons may be based on an informed assessment of the particular reform's expected life span, the presence (or absence) of resources to support its implementation, and/or potential student benefits, rather than on a blanket aversion to change.

Longtime central office middle management staff may publicly support a particular reform agenda but privately hedge their bets, knowing that they must be prepared to rapidly readjust their priorities and job responsibilities to maintain their positions in a changing organizational structure. This cynicism about the authenticity of reform rhetoric and policy pervades urban school districts. Combined with any large bureaucratic organization's inertia to change, this climate creates significant obstacles to sustained district progress towards a system of high-achieving schools. For these reasons, many failed reforms result more from the inability to gain a critical mass of effective implementation than from flaws in the innovation itself. Should we then abandon systemic change efforts, retreating to a focus on individual schools' improvement alone? Many reformers would argue that position. Yet the greater system, including the education political climate and policies, affects individual schools and classrooms, whether or not educators engage that system. The history of failed reforms includes myriad stories of effective programs and schools derailed by unexpected events. Assessment of the systemic forces that may impact – positively or negatively – middle-grades education reform will allow school-based leaders and their allies to proactively engage the drivers of the reform. In addition, they can anticipate and plan how to overcome potential barriers to the change effort.

> ...many failed reforms result more from the inability to gain a critical mass of effective implementation than from flaws in the innovation itself.

In districts with large numbers of students for whom the system does not work, the complete decentralization of education reform to individual schools may further exacerbate the inequities of opportunities to learn within the system. While small experimental schools flourish, the majority of students have no choice but to attend a school with inferior educational materials, facilities, and teaching, where the opportunities to excel are limited to a chosen few. The large numbers of children impacted daily by these inequities calls for urgent attention. We must learn how to effectively maximize the creative innovation that is unleashed under school-based planning, while maintaining an overall vision of one system, working together to effectively educate all its students.

## Common Lessons About Systemic Change at the District Level

Through our work with different districts we sought to move beyond the reform rhetoric and to gather practical strategies and meaningful examples that could inform other change leaders as they engage in district middle-grades reform. In these four cases, and from many recent studies of systemic change to improve student achievement, common lessons emerged. These lessons contribute to a growing understanding of how to effectively mobilize school systems to improve student achievement, and particularly how to address gaps in achievement across groups by race, socioeconomic status, and gender. The lessons derive as much from the mishaps and barriers overcome as from the successes. In this chapter, we summarize some of our common findings and describe promising practices, particularly those that address typical barriers to systemic change in urban and other large school systems.

These lessons are expressed as concerns, as questions. Each one is followed by a recommendation for how to address the concern, more details about its theme, and examples of how districts are addressing this question. Concerns 1-4 relate to key areas of leadership.

## LEADERSHIP

CONCERN 1 —

Where is the district site-based management group?

**RECOMMENDATION:**

***District leaders must provide significant roles and common work for all stakeholders in district planning, decision making, and in implementing changes to improve student achievement.***

The implementation of site-based decision making and autonomy varied greatly among the four sites, from very centrally managed to almost complete decentralization. In all the sites, however, few meaningful opportunities for participatory decision making existed at the district level. This causes a mismatch between the goals and practice of school decision making and accountability on the one hand, and the often arbitrary manner in which central decisions – which affect schools greatly – are made. This contradiction of governance feeds the long-held suspicions and distrust between the central office and the schools. Referring to the recent change in the district administrative organization from elementary, middle, and high school clusters to K-12 vertical clusters, one principal said:

> *This just came about from one day to the next. I'm not saying it's not the best decision for the district as a whole. I just wished we would have been consulted. When I want to make a decision, I need to include faculty, parents, and my governance committee. Where is the district site-based decision-making team?*

The central office, superintendent, and board can do much to break down the isolation and mistrust that school staff and parents feel through modeling significant opportunities for cross-role groups to work together and provide input on the system's goals and decisions. These initiatives must include real commitment to sharing decisions, or they will result in further apathy. One teacher who had just participated in a six-month district policy planning committee concerning grades, retention, academic acceleration, and attendance expressed it well. "Why didn't they just tell us at the beginning they were going to rewrite everything over the summer? They knew what they wanted from the beginning. They just were trying to get us to regurgitate it."

Participation in such showcase involvement initiatives causes more harm than good. Fullan and Steigelbauer (1991) explain in *The New Meaning of Educational Change*:

> *Since introducing innovations is a way of life in most school systems, districts build up track records in managing change. The importance of the district's history of innovation attempts can be stated in the form of a proposition: The more that teachers or others have had negative experiences with previous implementation attempts in the district or elsewhere, the more cynical or apathetic they will be about the next change presented regardless of the merit of the new idea....Districts...can develop an incapacity for change as well as a capacity for it.* — p. 74

The good news here is that many teachers, families, and community members in the districts we visited reengaged quickly and enthusiastically in the change effort once they understood through district actions that their input would be taken seriously and could impact important matters, such as budgets and teaching and learning. We need to redefine the district and leadership to include all the stakeholders. This redefinition requires changes in the district's culture as well as its structures. District leaders who model the behaviors that create experiences we want for students – such as respectful caring based on our individual strengths and needs, meaningful and challenging work that is related to real-life concerns, and opportunities to direct and take responsibility for our own learning – establish a new culture of "how we do things around here" – by example rather than exhortation. This new culture will fuel engagement, ensure that multiple viewpoints are heard and included in the reform, and help build a critical mass of people involved in the targeted change effort who believe they can make a difference for students.

Examples of significant roles for all stakeholders in district planning and implementation of middle-grades reform follow. Some are from systems other than the four case studies identified earlier.

- School improvement plans in Long Beach were critiqued by a team of "critical friends" from outside and inside the district. Suggestions for how to align the initiatives with goals for students were made.
- Milwaukee's middle grades coordinator, with the assistance of an outside "critical friend," convened representatives from all the departments, community agencies, funded projects and constituencies involved in middle schools. They shared their goals for students and created a map of all the middle school-related activities going on in the district to see their interrelationships and overlap. This led to a single consolidated plan that was monitored quarterly by a governance body.
- Teachers, superintendents, parents, and principals attend conferences and retreats together, providing time to form new relationships and to share common learning and experiences.
- Parents, teachers, and representatives of the general public take part in a meeting to review student work and what it tells us about the content standards, our teaching, and next steps for students.
- Parents and students take after-school classes together that are led by teachers.
- Diverse and representative parent leaders work with parent group leaders across the district on ways to effectively engage a diversity of parents in school improvement.
- A district steering committee made up of representatives of constituency groups provides leadership and coordination for reforms at the system level. The proceeds and agendas of these meetings are distributed freely.

## CONCERN 2 —

What is middle school reform, anyway?

**RECOMMENDATION:**

*District leaders should develop a clear vision and a plan for middle-grades education and student learning with all stakeholders involved.*

The early adolescent years are difficult for many families. As children approach adulthood they seem to be more influenced by peers than parents or other adults. In urban settings where safety is a primary concern, this causes families heightened anxiety about schools. In addition, many families, as well as school personnel, have a shallow understanding of middle school philosophy and practices, and how they will lead to the specific knowledge and skills that students need to succeed in high school and beyond. Unless middle school reform is proactively defined and the initiatives and successes shared broadly, middle schools often suffer from a negative reputation in the community. Sometimes this reputation is deserved; in schools where sixth grade performance dips, students are tracked into courses that may limit their future options, and students needing support are lost in the system. However, many middle-grades schools in urban districts do engage students in challenging learning while creating safe communities where everyone is cared for. These positive stories need to be shared along with a frank appraisal of the district's progress towards addressing public concerns about middle schools.

All stakeholders need opportunities to define and operationalize the vision for middle-grades education. This middle-grades vision should not be defined by grade configuration but must be based on the nature and needs of young adolescents and the district's goals for what they will know and be able to do by the end of eighth grade. Visions, plans, and standards that are defined without broad input do not become evident in classrooms. In addition, reform terms mean different things to different people. In-depth discussion of the purpose and process of middle school components, varied assessments of their use and results, site visits to exemplary schools, shared staff development and follow-up, along with ongoing reporting and making changes to the plan based on goals for students and lessons learned will demonstrate seriousness about providing effective schools for young adolescents. In California, particularly, this understanding of middle school reform was leveraged by a supportive state policy context, and the publicity generated around *Turning Points* (1989) and California's *Caught in the Middle*. (1987) reports.

Below are some additional ways that districts engaged stakeholders in the vision and plan for middle-grades education.

- District middle school conferences included parents and school board members in assessing and defining the promising practices in schools.
- Community partners, parents, and teachers conducted district and school assessments, analyzed the data based on common criteria, and participated in creating solutions to the problems surfaced in the assessments.

- School, central office staff, parents, and community organizations co-lead a series of seminars on "Living with and supporting the education of a young adolescent."
- District staff mobilized broad-based input on content standards as they were developed and implemented.
- Districts widely disseminated the results of system assessments, both positive and negative. They distributed the action plans that resulted and provided timely reports based on the plan's progress.

## CONCERN 3 —

Which of these top priorities am I supposed to do?

**RECOMMENDATION:**

***District leaders should focus initiatives on the heart of the matter – improving teaching and learning.***

The current pace and scope of innovation is often overwhelming for implementers. The demands for rapid results can lead to instant adoption of a new program with little preparation, follow-up, or evaluation of its success. If implementation does not lead almost immediately to gains in student achievement, the effort is abandoned, or another new program is tried, leading to layers of innovations, none of which were adequately tried out. This proliferation of programs without integration into the core operation of the school or system is so prevalent it is referred to as the *Christmas tree school* by Anthony Bryk in a study of schools in the Chicago School Reform (1994). In these schools, individual programs remain isolated and unrelated, much like the ornaments on a Christmas tree.

In a study of 44 site-based management (SBM) schools, Wohlsetter and Briggs (1994) found that some schools were successful in restructuring, while in others site-based processes did not affect teaching and learning. Those who failed adopted SBM as an end in itself, lodged the decision-making power in a small select group, and proceeded with business as usual – in other words, "SBM was layered on top of whatever else was happening." Successful schools established teacher-led decision-making teams, "focused on continuous improvement with school-wide training in functional and process skills and in areas related to curriculum and instruction," and "communicated with a broad range of constituents" (p. 14).

When an innovation affects one part of the system, other unanticipated parts of the system must change in order to realign the way that departments and functions work together, or contradictory policies will frustrate implementers. For example, one district moved to middle school implementation, but did not deal fully with the sixth grade at K-6 schools. This caused an unwitting competition for sixth graders between middle schools and K-6 schools. Another district spent extensive time training teacher teams to work together and integrate curriculum but neglected to inform and include the counselors who scheduled the students without considering the integrity of the team.

All of the case study districts conscientiously are trying to integrate innovations, implement them with depth, and to align middle-grades reform with other aspects of the system. Some of the ways this is working follow:
- San Diego's 16 expectations and five design tasks provide a framework to interrelate all its initiatives. The superintendent has stressed to funders, to assistant superintendents who work with school clusters, and to all departments that all district activity must relate to this framework. They have rejected technical assistance or funded innovations that do not fit the framework.
- The Advisory Council and a steering committee for the Middle Level Initiative in Atlanta coordinate the work of the committees; this ties the middle school reform to the larger strategic plan.
- Corpus Christi's interrelated strategic plan, action plans, staff development, and assignment of curriculum specialists to target middle schools reinforced the stated priorities at each level.

## Concern 4 —

Where are the students and family members who were invited?

**Recommendation:**

*District leaders should, together with parents and students, establish group norms and structures that facilitate their equal and active participation.*

While developing and conducting the district audit, some of our advisors questioned the need to interview students. We found that students contributed sensible, comprehensible, and powerful opinions about how to improve their schools. They provided some of the most important data. Middle school students are very capable of analyzing their school and making sound recommendations on how to improve their experiences and education. Unfortunately they are seldom consulted or involved when reforms are planned, ones ostensibly in their interest. We discovered that despite the reform efforts, most students still spend the majority of the school day listening to teachers. They are hungry for active, hands-on, significant projects that require real engagement and problem solving. They also recognize whether the primary atmosphere in the school is one of mistrust and control, or one of respect, caring, and challenge.

Families often feel unwelcome in school, or believe that school staff may accuse them of apathy or blame them for the conditions that often surround urban schools in impoverished settings. When they are contacted by the school, they are often given bad news about their child's behavior. Their own children, experiencing young adolescents' desire to be independent, may not tell them about invitations to the school or talk to them about how they are doing in school. Many parents of young adolescents suddenly feel left out, ignorant of important information about their child's life. Parents of immigrant students often do not speak the language or understand how to navigate in an unfamiliar school system. As previously mentioned, larger schools inevitably increase this feeling of anonymity.

Students and families bring unique and invaluable perspectives to the plan and implementation of middle school reform; for it is their own and their child's present and future at stake. Despite widespread attempts to involve parents in significant roles in each of the districts, we found that, with a few visible exceptions, both parents and students were involved in pro forma ways. They often recognized this and stopped attending meetings in which, as one parent told us, "I try to bring things up but the school people really have the floor. They just don't seem to listen, and they talk in all this alphabet jargon; you need a score card to understand. It's hard to tell if they really want parents involved or not." Students who participate on planning committees at the school and district level (when they are included) participate in ones or twos. As such they are supposed to represent "the student point of view," but do not necessarily have a means to represent or speak for anyone but themselves. This is often true for individual parent representatives as well. The language and prior knowledge of the school and middle-grades education assumed in these planning groups may also be a barrier to their participation.

Authentic involvement of students and families requires attention to differential power dynamics, investigating ways that traditional meeting norms may silence different constituencies, creating vehicles in which all participants are learners together, and providing multiple ways for parents and students to express their views, stay informed, and be involved. Through these changes in culture and structures of schools, valid engagement of parents and students can be arranged on committees, in the day-to-day business of running the school, and in working with the school and system towards shared goals for student learning.

---

Concerns 5 through 8 relate to support mechanisms for implementation of the proposed visions and plans.

## SUPPORT

**CONCERN 5 —**

Who has the time or support needed to implement these wonderful ideas?

**RECOMMENDATION:**

*District leaders should align district staff development with strategic plans and identified school improvement goals. With planning and delivery input from the schools, provide intensive and varied staff development activities that allow time for implementers to make their own meaning of the reform.*

New skills are required of all stakeholders under a participatory district middle school initiative. Too often the training and support provided for implementation consists of a training workshop with little follow-up. Classroom changes are frequently not linked to teams and/or school changes. The districts in the case studies all provided staff development related to middle schools, young adolescents, specific content, teaching strategies and assessment. However, they were just beginning to develop comprehensive means to provide implementation support and evaluation of an innovation's effectiveness, and to align district and school staff development needs. The professional development of principals has often been neglected once they take on the principalship. Support and classified are likewise often overlooked in staff development programs. In reviewing staff development, one district found staff development offered from 14 different sources. These needed to be reviewed and evaluated to assess their relationship to each other and to improving student achievement. In addition, the districts are beginning to view staff development more broadly than training – as an ongoing job-embedded involvement in action research, school improvement, or reflection with others. They link staff development to teacher preparation, hiring, and assignment. They work with local universities to prepare teachers for urban middle schools and principals who can facilitate change to improve instruction. Some of the promising practices tried:

- Planning teacher-led staff development that includes intensive training and once-a-month follow-up with implementers at their schools.
- Organizing study groups for all school personnel to learn more about a topic related to the school or district's improvement goals.
- Providing a seminar and discussion series for parents on "Living with and Supporting the Achievement of Young Adolescents" planned by central office staff, parents, teachers, and community partners with expertise in adolescent development.
- Coaching, class visitations, and other means of bringing teachers into each others' classrooms and sharing how new skills work with students.
- Involving parents, community partners, students, principals, support staff, board members and central office staff, as well as teachers in staff development sessions.
- Engaging central office staff, teachers, university partners, and parents as coaches and advocates for individual schools.
- Using time creatively, such as a minimum work day following days with banked minutes, restructured faculty and team meetings to provide time for teachers to plan and work together, or partial days in which students engage in service learning or other activities in the community while teachers meet together.
- Recognizing the ongoing need for professional development and building pupil-free time into the official school calendar.
- Conducting public referendum campaigns to secure additional funds for staff development linked to improved student achievement.

| | |
|---|---|
| **CONCERN 6 —**<br><br>How can we take responsibility for the achievement of all students? | **RECOMMENDATION:**<br><br>*District leaders should create small accountable communities out of a large system with its many schools.* |

As Sizer (1992) and others (Carnegie Council on Adolescent Development 1989; Lee & Smith, 1993; Newmann & Wehlage, 1991) have pointed out, personalization of the learning environment reduces the anonymity and disaffection that often occurs in large schools. This personalization can be created through interdisciplinary teams that share a common group of students, fewer teacher/student contacts daily, multiple small teacher-led schools in a single building and with K-12 articulation, and systems to track and support student progress. Lessons about creating small communities for children apply to creating manageable-sized systems for adults in the district to interact and to impact on a group of schools. Vehicles such as district study groups to discuss portfolio implementation, retreats and activities that allow teachers and others to learn about each other and to complete a common task, and K-12 clusters that plan for a group of students can contribute to a feeling of "team" and ownership of the system. This personalization can help both adults and children to engage more fully in school and the system. The networks make it more difficult to remain isolated to what is going on outside of individual classrooms or in different schools. The goals and purposes for the small communities should be continuously revisited lest these avenues for personalization and accountability for students and adults devolve into a meaningless bureaucratic structure. In addition, mechanisms to communicate across the smaller groups should be planned to avoid the typical isolation that can occur in departmentalized settings. Examples of making smaller communities out of the whole follow:

- San Diego established clusters of elementary, middle, and high schools that share feeder patterns and students. These clusters review academic content standards and how to reach them, school-to-work issues, and how to address the social needs of families and students.
- In some schools teachers spend multiple years with students to establish strong long-term bonds of support. The ongoing relationship allows teachers to minimize the time spent in norm-setting and diagnosis each year. They can work with students on improvement of skills based on experience with individuals the prior year.
- Small schools, schools with block time, and those experimenting with two- or three-person teams are evaluating how reducing numbers of teacher/student and teacher/teacher contacts affects school climate and students' performance.
- School partnership and visitation support networks, conducting action research across job roles, and other networking opportunities outside of the formal organizational structure generate powerful relationships and shared commitment to implement changes.

| | |
|---|---|
| **CONCERN 7 —**<br><br>Why didn't anyone tell me about this project? | **Recommendation:**<br><br>*District leaders should continuously communicate with all stakeholder groups and invite new participation.* |
| | Moving from small pockets of pioneers to a critical mass of supporters who will make the middle school reform part of the everyday life of the classroom, school, and system requires careful attention to communication. In addition, plans for how to go from pilots or initial implementers to full-scale adoption need to be thought through in the beginning of the change. Even if the whole system has engaged in common learning or training, new teachers and incoming parents need to learn about the middle school plans and promising practices. Multiple opportunities to participate should include options for varied levels of time and interest. Multiple vehicles to learn about progress, challenges, and new plans increase the awareness and interest level of those not immediately involved as change agents. Some of the communication strategies being tried by the case study districts are:<br>• Student-led conferences and culminating performances that showcase new skills and abilities;<br>• Student and teacher presentations to the school board to discuss the middle school reform changes and their benefits;<br>• World Wide Web pages, radio shows, newsletters, and other multimedia approaches to reach the community with reform descriptions;<br>• Community members shadow a principal, teacher, or student for a day;<br>• Parent/community rooms, volunteer mentors in schools, and after-school opportunities in the schools for community members;<br>• Proactive communication about the system's performance beyond reporting of standardized tests, and vehicles to explain their significance;<br>• Inviting parents to attend staff development sessions and learn about the reforms first hand; and<br>• Gathering and disseminating opinions of stakeholders and adjusting plans based on their feedback. |
| **CONCERN 8 —**<br><br>What about equity issues for students from diverse cultures and for those with special needs? | **RECOMMENDATION:**<br><br>*District leaders should include specialists and families of bilingual, special, and gifted and talented students to ensure that reforms for all meet the needs of individual students.* |
| | Until recently, while the middle-grades reform movement focused on improved performance and learning for all students, the specific needs of students based on cultural diversity, language, and special education were frequently left out of the picture. These case study districts are no exception. Particularly in sites where school-based autonomy is high, the school staff, while well meaning, may not possess the knowledge of how best to meet |

the needs of a diverse population. According to a California Tomorrow study (Olsen et al., 1994) on restructuring schools:

> *Though the rallying cry of 'all children' is important and worthy of praise, it mistakenly glances over students' specific needs. Most of the coaches and projects/models we observed demonstrated little or no expertise in the area of effective learning and teaching for language and cultural minority students. Coaches without the focus or expertise on issues of diversity and equity are not able to encourage such a focus at the school site or to provide the essential research or knowledge base.* — p. 245

The report goes on to discuss important roles that district level staff have played to assure equity and access in education.

> *Compliance has become a dirty word – associated with bureaucracy, over-control and conformity. Yet the entire apparatus of compliance and monitoring exists because historically schools left on their own have not met their legal obligations with regards to access and equity.* — p. 263

The following examples show how systems can address the needs of diverse students in their middle school reform plan:

- San Diego has developed inclusion demonstration sites to work on models of inclusive programs for special education. The directors of special and exceptional education and for bilingual education are also working with the middle-grades reform planning group to provide expertise related to some of the reform goals for heterogeneous grouping.
- In one San Diego school, the core academic staff became certified in English as a second language and sheltered instruction, and in another, they all studied for gifted and talented education certification. This gave many of the faculty a common language and strategies to discuss improvements for these students.
- In Corpus Christi, several schools are becoming laboratories for second language learning. Action research and varied strategies will be demonstrated at the schools and then disseminated throughout the system.
- In most of the districts, disaggregation of student data by race, gender, SES, and program status allows school faculty to look for patterns of class assignment, achievement, attendance, and disciplinary action that may indicate equity problem areas in the school.
- Bilingual parents in one district became much more active in raising their concerns for their children's education after attending parent information and training sessions sponsored by various community agencies. After some initial resistance and the facilitation by a district mediator, one school implemented many of their suggestions. This has provided a great increase in support from bilingual parents and helped develop a more unified school community.

### The special importance of accountability

The last group of concerns relates to the issue of accountability. Increased public dissatisfaction with schools and school systems' results has brought calls for accountability for student performance to the forefront of the reform agenda. Accountability is a cornerstone of state and local standards development and implementation. Most accountability systems seek ways to institute challenging core academic standards for all students, while preserving local flexibility in how students will meet the standards. This accountability for results centers around performance, content, and delivery standards. While content standards and state accountability systems proliferate, few delivery or opportunites to learn standards have been adopted. More fundamentally, accountability requires a change in attitude and beliefs about who is responsible for student success. It also requires a belief in the ability of diverse students to meet rigorous standards when provided with high content curriculum and proper support mechanisms. High stakes accountability systems that set single measure performance goals with limited input of school personnel, parents, and students and that include sketchy plans for how to provide additional resources and support to low-performing schools reinforce school personnel's fear of risk taking, rather than spur innovation. Three main themes related to accountability in the districts studied were: (1) ensuring that accountability involves shared responsibility, multiple benchmarks, and adequate support systems; (2) learning to conduct research and to use data to inform school planning; and (3) modeling system self-assessment.

## ACCOUNTABILITY

**CONCERN 9 —**

How can I afford to try new things? We have to improve our test scores this year.

**RECOMMENDATION:**

*District leaders should ensure that assessment and accountability mechanisms involve shared responsibility, multiple benchmarks, and adequate support systems.*

Changing practice requires risk taking and learning new skills. Test results may decline before they improve. If standardized test scores are viewed as the sole measure of improvement, many teachers and principals will be afraid to take on changes that they do not see as immediately leading to improvement of scores. In many schools visited, improving test scores became the school mission, not a vehicle to assess the school's progress in increasing student learning. When the test involves multiple choice answers to basic skills questions, teachers will focus their teaching on the same outcomes. The cases illustrate the problems that occur when the academic content standards and benchmarks created in the district no longer align with the state tests or other accountability measures used. Finding multiple ways to assess implementation of reforms and their impact on student performance that are understandable and meaningful to the community helps standardized test scores to become just one of a multiple group of progress indicators for a school, rather than the sole measure of its success.

Defining accountability so that it means that all stakeholders share responsibility for students' learning and for providing learning environments that enable students to meet high academic standards can short-circuit the blame game in which teachers see the problem as students' families and community, families blame teachers and the schools for students' failure, and the central office blames the principals. Meaningful accountability mechanisms involve school communities, teachers, students, and families in reviewing the school's current state and linking staff development and school improvement plans to student performance goals. Open discussion of the strengths and challenges of schools and the system as a whole should lead to shared priorities for change. Each constituency's role in improving student learning will be different, but they will all be responsible for improvement. When improvement does not occur, the process by which low-performing schools and central office departments are identified for and receive special assistance or are reconfigured should be made clear.

External partners can provide the pressure and support to help the school and system continue the reform effort, even when the going gets rough. A mobilized community constituency can help the system to stay focused on its goals and be accountable for its plans and for results.

## Concern 10 —

Why do we need to reform? Everyone enjoys our new program. Our parents, staff, and students are very happy.

### Recommendation:

***District leaders should establish mechanisms for the district and schools to effectively gather, manage, and interpret data on student performance and program effectiveness and assist staff in utilizing the data to inform program planning.***

Data-based decision making has become an axiom in the literature of education reform. The case studies of districts illustrate how fundamental a change this required in the culture and operation of schools and districts. Each district collects enormous amounts of data on student performance, attendance, dropouts, suspension, and expulsion. Until recently these data may have been distributed to principals, but without much interpretation or guidance. With the rise of accountability, most states and districts prepare some form of school report card or student performance description to distribute to their communities and schools. This information is often disaggregated by race and socioeconomic status, and is intended to be used to develop school improvement plans. Only in the past several years, however, has attention gone to systematically bringing together principals, school staff, and members of the research and evaluation departments to interpret these data. In even fewer cases does the system discuss how the school staff can work with the central office and other partners to gather and interpret specific data related to implementation of a reform strategy.

Numerous restructuring studies illuminate the power of data to build a common perception of student and school performance, to assist in developing strategies to meet the needs of particular students, and to trace progress over time (Fullan, 1991; Olsen, 1995). These data may be provided externally, as with test scores, or gathered internally, through surveys, interviews, observations, review of documents, and review of student work. Data should be seen broadly, as measures that meaningfully provide information to answer specific questions. This requires a research design, data collection methods, and the skill to interpret various forms of data. School staff can use assistance from the district and other support groups to conduct effective research, and they look to the central office for an effective data management and interpretation system. In addition, they need time to review, raise questions, analyze, and interpret the meaning of the data. Once that is clear, the search for an appropriate solution begins. Often the school and district plans do not adequately or powerfully address the challenges posed by the data. These plans need to reflect a whole school mobilization to address problems that surfaced from the data.

The skills of data-based planning are new to most school-based personnel. They may be new to district administrators. Those in the research and evaluation department may know how to interpret the data, but not how to research the solution to the problem. In addition, they may not know how to teach others. This is a case where those with varied types of expertise need to come together and design a system that provides both pressure and support to schools and the system. Plans need to be based on data and programs evaluated on their effects rather than on positive participant responses.

Data-based decision making has been a priority in some of the districts studied. However, support to schools and alignment of data collection and management systems still present a challenge. Some promising examples follow:

- Leaders in accountability demonstration sites in San Diego receive coordinated training and ongoing support on how to use school data, student work, and performance and portfolio assessments to develop and monitor their school's comprehensive plan. A trained "critical friend" provides ongoing external feedback, encouragement, and assistance.
- Working with Boston College faculty, several districts are experimenting with a variety of unique assessment tools such as student drawings and narratives about their classes to provide insight into students' views of classroom changes.
- Paired schools decide on the innovations they want to examine, develop criteria that they will look for, and then visit each other's schools. Feedback is provided related to each school's questions and criteria.
- School and district assessments – such as the Middle-Grades Reform Audit process in Atlanta or the Middle Grades Assessment Program which was used by schools in Minneapolis and San Diego – in which teachers and other stakeholders participate in data gathering and analysis and create local ownership of the data. They also provide a planned vehicle

in which participants enhance skills in conducting interviews, interpreting student performance data, observing classes, and synthesizing data.

## Concern 11 —

Why does the buck stop at the principal? Shouldn't the whole system be accountable?

**Recommendation:**

***District leaders should model system accountability for effective functioning and for facilitating student success.***

> *At the deepest level, the enemy of high performing systems is the feeling of helplessness that so many of us in organizations seem to experience....The core of the bureaucratic mind-set is not to take responsibility for what is happening. Other people are the problem.* — Block 1987, pp. 1, 6

Mistrust for the intentions and capabilities of those at every level of the system abounds in urban districts and schools. In traditional hierarchical districts, administrators create structures aimed at safeguarding against the incompetence and insubordination of those at schools. In more decentralized systems, "if power and resources can be shifted to the school level, central authorities may also be able to shift most or all of the responsibility for failure to improve student performance to teachers and administrators in the school" (Levine & Eubanks, 1989, p. 21). Neither stance encourages or supports risk taking, continuous improvement, or open discussion of challenges. In this model, individuals, specific schools, or students are seen as the source of the problem and receive blame and sanctions. Those that improve results are elevated and championed, causing competition rather than collegiality between schools, administrators, and teachers.

Despite strong accountability measures at the school level in the case study districts, only one had fully enacted system assessment and accountability as part of the change. When the district staff and school board openly discuss and share the problems in the system, engage various stakeholders in addressing them, and encourage schools and the community to evaluate the effectiveness of the central office services, they model continuous improvement and responsible accountability. In most cases, however, reform still means changing schools, not the central office or system as a whole. Some initial methods by which the central office engages in system accountability follow:

- Minneapolis Superintendent Peter Hutchinson's pay is partially tied to improvements in indicators of student achievement, parent and community satisfaction, and school personnel's assessment of central office services.
- San Diego instituted parent satisfaction surveys and conducted several system management and organization audits to assess the expectations related to high-performing system.
- Minneapolis' Quality School Study spoke openly about the negative ef-

fects of the system's lack of leadership in curriculum as well as other concerns in the system. The study was distributed widely in the media as well as by the system.

## Overarching Implications for Leaders of District-Wide Middle-Grades Reform

One challenge to making sense out of the myriad, interweaving stories that comprise district-wide middle-grades reform is the complexity of looking at the whole system. When examining the reform up close and specifically, one is constantly in danger of making the mistake highlighted in the fable of the blind men and the elephant, who lost the big picture by focusing only on one part. When synthesizing the depth, interconnectedness, and ambiguity of the whole system into a few overarching implications, one faces the danger of distilling this complexity into overly simplistic models.

The work reported in this volume grew out of a troubling issue in education reform, "How do we go beyond individual excellent schools to a system of schools in which all students achieve at high levels?" In our work in urban districts to improve student achievement we saw the powerful role of external consultants and networks in facilitating change at the school site, and experienced the positive engagement of teachers and principals with these change initiatives. At the same time, in the relationships between the schools, central office, the community, parents, and students, the other groups were often perceived as the source of the problems, rather than allies critical to the problems' effective resolution. Individuals wasted precious time blaming other groups and either trying to get them to change or feeling hopeless. They rarely focused on the area over which they did have control and asked, What can I do to improve teaching and learning for students? From the boardroom to the classroom, the bureaucratic culture stifled attempts to work together to improve schools, and encouraged contentious factions with little understanding or empathy for each other's perspectives, skills, or barriers. However, for a system to support and challenge all schools to continuously grow as places of learning for adults and students, each aspect of the system must continuously grow and improve. To sum up the main finding about district-wide middle-grades reform:

**Reforming middle-grades education to improve student achievement means changing the whole system, not just schools. Central office staff (and leaders from every constituency) can best facilitate reform by *themselves* modeling the beliefs, practices, and shared power relationships that we want to see in reformed schools, and by creating environments and networks that foster the growth of a community of learners and leaders across the system.**

What does this mean? It means that actions speak louder than words. Those enmeshed in the bureaucracy will skeptically examine words for the substance that lies within. This means that district-wide middle-grades reform depends on establishing a new culture as well as new structures and practices. Peter Senge in *The Fifth Discipline Fieldbook* (1994) describes disbursing power as the number one ability that organizations need to possess to successfully cope with the rapid changes in society.

> *Right now the word 'empowerment' is a very powerful buzzword. It is also very dangerous. Just granting power, without some method of replacing the discipline and order that come out of a command-and-control bureaucracy, produces chaos. We have to learn how to disperse power so self-discipline can replace imposed discipline. That immerses us in the area of culture: replacing the bureaucracy with aspirations, values, and visions.* — p. 14

This disbursement of power requires new *roles and relationships* (Schlechty, 1991; Fullan, 1993) between schools and the districts and the community. Fullan describes this as "coordinated co-development of schools and the district" (p. 147). Sergiovanni (1995) calls for schools to be "managerially loose, but culturally tight"(p. 46). To remake culture, districts need to demonstrate and sustain the system's values and purpose. Many informal, symbolic, and implicit things convey those values more strongly than mission statements on the walls or board resolutions. For example, the way budget decisions are made and resources allocated conveys a great deal about the system's values. Does the informal structure of the system, including how policies are actually enacted, the grapevine, and the stories we tell about the organization, support or undermine these values? Are newcomers to the system socialized in ways that reinforce or contradict the values?

These values and purpose can be reinforced through rituals, symbols, stories, and the "way things are done." In this way the system binds its constituencies through their identification with a common purpose, their importance to achieving that purpose, and their sense of belonging to a community. In the practice of cultural leadership, very often "it is the little things that count. One does not have to mount a white horse and charge forward in a great dramatic event in order to be a symbolic leader. Simple routines and humble actions can communicate very important messages and high ideas" (Sergiovanni, p.91).

In the case study districts, leaders engaged in reforms to change the culture and structures of the district and school to one of continuous improvement and ownership for the education of all students. So far, the changes in culture are tentative and are still located in pockets of those closest to the reform implementers. However, attempts to go beyond individual implementers and excellent schools will depend on leaders' ability to model and nurture the values and actions that foster high achievement for all. Central office staff because of their strategic vantage point and ability to look at the whole system, their ability to engage external resources in the reform, and their authority to establish districtwide structures and initiatives are in a pivotal position to facilitate this reform effort.

The lessons learned from attempts at large-scale school reform are beginning to sound the same. They point to solutions that are imbedded in people: such as building effective relationships; clarifying the meaning and goals of the middle-grades reform process; providing pressure and support for change from inside and outside the system and schools; establishing respect and caring for students, families, and staff; and providing real roles for all the stakeholders. They are imbedded in the heart of schooling; focusing on first things first – teaching and learning. They do not provide a recipe, but a general map of the infrastructure and culture necessary to engage the minds and hearts of a critical mass of implementers in the reform process. If reformers hope to move beyond ephemeral pockets of success, these hard-learned lessons must be studied and shared.

# References

Block, P. (1987). *The empowered manager.* San Fransicso: Jossey Bass.

Bryk, A.S., Easton, J.Q., Kurbow, D., Rollow, S.G., & Sebring, P.A. (1994). The state of Chicago school reform. *Phi Delta Kappan, 76* (5), 74.

Carnegie Council on Adolescent Development (1989). *Turning points: Preparing American youth for the 21st century.* New York: Carnegie Corporation of New York.

California State Department of Education. (1987). *Caught in the middle.* Sacramento, CA: Office of Middle Grades Support Services.

Fullan, M. (1993). Coordinating school and district development in restructuring. In J. Murphy & P. Hallinger, (Eds.), *Restructuring schooling: Learning from ongoing efforts.* Newbury Park, CA: Corwin Press.

Fullan, M., & Steigelbauer, S. (1991). *The new meaning of educational change.* New York: Teachers College Press.

Lee, V., & Smith, J. (1993). Effects of school restructuring on the achievement and engagement of middle-grade students. *Sociology of Education, 66* (July), 164-187.

Levine, D., & Eubanks, E. (1989). *Site-based management: Engine for reform or pipedream? Problems, pitfalls, and prerequisites for success in site-based management.* Manuscript submitted for publication.

Newmann, F., & Wehlage, G. (1995). *Successful school restructuring: A report to the public and educators by the Center on Organization and Restructuring of Schools.* Madison, WI: Wisconsin Center for Education Research, University of Wisconsin-Madison School of Education.

Olsen, L., Chang, H., De La Rosa Salazar, D., Leong, C., McCall Perez, Z., McLain, G., & Raffel, L. (1994). *The unfinished journey: Restructuring schools in a diverse society.* San Francisco: California Tomorrow.

Senge, P. (1994). *The Fifth Discipline Fieldbook.* New York: Doubleday.

Sergiovanni, T. (1995). *The principalship: A reflective practice perspective.* Needham Heights, MA: Allyn and Bacon.

Sizer, T. (1992). Horace's school: Redesigning the American high school. Boston: Houghton Mifflin Company.

Wohlsetter, P., & Briggs, K. (1994). The principal's role in school-based management. *Principal, 74* (2), 14-17.

# II.
## Resources and Tools for Change

Some specific tools to use in carrying out district-wide reform efforts are included in this functional section. For each of the eighteen standards the following materials are provided:

- **Questions for Gathering Data on Your District** – to guide a group in determining the current status of the district related to this standard.

- **Suggested Activities** – to further this standard in the district. In some cases, workshop outlines and handouts are included; in others, the suggested activities are more truncated.

- **Additional Resources** – books, activities, articles, and audiovisual material that provide more theoretical and research background related to the standard and sometimes additional activities to carry out related to the standard.

This section can be used in a variety of ways based on your local needs. If you are in the needs assessment stage of your change initiative, you can utilize the audit and/or the self-study questionnaire (at the opening of this section) to help identify and prioritize areas for more intensive work. You may, however, already be engaged in reform activities and know of areas where you could use assistance, such as the development of a vision, adoption of academic content standards, or development of a comprehensive staff development plan. In this case the title of the specific standard and its ideal will lead you to the resource section you may need.

In general the *leadership* standards relate to the development of vision, policy, roles, and structures to guide the district middle-grades education reform initiative. The *support* standards relate to the kinds of district initiatives that will help scale up the implementation of reforms to improve student achievement. In the *accountability* standards, means to assess the results of the reform effort for students, schools, and programs, and for the system as a whole are discussed.

These resources should help you think holistically about your reform effort. Use them as a reference point in the development of your own framework for middle-grades education reform.

# District Middle-Grades Reform Self-Study Questionnaire

The following self-assessment questionnaire can be used by district stakeholders (central office staff, teachers, school administrators and staff, school board members, community advisory boards, etc.) to assess the current levels of leadership, support, and accountability provided in the district that are necessary to sustain middle grades reform. The assessment will reveal both district strengths and areas where improvement efforts can be targeted. The assessment is most valuable if completed by a number of different district stakeholders, who then can compare perspectives to determine areas of most need.

For maximum effectiveness, the following steps are suggested:

1. Make copies of the assessment for all members of stakeholder groups. Ask each member to carefully complete the questionnaire, working alone.

2. Using the scoring grid that follows, have each group member place his/her scores in the grid and calculate the average score for each of the 18 question areas.

3. Individuals in the group should then compare scores and discuss similarities and differences and the criteria they based their choices on. Scores should be compared both based on individual questions and question area averages. Any item receiving a score of 3 or less by the majority of the group should be of particular concern.

4. Group members should then try to reach consensus on which of the specific areas the district most needs to work on, and then develop an action plan for how to address district needs.

| LEADERSHIP | Strongly Disagree | Disagree | Somewhat Agree | Agree | Strongly Agree |
|---|---|---|---|---|---|
| 1a. The district has a clearly defined and articulated middle-grades vision. | 1 | 2 | 3 | 4 | 5 |
| 1b. All key stakeholders (administrators, teachers, parents, students, community members) were involved in the development and ratification of the middle grades vision. | 1 | 2 | 3 | 4 | 5 |
| 1c. The district middle grades vision underlies all planning, decision making, and programs at the middle level. | 1 | 2 | 3 | 4 | 5 |
| 1d. An up-to-date understanding of effective middle-grades practices informs the district middle-grades vision and guides decision making. | 1 | 2 | 3 | 4 | 5 |
| 2a. Knowledge of early adolescent development is pervasive in the district and serves to support middle-grades programming. | 1 | 2 | 3 | 4 | 5 |
| 2b. The district staff and schools uphold high expectations for all middle-grades students. | 1 | 2 | 3 | 4 | 5 |
| 3a. Content standards for what students should know and be able to do by eighth grade have been developed with school and community input. | 1 | 2 | 3 | 4 | 5 |
| 3b. District content standards are aligned with state and national frameworks. | 1 | 2 | 3 | 4 | 5 |
| 4a. District policies are the result of shared decision making of all constituents. | 1 | 2 | 3 | 4 | 5 |
| 4b. District policies are consistent with the district middle-grades vision and are based on research on best practices. | 1 | 2 | 3 | 4 | 5 |
| 4c. District policies focus on outcomes and on flexibility, rather than inputs and compliance. | 1 | 2 | 3 | 4 | 5 |

| LEADERSHIP | Strongly Disagree | Disagree | Somewhat Agree | Agree | Strongly Agree |
|---|---|---|---|---|---|
| 5a. A strategic plan for middle grades improvement, with clear outcomes and timelines, exists. | 1 | 2 | 3 | 4 | 5 |
| 5b. District strategic plans include both alignment between elementary, middle and high school programs and a specific focus on the unique place of middle grades. | 1 | 2 | 3 | 4 | 5 |
| 5c. Site specific school plans are aligned with a wider district middle-grades strategic plan. | 1 | 2 | 3 | 4 | 5 |
| 6a. District leadership engages parents, teacher, community members, and administrators in improving middle level education. | 1 | 2 | 3 | 4 | 5 |
| 6b. Parents are viewed as partners in the children's education. | 1 | 2 | 3 | 4 | 5 |
| 6c. Strong links exist between the school and the community. | 1 | 2 | 3 | 4 | 5 |
| 7a. The central office has a service orientation - engaged in and active in schools. | 1 | 2 | 3 | 4 | 5 |
| 7b. Decision making at district and school levels is focused on what is best for students. | 1 | 2 | 3 | 4 | 5 |
| 7c. A committee is responsible for charting and assessing district middle grades plans. | 1 | 2 | 3 | 4 | 5 |
| 7d. District staff model desired behaviors, beliefs and values. | 1 | 2 | 3 | 4 | 5 |
| 7e. Middle-grades students are involved in decisions that affect them and maintain leadership roles in the school and district. | 1 | 2 | 3 | 4 | 5 |
| 7f. The district focus is on coaching and facilitating, as opposed to mandating and supervising. | 1 | 2 | 3 | 4 | 5 |

| SUPPORT | Strongly Disagree | Disagree | Somewhat Agree | Agree | Strongly Agree |
|---|---|---|---|---|---|
| 8a. The district allocates financial and human resources on the basis of school needs and improvement plans. | 1 | 2 | 3 | 4 | 5 |
| 8b. Schools control their budgets. | 1 | 2 | 3 | 4 | 5 |
| 8c. Schools have significant input into personnel hiring and configuration at their sites. | 1 | 2 | 3 | 4 | 5 |
| 8d. The district provides adequate resources for professional development and exchange. | 1 | 2 | 3 | 4 | 5 |
| 9a. Networks for professional discussion and dialogue are in place in the district and in the schools. | 1 | 2 | 3 | 4 | 5 |
| 9b. Clear plans exist for student transition between grades and for K-12 articulation. | 1 | 2 | 3 | 4 | 5 |
| 10a. The district provides schools access to current research on teaching and learning and on successful school practices for young adolescents. | 1 | 2 | 3 | 4 | 5 |
| 10b. District and school-based decisions are guided by research on best practices. | 1 | 2 | 3 | 4 | 5 |
| 10c. Faculty members are engaged in action research throughout the district. | 1 | 2 | 3 | 4 | 5 |
| 11a. The district culture supports continuous improvement. | 1 | 2 | 3 | 4 | 5 |
| 11b. District staff encourage collegial structures and sharing and model lifelong learning. | 1 | 2 | 3 | 4 | 5 |
| 11c. The district encourages cross role sharing of ideas and practices. | 1 | 2 | 3 | 4 | 5 |

| SUPPORT | Strongly Disagree | Disagree | Somewhat Agree | Agree | Strongly Agree |
|---|---|---|---|---|---|
| 12a. Staff development is based on district strategic plans and school improvement plans. | 1 | 2 | 3 | 4 | 5 |
| 12b. School improvement plans are aligned with district goals. | 1 | 2 | 3 | 4 | 5 |
| 12c. Adequate time and resources are provided for staff development. | 1 | 2 | 3 | 4 | 5 |
| 12d. Various approaches to staff development exist, including study groups, action research, workshops with follow-up, coaching and peer interaction. | 1 | 2 | 3 | 4 | 5 |
| 12e. A coordinated district staff development plan exists, with decisions made by a cross role governance group. | 1 | 2 | 3 | 4 | 5 |
| 13a. Schools are provided assistance to assess their current state and develop and implement improvement plans. | 1 | 2 | 3 | 4 | 5 |
| 13b. Data for school improvement plans is collected at all levels, not just by the central offices. | 1 | 2 | 3 | 4 | 5 |
| 13c. Data for school improvement planning is multi-sourced, not simply focused on test scores. | 1 | 2 | 3 | 4 | 5 |
| 13d. Low performing schools are targeted for additional district assistance. | 1 | 2 | 3 | 4 | 5 |
| 14a. The middle-grades curriculum provides core content frameworks which enable student to meet eighth grade content standards. | 1 | 2 | 3 | 4 | 5 |
| 14b. Curriculum support is provided by content specialists and by school study. | 1 | 2 | 3 | 4 | 5 |
| 14c. The middle-grades curriculum is developmentally appropriate and integrated. | 1 | 2 | 3 | 4 | 5 |

| SUPPORT | Strongly Disagree | Disagree | Somewhat Agree | Agree | Strongly Agree |
|---|---|---|---|---|---|
| 14d. The middle-grades curriculum reflects cultural, racial, and gender diversity. | 1 | 2 | 3 | 4 | 5 |
| 14e. A variety of teaching strategies are used and discussed throughout the district. | 1 | 2 | 3 | 4 | 5 |
| 14f. Curricular continuity exists between grade levels in the district. | 1 | 2 | 3 | 4 | 5 |
| 15a. Mechanisms exist to assist students that cannot meet performance standards. | 1 | 2 | 3 | 4 | 5 |
| 15b. Exceptional education services (second language learning, gifted and talented, special education) are integrated into the curriculum and school reform planning. | 1 | 2 | 3 | 4 | 5 |

| ACCOUNTABILITY | Strongly Disagree | Disagree | Somewhat Agree | Agree | Strongly Agree |
|---|---|---|---|---|---|
| 16a. Student performance is assessed by multiple sources and compared to benchmarks. | 1 | 2 | 3 | 4 | 5 |
| 16b. Multiple sources of assessment are used, including portfolios, qualitative narratives, student self assessments, and tests which measure higher order thinking skills. | 1 | 2 | 3 | 4 | 5 |
| 16c. Standards for student performance are articulated for the middle grades. | 1 | 2 | 3 | 4 | 5 |
| 17a. The district works with schools to set benchmarks for student performance improvement. | 1 | 2 | 3 | 4 | 5 |
| 17b. Schools gather and analyze data with district staff and use it to evaluate programs and school environments for the purpose of continuous improvement. | 1 | 2 | 3 | 4 | 5 |
| 17c. The district works with schools to establish assessments, and to gather and interpret data. | 1 | 2 | 3 | 4 | 5 |

| ACCOUNTABILITY | Strongly Disagree | Disagree | Somewhat Agree | Agree | Strongly Agree |
|---|---|---|---|---|---|
| **17d.** State and district assessments align with content and performance standards and school goals. | 1 | 2 | 3 | 4 | 5 |
| **17e.** Both qualitative and quantitative assessment measures are used. | 1 | 2 | 3 | 4 | 5 |
| **18a.** District practices are reviewed and aligned with vision, plans and accountability mechanisms. | 1 | 2 | 3 | 4 | 5 |
| **18b.** The whole school system is assessed by all stakeholders, including the district's services. | 1 | 2 | 3 | 4 | 5 |
| **18c.** Schools set individual benchmarks and targets with district input. | 1 | 2 | 3 | 4 | 5 |
| **18d.** The district emphasizes equity of resources and performance. | 1 | 2 | 3 | 4 | 5 |
| **18e.** Mechanisms exist for school staff and families to evaluate district support services. | 1 | 2 | 3 | 4 | 5 |
| **18f.** All stakeholders review and provide input to district plans for middle grades based on evaluation data. | 1 | 2 | 3 | 4 | 5 |
| **18g.** District services/activities can be selected/reviewed by schools. | 1 | 2 | 3 | 4 | 5 |

## SCORING

Plot individual scores in the box corresponding to each question. Then calculate the average score for each of the 18 questions.

### LEADERSHIP

| Score | | | | | | | | | | | |
|---|---|---|---|---|---|---|---|---|---|---|---|
| 5 | | | | | | | | | | | |
| 4 | | | | | | | | | | | |
| 3 | | | | | | | | | | | |
| 2 | | | | | | | | | | | |
| 1 | | | | | | | | | | | |
| Question | 1a | 1b | 1c | 1d | 2a | 2b | 3a | 3b | 4a | 4b | 4c |

### LEADERSHIP

| Score | | | | | | | | | | | |
|---|---|---|---|---|---|---|---|---|---|---|---|
| 5 | | | | | | | | | | | |
| 4 | | | | | | | | | | | |
| 3 | | | | | | | | | | | |
| 2 | | | | | | | | | | | |
| 1 | | | | | | | | | | | |
| Question | 5a | 5b | 5c | 6a | 6b | 6c | 7a | 7b | 7c | 7d | 7e | 7f |

Estimate the average score for each of the question. List the averages below.

| 1. Middle Level Vision | average score of questions 1a-1d = |
|---|---|
| 2. Beliefs | average score of questions 2a-2b = |
| 3. Content Standards | average score of questions 3a-3b = |
| 4. Policies | average score of questions 4a-4c = |
| 5. Strategic Plan | average score of questions 5a-5c = |
| 6. Parent/Community Involvement | average score of questions 6a-6c = |
| 7. New Leadership Roles | average score of questions 7a-7f = |

### SUPPORT

| Score | | | | | | | | | | | | | | |
|---|---|---|---|---|---|---|---|---|---|---|---|---|---|---|
| 5 | | | | | | | | | | | | | | |
| 4 | | | | | | | | | | | | | | |
| 3 | | | | | | | | | | | | | | |
| 2 | | | | | | | | | | | | | | |
| 1 | | | | | | | | | | | | | | |
| Question | 8a | 8b | 8c | 8d | 9a | 9b | 10a | 10b | 10c | 11a | 11b | 11c | 12a | 12b | 12c |

## SUPPORT

| Score | | | | | | | | | | | | | | |
|---|---|---|---|---|---|---|---|---|---|---|---|---|---|---|
| 5 | | | | | | | | | | | | | | |
| 4 | | | | | | | | | | | | | | |
| 3 | | | | | | | | | | | | | | |
| 2 | | | | | | | | | | | | | | |
| 1 | | | | | | | | | | | | | | |
| Question | 12d | 12e | 13a | 13b | 13c | 13d | 14a | 14b | 14c | 14d | 14e | 14f | 15a | 15b |

Estimate the average score for each of the question. List the averages below.

| | |
|---|---|
| 8. Provide Resources | average score of questions 8a-8d = |
| 9. Coordination/Communication | average score of questions 9a-9b = |
| 10. Information/Research | average score of questions 10a-10c = |
| 11. Culture | average score of questions 11a-11c = |
| 12. Staff Development | average score of questions 12a-12e = |
| 13. School Improvement Planning | average score of questions 13a-13d = |
| 14. Core Curriculum and Instruction | average score of questions 14a-14f = |
| 15. Student Services | average score of questions 15a-15b = |

## ACCOUNTABILITY

| Score | | | | | | | | | | | | | | |
|---|---|---|---|---|---|---|---|---|---|---|---|---|---|---|
| 5 | | | | | | | | | | | | | | |
| 4 | | | | | | | | | | | | | | |
| 3 | | | | | | | | | | | | | | |
| 2 | | | | | | | | | | | | | | |
| 1 | | | | | | | | | | | | | | |
| Question | 16a | 16b | 16c | 17a | 17b | 17c | 17d | 17e | 18a | 18b | 18c | 18d | 18e | 18f | 18g |

Estimate the average score for each of the question. List the averages below.

| | |
|---|---|
| 16. Student Assessment | average score of questions 16a-16c = |
| 17. Program Assessment | average score of questions 17a-17e = |
| 18. Systems Assessment | average score of questions 18a-18g= |

## 1. Middle grades vision

**LEADERSHIP STANDARD**

Establish and model a shared district vision based on goals for what students should know and be able to do.

Please circle a number on the scale below that best represents the status on this standard

1 .................... 2 ..................... 3 ................... 4 ..................... 5

**Not Present**          **Somewhat Present**          **Clearly Visible**

### EXAMPLES

| | | |
|---|---|---|
| No overall vision | → | Vision clearly visible in practice |
| Vision handed down to constituents | → | Vision developed and ratified with all stakeholder groups |
| Multiple (and conflicting) visions for different programs | → | Systemic vision apparent in all program areas of district |
| Limited vision of effective middle-grades practice | → | Vision based on research of effective middle-grades practice and application to local conditions |

## QUESTIONS FOR GATHERING DATA ON YOUR DISTRICT

Gather artifacts, policies, and reports produced by the district over the past 5-10 years. In addition, take a tour of schools, the central office, and when possible, attend school board meetings, looking for actions, artifacts, and language that illustrate the underlying vision. Ask committee members to bring back information and artifacts that provide evidence to answer the following questions:

1. Does the district have a board policy or other written and articulated vision for middle-grades education? If not, is there an "unwritten" vision?
2. What is the vision for middle-grades education in the district? How was it developed and communicated to the community and families? Who was involved in the research, development, and adoption of the vision?
3. How is the vision articulated in day-to-day operations at the district, in the schools, and in the community?
4. Does the district have an overall strategic plan? If yes, how does the vision for middle-grades education fit in with the goals and objectives of the strategic plan?
5. What is the alignment between the vision for middle-grades education and that of other district departments or areas such as curriculum and instruction, elementary, and high school?
6. Does the district vision for middle-grades education align with each middle-grades school's vision?

## SUGGESTED ACTIVITY:

*Envisioning Success*

A clearly articulated and widely shared vision is at the heart of district-wide middle-grades improvement efforts. Establishing consensus about what it is that students should know and be able to do in the middle grades and how middle-grades education should be organized is equally important. The goal of this activity is to clarify and make explicit the personal visions of district staff and then to use these to develop greater district-wide consensus about goals and directions for middle-grades education using form on p. 83. This activity can be undertaken with different district stakeholders, including district staff, teachers, parents, students, and community members. After groups complete this activity, use their personal reflections to examine existing visions and as springboards for establishing consensus on a shared district vision for middle-grades education.

When individuals have finished with their responses, gather together in a group of like-role individuals. Create a visual representation of your vision of success. Share with the whole group. Explore these questions:
- How are the visions similar for each group? What is the most frequently mentioned success?
- How do the visions differ across groups?
- What current practice and/or policy in the district shows the greatest discrepancy from the vision?
- What would it take to change this?

## ENVISIONING SUCCESS

Today is (pick a date in the future when you hope to have achieved some future goals, i.e. three or five years from today). We have gathered together to reflect on the process we have taken to create a system of effective middle schools that reflect the best that is known about teaching and learning. Thus far, we have been extremely successful in bringing this vision to fruition in the district. Think about the accomplishments we have made as a district. Select the one accomplishment you are most proud of and describe it below.

_____
_____

Now reflect on the following questions and write some comments on each:

1. What type of teaching and learning is occurring in the middle schools in this district? What are students doing and learning?

_____
_____

2. What are the most effective structures and practices that exist in middle schools in the district?

_____
_____

3. How are successes at particular middle schools shared with other middle schools in the district?

_____
_____

4. What materials, equipment and resources are available to middle school teachers in the district?

_____
_____

5. What are teachers, staff, school, and district administrators doing? What are their roles?

_____
_____

6. How are families and community agencies involved in the schools? At the district level?

_____
_____
_____

This activity is adapted from the "Helicopter Activity" in *Kindle the Spark*.

## ADDITIONAL RESOURCES FOR ACTIVITIES:

*Tools for Change Workshops*

Produced by the National Staff Development Council, Robby Champion's *Tools for Change Workshops* (1993) provides guidelines and activities for successfully undertaking organization change. In her section on managing change, Champion offers several workshops relevant to creating and establishing vision, including ones dedicated to: prioritizing goals, getting to the business of shared vision, dealing with the inevitable group conflicts, and building group consensus. She also offers the following ten tips on the business of creating a shared vision (pp. 216-7):

1. A primary role of leadership in an organization is to provide a vision that can serve as a guiding light in developing the organization. The process of transforming an organization requires tremendous commitment on the part of the stakeholders who share the vision. The connection between the organization's beliefs, vision, and mission needs to be explicit, logical, and useful, and it must be clearly communicated.

2. People need time to reflect on the vision.

3. People need numerous opportunities to have input into the vision. It cannot become a shared vision in one faculty meeting or in one retreat.

4. To avoid slipping into an everyday operational thinking and problem-solving mode, people need to know the expectations for them in this process. Are they to help refine the vision from the leader or organization? Are they to point out problems? Are they to say where they agree? Will they create a vision for their own sub-unit (department, school, grade, etc.) that is congruent? What will happen next?

5. People need to be in the right frame of mind. To place a visioning session in a 45-minute time slot in a meeting is to imply that it's just another business item, like finding a place for the copy machine key. Music, plenty of time to be heard, a relaxing setting, opportunities to try out ideas in safe, small groups, and imaginative group processes can help pull out the best ideas.

6. People need to be encouraged to think aloud even if ideas are not completely formed. They need to be encouraged to think broadly, to dream (building new adjectives, new metaphors, new slogans, new pictures of our group at work, new products, etc.).

7. "Ahaas" need to be encouraged. Innovative thinking needs a climate in which flashes of insight are valued.

8. Patterns in viewpoints need to be clustered, examined, recognized, and acknowledged. People need opportunities to connect with each other and reach consensus. Often differences in vocabulary make distances seem greater than they really are.

9. People need to know that the vision being built will really count. The leader's behaviors while a group works on creating a shared vision and following the meetings are crucial. Leaders need to become adept at the care and feeding of the vision if it is to be kept alive. A vision statement needs to guide organizational decisions at all levels.

10. People need to know that creating a shared vision is only one step in the process of creating a new organization or renewing an existing one. What happens next? What's going to change? How will the vision become the beacon in a lighthouse?

—from Champion, R. (1993). *Tools for Change Workshops.* Oxford, OH: National Staff Development Council.

## RESOURCES

**Barker, Joel.** *The Power of Vision.*

This video presents several vivid historical examples that illustrate how a vision sustains individuals and groups through hardship by providing a reason to keep going -- to make the vision a reality. Based on concentration camp survivor Victor Frankl's book, *Man's Search for Meaning*, Barker's video provides an excellent introduction to the development of a vision.

**Senge, Peter M. et al. (1994).** *The Fifth Discipline Fieldbook: Strategies and Tools for Building a Learning Organization.* **New York: Bantam Doubleday Dell Publishing Group, Inc.**

This field book is filled with strategies to develop a "learning organization." Shared vision occupies a central place in that organization. Pages 297-347 address this need. "What Do We Want to Create?" (pp. 337-339) provides an additional activity for defining the vision of the organization. This book is focused more towards business than to education, but the activities and concepts are rich, practical, and easily transferrable.

**Shockley, Robert. (1992). Developing a Sense of Mission in Middle Schools in Judith L. Irvin (Ed.),** *Transforming Middle Level Education: Perspectives and Possibilities* **(pp. 93-101). Boston: Allyn and Bacon.**

2. BELIEFS

**LEADERSHIP STANDARD**

# 2. Beliefs

**Define core values and beliefs about student learning based on knowledge of the age group.**

Please circle a number on the scale below that best represents the status on this standard

1 .................................. 2 ................................... 3 ................................... 4 ...................................... 5

**Not Present**　　　　　　　　**Somewhat Present**　　　　　　　　**Clearly Visible**

### EXAMPLES

| | | |
|---|---|---|
| Erroneous or inconsistent beliefs/actions undermine reform | ····················→ | Beliefs align with vision and research and serve as a guide to change |
| Little knowledge of adolescent needs | ····················→ | Knowledge of adolescent development guides practice |
| Limited expectations for some students. High for a few "academically gifted." | ····················→ | Demonstrated high expectations for all students. |

**QUESTIONS FOR GATHERING DATA ON YOUR DISTRICT**

Uncovering fundamental beliefs about young adolescents and middle-grades education may take some detective work. Currently, most official documents declare high expectations for learning for all students. They state a focus on healthy growth and development and achievement. However, practices and informal statements may uncover different beliefs. As Rick Ross states (Senge, 1994):

*We live in a world of self-generating beliefs which remain largely untested. We adopt those beliefs because they are based on conclusions, which are inferred from what we observe, plus our past experience. We are often stuck in the feeling that :*
- *Our beliefs are the truth.*
- *The truth is obvious.*
- *Our beliefs are based on real data.*
- *The data we select are the real data.* — p. 242

This is described as the ladder of inference. In order to improve the results of middle-grades education, your district will need to explore the current beliefs and how the data do or do not support these beliefs. Visits to schools and districts outside your own can provide new data to challenge beliefs. Gather data based on observation, interviews, and through participation in new experiences.

1. What beliefs about adolescent development undergird middle grades decision making, planning, and program development in your school and/or at the district level?

2. Is time set aside for teachers and other stakeholders to discuss beliefs and core values about early adolescence and to share strategies for student learning?

3. How are middle grades practices in your school and/or district consistent with research-based beliefs about early adolescence?

4. What are the most effective practices in middle-grades education in your school? In the district? How do they improve student learning and reflect the developmental needs of early adolescents?

5. How do your students view the beliefs that adults have about them and their abilities to learn? Does this vary across groups of students?

6. What beliefs/values are communicated to parents about middle school students and their ability to learn?

## SUGGESTED ACTIVITY:

*Adolescent Development – Myth or Reality?*

In order to create meaningful learning experiences for young adolescents, a background knowledge about adolescent growth and development is essential. The purpose of the activity on the following page is to review information on early adolescent development to ensure that those involved with middle grades education hold valid beliefs about this age group and about normal growth and development. A second purpose is to provide a forum for discussion of topics related to adolescent development and how changes that occur during this age impact the classroom. The participants should be divided into small groups to complete the quiz, assuring them that it is not a test but a springboard to discussion. Each answer should then be discussed, along with the supporting research. Further, participants may discuss how the myth and reality statements impact classroom planning and decisions.

## RESOURCES

**Senge, P. M. (1994).** *The Fifth Discipline: The Art and Practice of the Learning Organization.* **New York, New York: Doubleday.**

Senge provides practical strategies to utilize "new mental models." These models help surface underlying beliefs and assumptions which may interfere with the organization's stated goals, and ways to explore how the various systems may reinforce these beliefs and practices. (pp 242-253).

A prioritization activity for individuals and the whole group – helps to prioritize the level of agreement of three or four core beliefs for the organization.

**Cisneros, S. (1991). Eleven.** *Woman Hollering Creek and Other Stories.* **New York: Random House Press.**

This chapter is told from the point of view of a girl on her eleventh birthday. The author describes the shame and conflict she feels when the teacher forces her to claim a tattered sweater. It helps adults see the power we have to influence young adolescents and to understand the fragility of their self-concept during this changing time.

**National Middle School Association. (1995)** *This We Believe: Developmentally Responsive Middle Level Schools.* **Columbus, OH: Author.**

This recent version of the organization's statement of beliefs can be used as a springboard for discussions on beliefs for your school and/or district.

**Carnegie Council on Adolescent Development. (1989).** *Turning Points: Preparing American Youth for the 21st Century.* **New York: Carnegie Corporation.**

The *Turning Points* recommendations provide a starting point for discussion on the goals and beliefs about middle-grades education in your district.

**Lewis, Anne. (1990).** *Making It in the Middle: The Why and How of Excellent Schools for Young Urban Adolescents.* **New York: The Edna McConnell Clark Foundation.**

This volume summarizes research and experience for schools that promote success for all students, particularly those in poverty.

## ADOLESCENT DEVELOPMENT — MYTH OR REALITY?*

**Directions:**
1. Place an *M* for Myth beside each statement that is false although it may be widely accepted as true.

2. Place an *R* for Reality beside each statement that is true.

_____ 1. Human beings grow more rapidly during their adolescent growth spurt than during any other time in their lives except infancy.

_____ 2. It is abnormal for an 11-year-old girl to have begun to menstruate.

_____ 3. In an 8th grade classroom you could see a six- to eight-year span in physical development among the students.

_____ 4. Adolescence is characteristically a stormy period marked by rebellious, acting-out behavior.

_____ 5. About 80% of all adolescents make it through adolescence without pathological storm and stress.

_____ 6. During early adolescence, the peer group replaces the family as the most important people in the adolescent's life.

_____ 7. Periods of disequilibrium are typical in families as young teens and parents work out mutually acceptable ways to accommodate teens' new concerns and parents' continuing responsibilities.

_____ 8. When young adolescents request increasing levels of autonomy in areas like dress, curfew, and selection of friends, they are demanding complete independence from parents.

_____ 9. It is normal for young adolescents to appear at times to be self-centered and preoccupied with themselves, often to the exclusion of thoughts or concerns about others.

_____ 10. Young adolescents usually know and can apply to themselves the personal consequences of such risk-taking behavior such as driving or riding in a speeding car, engaging in unprotected sexual intercourse, or hitchhiking on a busy highway.

_____ 11. Young adolescents tend to have bouts of low self-esteem and self-doubt as they adjust to the rapid and pervasive changes in their bodies and their social relationships.

_____ 12. Young adolescents have the same thinking and reasoning skills as adults do.

_____ 13. Young adolescents' questioning of formerly accepted rules and beliefs may be a sign that they are using their new cognitive abilities.

_____ 14. Seeking behavioral independence is a new issue for children during adolescence.

_____ 15. Most young adolescents are concerned about understanding their body changes and incorporating their new physical capabilities and sexual interests into a set of sexual values they have already learned during childhood. While they are curious about the physical sex act, that is not their only sexual concern or interest.

_____ 16. All young adolescents think and learn the same way.

_____ 17. Because they are irresponsible, young adolescents are not capable of or interested in having a role in making decisions that affect them, or in helping other people.

_____ 18. Young adolescents do not want to be separated from the adult world. They need and want opportunities for positive social interaction with adults.

_____ 19. It is important to young adolescents to know that they have done something well. They want to be successful.

_____ 20. While they may need them, young adolescents no longer want rules and limits.

---

*Activity taken from Dorman, Gayle (1996). *Middle Grades Assessment Program: Leaders Manual (pp. 53-54).* Carrboro, NC: Center for Early Adolescence.

3. ACADEMIC CONTENT STANDARDS                                                               91

**LEADERSHIP STANDARD**

# 3. Academic standards

Develop with school and community involvement academic and performance standards for what students should know and be able to do by the end of eighth grade.

Please circle a number on the scale below that best represents the status on this standard
1 .................................. 2 .............................. 3 ................................ 4 ................................ 5

**Not Present**　　　　　　　　　**Somewhat Present**　　　　　　　　　**Clearly Visible**

### EXAMPLES

| | | |
|---|---|---|
| Focus on courses taken, time enrolled | ⟶ | Focus on key content/learning. Alignment with national standards |
| Standards created centrally with little community or teacher input | ⟶ | Standards based on discussion of student work and desired outcomes for students |
| Differential standards based on race, language, special needs | ⟶ | Focus on equity and using standards to benchmark improvement |

## QUESTIONS FOR GATHERING DATA ON YOUR DISTRICT

1. Has the district developed academic standards in the core subject areas? If so, what is the level of implementation and understanding in the schools and the community of the content and performance standards?

2. How were district academic standards established? How are or were all district stakeholders (including school staffs, families, and community members) involved in this process? What is the level of staff development and teacher input into the standards?

3. Does the middle-school curriculum align with established content standards? How is curriculum and instruction being examined to see if it provides opportunities for students to do work that will help them meet the standards?

4. Do district and school mechanisms exist to assess the levels of use of standards-based curriculum and instruction? How is support provided to teachers who must change their practice?

5. How is student achievement of content standards assessed? How are supports provided to students who may struggle to meet the standards, or may have special needs?

6. How does interdisciplinary instruction and teaming at the middle level interact with specific subject content standards and content accountability in the middle schools?

7. Have district and school policies, organization, and structures been examined for how they may enhance or detract from students' opportunities to learn and achieve the content standards? How will they be addressed to ensure that some students do not get left behind as standards are raised?

## SUGGESTED ACTIVITIES/ RESOURCES

## Learning Together About Standards-Based Reform

The field of education reform is packed with new vocabulary. Academic standards and standards-based reform are no exceptions. The first step in standards-based reform is understanding the terms. The "new standards" movement, rather than setting the bar higher in order to sort out students, focuses on standards as a means of clarifying key knowledge goals for students, and as a guide to curriculum, pedagogy, school and student assessment, and professional development.

Three kinds of standards are discussed in the new standards movement: content, performance, and opportunity to learn standards. Your team can hold standards forums for families, students, community members, teachers, and administrators so that everyone will be speaking the same language. Some resources to read and review together:

**Wheelock, A. (1995)** *Standards-based Reform: What Does it Mean for the Middle-Grades?* **New York: Program for Student Achievement, Edna McConnell Clark Foundation.**

This report unravels the sometimes confusing policy debate, terminology, and status of national content standards development. In addition, Wheelock addresses the potential of the "standards movement" for middle school reform to improve student achievement.

**The Education Trust (1996)** *Front End Alignment.* **Washington, DC: Author.**

This publication explains how to carry out a local standards-setting process involving teachers, higher education faculty, parents, and business representatives. It provides useful examples and a step-by-step guide to developing standards and putting them to use in the classroom.

*The Harvard Education Letter*, **XII (5) (1996). Cambridge, MA: Harvard University.**

This issue is devoted to standards in the middle grades.

**The Business Roundtable. (1996).** *A Business Leader's Guide to Setting Standards.* **Washington DC: Author.**

This publication explains standards-based reform, and describes the role that business can play in standards-setting. Copies available for free.

Framing the Debate: A Special Commentary Report. The Politics of Standards. *Education Week*, June 5, 1996, pp. 39-42. Includes articles by: Margaret S. Branson, Roy Romer, Robert G. Morrison, Joyce Elliot, and Diane Ravich.

U.S. Department of Education (1994). *High Standards for All Students.* Washington, DC: Pamphlet produced by the U.S. Government Printing Office: 377-187/10486.

Wiggins, Grant. (1991). Standards, Not Standardization: Evoking Quality Student Work. *Educational Leadership 48* (5), 18-25.

MiddleWeb > www.middleweb.com <  A web site dedicated to urban middle school reform.

This site includes lots of stories and examples from districts engaged in standards-based reform.

## 4. Policies

**LEADERSHIP STANDARD**

Base policies on research-based practices that support student learning and growth and align with the district middle-grades vision, plans, and academic standards.

Please circle a number on the scale below that best represents the status on this standard

1 .................... 2 .................... 3 .................... 4 .................... 5

**Not Present**  **Somewhat Present**  **Clearly Visible**

### EXAMPLES

| | | |
|---|---|---|
| Policies made by board and handed down | Stakeholders involved in development/ratification | Shared decisions on policies including student voice. Waivers available to school sites |
| Policies focus on compliance/inputs | ⟶ | Policies focus on outcomes/flexibility of methods |
| Policies are often contradictory/arbitrary | ⟶ | Policies aligned with vision and plan and based on research |

## QUESTIONS FOR GATHERING DATA ON YOUR DISTRICT

1. Does the district have an overall improvement vision for middle grades education? What policies are integral to supporting this vision?

2. How are district policies decided? How are all key stakeholders involved in policy discussions and decisions? What principles guide policy-making at the district and school levels?

3. How are district policies articulated to stakeholders and the community?

4. At what level are policy decisions made? How much autonomy is afforded to the schools and to the district? Are there state and federal level policies that impact middle grades education?

5. How are school, district, state, and federal policies aligned in practice? Which policies are no longer useful, not implemented, or implemented quite differently than their intent?

6. When were policies last reviewed for their relevancy to current school and district goals? How were stakeholders involved in this review?

7. What provisions exist for schools to obtain waivers to specific state and/or district level policies? If provisions exist, do schools take advantage of the waivers?

## SUGGESTED ACTIVITIES/ RESOURCES

**1. Aligning policies, goals, beliefs, and standards.**

Conventional "wisdom" may result in policies that are in conflict with, undermine, or actually prevent achievement of a district's education goals. Negative results may be unforeseen or unintentional, however, each policy and its impact **in practice** must be examined for alignment. An example of this policy impact analysis that is unfortunately still relevant is *The Way Out: Student Exclusion Practices in Boston Middle Schools*. Written in 1986 by Anne Wheelock at the Massachusetts Advocacy Center, its findings and recommendations are very relevant today. This report is an excellent example of how a community coalition can analyze policy impact.

**2. Engaging policy makers at the district, state, and national level.**

It is crucial that policy makers hear the views of educators, parents, and students and how policy impacts them. A committee to engage policy makers can develop a proactive strategy to inform policy in the development stages. The following resources may help:

**Richardson, J. (1997). Policies that support staff development can help improve student learning.** *The Developer, 1,* (4)

**Council of Chief State School Officers (1992).** *Turning Points: States in Action.* **Washington, DC: Author.**

### General policy resources:

**Brown, R. (1991).** *Schools of Thought.* **San Francisco, CA: Jossey Bass Inc.**

This book examines how policy environments affect teachers and administrators and examines specific policy barriers to thoughtful teaching for improving literacy.

**Education Commission of the States. (1991, March).** *Exploring Policy Options to Restructure Education.* **Denver, CO: Author.**

**Kirst, M. W., & Mazzeo, C. (1996). The Rise, Fall, and Rise of State Assessment in California 1993-96.** *Phi Delta Kappan.* **78 (4). 319-324.**

This case study provides an analysis of forces for policy enactment, by looking at the CLAS.

**Glickman, Carl D. (1993).** *Renewing America's Schools: A Guide for School-based Action.* **San Francisco: Jossey-Bass Publishers.**

Chapter 8, pp. 110-131, discusses the district's role with an emphasis on policy changes and waivers to support student learning and site-based decision-making teams.

**Olsen, Laurie et al. (1994).** *The Unfinished Journey: Restructuring Schools in a Diverse Society.* **San Francisco: California Tomorrow**

Chapter 15 gives specific guidelines on how to gather and use data to inform school plans and policies. Pages 302-303 provide suggestions for establishing a student data and information system. Policy Recommendations for Restructuring (pp. 309-320) illustrates how these data can lead to a specific policy agenda.

## 5. Strategic plan

**LEADERSHIP STANDARD**

Develop a plan to improve student learning that includes goals and timelines and involves schools and community fully.

**Please circle a number on the scale below that best represents the status on this standard**

1 .................... 2 .................... 3 .................... 4 .................... 5

**Not Present**          **Somewhat Present**          **Clearly Visible**

### EXAMPLES

| | | |
|---|---|---|
| No overall plan<br>Plan on paper: no evidence of action/involvement | → | Plan and vision guide all actions and decisions |
| Contradictory plans | → | Plans aligned K-12 and beyond but also focus on the middle-grades unique place/role |
| Unrealistic time lines | → | Long range strategic plan |
| School plans do not align with district plan | → | School plans aligned with district plan |
| No regular review of plan | → | Plan frequently reviewed and revised as conditions change |

## QUESTIONS FOR GATHERING DATA ON YOUR DISTRICT

1. Does an overall strategic plan for the district exist? How does the overall plan relate to the middle-grades? How and when was the plan developed? Who was involved in the plan's development?

2. If a plan exists, how has it been implemented, monitored, evaluated, and modified? Who is responsible for keeping the plan updated?

3. Do the plans and activities of various departments, clusters, grade levels within the district relate to the overall priorities in the district plan? How are different constituencies involved in the plans of various departments?

4. What evidence do you find that the plan is a living document that is used and modified as conditions change? How does the plan guide action at the district level? At the schools? How is the plan communicated to the public? To families and students?

5. Compare the goals, objectives, target dates, resources, and timelines of various plans in the district. Do they reinforce each other, contradict, or operate in isolation from each other? Whose needs do the plans serve? Are the plans useful to the both the implementers and those who need reports of activities?

## 5. STRATEGIC PLAN

**SUGGESTED ACTIVITIES:**

*Planning to Overcome Barriers*

Many detailed plans never make it to the implementation stage, despite research-based activities and timelines. Often this is because the plan does not specifically address the local conditions, including the factors which will block or facilitate the implementation. In order to effectively implement the change to the desired future, the strategic plan must address the key barriers to the change. This can be accomplished with a forcefield analysis. This activity can be done with a district planning group, in a school, or within specific constituency groups. Planning to overcome the barriers will require the group to focus on how to move from the current state to the desired future, based on your context. This can help mobilize commitment to the plan.

Conduct the forcefield analysis after the district has developed a vision and academic standards, and during the strategic planning process.

1. Display the current status, goals and vision, and other key strategic planning documents for the group to see. Ask the group to look at the current status and compare it to the desired future.
2. A succinct sentence summarizing the current status and the desired future should be placed on the forcefield analysis chart.
3. Each member of the group then should individually identify the forces that will drive the change toward the desired future, and those that are barriers to the change.
4. Share the results with the group and create a large forcefield analysis chart on chart paper that includes each member's input.
5. With 1/4" sticky circle labels, each member will vote for the most important barriers.
6. Take the top priority barrier and rephrase it as a problem. Begin the phrase with ("How to...) and then use an action verb with a desired state.
7. Brainstorm solutions to the problem.
8. Evaluate and combine options and choose one or two.
9. Develop an action plan.
10. Build into the strategic plan.
11. Build in evaluation benchmarks and times to review the plan.

*Strategic Visioning — Anticipating and Co-creating the Future*

Developed by the Bailey Alliance, the "Gameboard for Assessing & Strengthening the Change Infrastructure" is a visual template that holds a one page strategic plan summary. It helps the group to see the big picture and stay oriented as they engage in the planning process. At the same time the single visual allows planners to see the connections between the information collected. The chart holds the Vision, Mission, Indicators of Success, Guiding Values & Principles, Open System Involvement, Current Situation Assessment, Strategies to Close the Gap, Potential Barriers and Action Plans. They describe how to work with a group of stakeholders to design large events to carry out the strategic visioning process. This and other visual templates to guide systems change are available from the Bailey Alliance, 778 Brookside Drive, Vacaville, CA 95688. (707) 448-1520. They also offer training for facilitators and leaders of organizational change.

## RESOURCES

*Educational Leadership.* (1991). Strategic Planning Issue 48:7. Alexandria, VA: Association for Supervision and Curriculum Development.

This issue includes 11 articles on strategic planning which range from models for the planning process to stories from school districts around the country. The stories give a particularly good picture of various approaches to strategic planning.

**MCREL.** (1991). *A+chieving Excellence: An Educational Decision-making and Management System.* Kansas City, MO: Midcontinental Regional Educational Laboratory.

This system provides a framework for site-based management, school improvement, and outcomes-based performance. Four main sections address Leadership and Organizational Development, Efficiency, Effectiveness, and Excellence. The needs assessment tools which include surveys and other means to gather and analyze data, and the strategic analysis tactics in the excellence section are particularly relevant to strategic planning at the school or district level.

**Schmuck et al.** (1977). *The Second Handbook of Organization Development in Schools.* Palo Alto, CA: Mayfield Publishing Company.

This book is filled with practical strategies for organizational development. Chapters 7 on various problem solving strategies, 11 on evaluating outcomes, and 12 on institutionalizing organization development in school districts provide specific suggestions for long-range planning.

6. FAMILY/COMMUNITY INVOLVEMENT

LEADERSHIP STANDARD

# 6. Family/community involvement

Engage families and community members in all efforts to improve education at the middle grades.

Please circle a number on the scale below that best represents the status on this standard

1 .................... 2 ........................ 3 ........................ 4 ........................ 5

**Not Present**  **Somewhat Present**  **Clearly Visible**

### EXAMPLES

| | | |
|---|---|---|
| Little involvement and limited understanding– blaming prevalent. | ············→ | All stakeholders work together. Joint responsibility b for student performance. |
| Fragmented/limited services | ············→ | Plan to coordinate services |
| School shut off from community | ············→ | Community as classroom. Community actively engaged in schools |
| Parental alienation | ············→ | Parents as partners |

## QUESTIONS FOR GATHERING DATA ON YOUR DISTRICT

1. What are the community and family perceptions of schools and middle grades education in the district? How does the district gather and analyze data on these perceptions? How is this information used to inform practice?

2. Do parents and community members know the district's goals for what students will know and be able to do by the end of 8th grade? How does the system communicate with the public about its goals and progress towards achieving them? How were families and the community involved in shaping these goals?

3. Do the district and individual school sites have specific goals for family involvement to improve student learning? How are these goals set and communicated to families?

4. How are parents involved in school and district activities? Does a plan for parent outreach exist? Are parents on district and school committees and active in decision-making roles? If not, what are the barriers to this involvement?

5. How does the district involve traditionally under-represented families in middle-grades education and reform? Are strategies in place to reach families who do not speak English?

6. What is the relationship between the schools and the community? How are community agency partners engaged? How do they play a role in school and district improvement efforts? What are the guidelines and goals for community participation in the schools?

7. How are community resources identified and used to extend classroom learning? How are these resources coordinated and linked to schools?

8. Are universities connected to the middle grades reform effort? What informs and guides these partnerships?

## SUGGESTED ACTIVITIES

1. **Utilize standards for parental involvement to assess current practices and brainstorm new ones.**

   The National PTA has developed standards for parental involvement. Use these standards as a benchmark to assess parental involvement in your district. *The School Team Innovator*, May 1997, developed a planning activity using 50 ways to boost family involvement from the Wisconsin Department of Public Instruction suggestions.

2. **Initiate an outreach campaign to better communicate with community members.**

   In the current era of media sophistication, the district must be proactive in communicating the goals and progress of schools clearly with families and the community. Some ideas:

   - Distribute a visually inviting newsletter about education reforms in heavily visited neighborhood stores.
   - Bring in parents and community members to look at student work and compare to the academic standards.
   - Hold a "shadow a middle school student" day. Seek feature stories on the visits, which include profiles of a cross-section of students.
   - Develop and air a cable TV show on a key middle school priority for parents and the community co-hosted by students.

3. **Provide inviting avenues for input from parents and community members.**

   - Hold parent and community breakfast chats with the superintendent and principals.
   - Initiate parent of the month celebrations in each school for parents nominated by student essays.
   - Work with community agencies to sponsor parent seminars for under-represented groups and second language parents on supporting your child's education.

## RESOURCES

## Family Involvement

**Garlington, J. A. (1991)** *Helping Dreams Survive: The Story of a Project Involving African American Families in the Education of Their Children.* **Washington, DC: National Committee for Citizens in Education.**

This book is a story of the "With and For Parents" program in Baltimore as told through the eyes of the assistant director. It combines interviews, documents, journal entries, and recommendations from the carefully examined program. Practical suggestions for meetings, involving students, working with the school, finding community partners, reaching out to parents, understanding the neighborhood, and homes are included.

**Henderson, Anne T., Marburger, Carl L., & Ooms, Theodora. (1986).** *Beyond the Bake Sale: An Educator's Guide to Working With Parents.* **Columbia, MD: National Committee for Citizens in Education.**

This is a practical guide that clarifies five types of parental involvement: as partners; collaborators; audience; supporters; and advisors and co-decision makers. It then provides a way to profile parent involvement in the school and examine the school staff's attitudes about parent involvement. The next section explores basic principles of family-school partnerships and how to take the next steps and overcome barriers to collaboration. Chapter 7 provides four checklists for self-assessment in parent involvement based on characteristics of the school, characteristics of families in the school community, the family-school relationship, and the parent-teacher relationship. It concludes with recommendations for educators, parents, and policymakers.

**Kochan, Frances K. (1992). A New Paradigm of Schooling: Connecting School, Home, and Community. In Irvin, Judith L. (Ed.),** *Transforming Middle Level Education: Perspectives and Possibilities.* **Boston, MA: Allyn and Bacon.**

**Marburger, Carl L. (1990). The School Site Level: Involving Parents in Reform. In Bacharach, Samuel B. (Ed.).** *Education Reform: Making Sense of It All.* **Boston, MA: Allyn and Bacon.**

**Olson, Lynn. (1990). Parents as Partners: Redefining the Social Contract Between Families and Schools.** *Education Week 9*(28).

**Rioux, William J., & Berla, Nancy. (1993).** *Innovations in Parent & Family Involvement.* **Princeton Junction, NJ: Eye On Education, Inc.**

Two main barriers hamper parent-school involvement: school personnel often have not been trained to work with families, and parents are often unsure of themselves and not informed of their rights and what roles they can play in schools. Responding to these two issues, Rioux and Berla describe a wide range of different operational parent-family involvement programs at all different educational levels, including five different programs in middle schools. The authors also profile a number of district-wide initiatives, explore common characteristics of effective programs, and detail what recent research says about parent involvement.

## Community/University Partnerships

**Carpenter, Lynn. (1993).** *Critical Issues in Middle School Reform: School Community Partnerships.* **Philadelphia: PATHS/PRISM: The Philadelphia Partnership for Education.**

**Policy Studies Association. (1996).** *Learning to collaborate. Lessons from School-College Partnerships in the Excellence in Education Program.* **Miami, FL: John S. and James L. Knight Foundation.**

This monograph uses cases from 15 middle school-college partnerships to illustrate lessons learned about project design, implementation, and evaluation. Contact names and numbers are provided as are topics and issues addressed by each of the projects.

**Olsen, L. et al. (1993).** *Restructuring Schools for a Diverse Society.* **San Francisco, CA: California Tomorrow.**

Chapter 6, pp.112-136, "Community Forces for Change" gives a case study of a community coalition for positive change in Oakland, CA. Chapter 5, pp. 92-106, discusses parental involvement.

**Mackinnon, A. (1997).** *Working Together: Harnessing Community Resources to Improve Middle Schools.* **New York, New York: Edna McConnell Clark Foundation. (Available at no cost from the foundation).**

This document describes the development of a community coalition to support and improve middle schools. The author defines a community coalition as "a group of individuals who organize to learn more about the education of young adolescents and engage community resources to improve local schools. It brings together concerned people from inside and outside the school system. Each coalition should be geared to the unique needs and strengths of its school system and its community." The book describes potential accomplishments of a community coalition as well as the nuts and bolts of getting a coalition started and keeping it going. Mackinnon provides case studies from urban districts.

## LEADERSHIP STANDARD

# 7. New leadership roles

**Develop a central office climate that engages staff in the schools and encourages leadership from all stakeholders.**

**Please circle a number on the scale below that best represents the status on this standard**

1 .................... 2 ........................... 3 ......................... 4 ......................... 5

**Not Present**　　　　　　**Somewhat Present**　　　　　　**Clearly Visible**

### EXAMPLES

| | | |
|---|---|---|
| School shut off from community | →  | Community integrally connected |
| Leadership focused on compliance | → | Leadership focused on outcomes/vision inspiration |
| Top-down leadership | → | Shared decision making |
| Focus on the "way we do things around here" | → | Focus on what is best for students |
| Operate in isolation | → | District-level staff actively involved at school sites |
| No leadership structures for teachers/parents | → | Parents/teachers involved as leaders of change |
| Focus on supervision | → | Focus on coaching/facilitating |

**QUESTIONS FOR GATHERING DATA ON YOUR DISTRICT**

1. What is the overall mission of the central office in the district? How does this mission support student learning? How does it support school improvement?

2. How do central office staff define their roles? How do they interact with principals, teachers, and school staff?

3. How is the role of central office staff perceived in the schools and community? Does this mesh with the mission and self-defined role of the central office?

4. Who is responsible for middle-grades reform in the district? What mechanisms are in place to ensure that school staffs, families, and community members are involved in decisions and plans for middle-grades reform?

5. What leadership roles exist for middle-grades stakeholders in the district? How are individuals and groups prepared for these roles?

6. How do district and school leaders demonstrate facilitative and participatory leadership?

7. Where does the authority for important decisions on staffing, budget, and program reside? Do stakeholders feel they have a real role in making important decisions that affect student learning?

8. How well do the existing groups work together as a team? Has guidance or training been provided in team building, meeting management, and facilitation?

## SUGGESTED ACTIVITIES/ RESOURCES

1. **Provide team-building activities for decision-making groups.** The following resources will provide excellent suggestions for conducting team-building activities.

**Lyman, L., & Foyle, H. C. (1990).** *Cooperative Grouping for Interactive Learning: Students, Teachers, and Administrators.* Washington, DC: National Education Association of the United States.

This slim volume is filled with concrete methods to build cooperative groups while engaged in real problem solving to improve the school. The rationale, references, step-by-step instructions for specific activities are all included as are methods to assess the outcome of the cooperative groups. A useful volume for facilitators of a school or district retreat.

**Richardson, Joan. (1996, November).** *The Team Innovator.* Oxford, OH: National Staff Development Council.

This entire issue is devoted to team building for school planning groups. Resources are provided, including a bibliography of more energizers and team-building activities.

2. **Understand the change process and how to facilitate groups.**

Very few members or leaders of school and district improvement committees have had specific training to lead adults in a change process. The following resources help to prepare change leaders.

**Saxl, E. R., Miles, M. B., and Lieberman, A. (1989).** *Assisting Change in Education: A Training Program for School Improvement Facilitators. Trainer's Manual.* Alexandria, VA: Association of Supervision and Curriculum Development.

This training program is based in research on the skills of effective school improvement facilitators in New York City. The training program was then field tested with other facilitators. It contains a series of skills assessments, training modules, and tools to use with school staff in the areas of trust and rapport building, organizational diagnosis, dealing with the process, resource utilization, managing the work, and building the capacity to continue. Case studies, role plays, overhead masters, and planning tools are included.

**Hord, S., Rutherford, W.L., Huling-Austin, L., and Hall, C.E. (1987)** *Taking Charge of Change.* Alexandria VA: Association for Supervision and Curriculum Development.

This book provides insights about the school change process and about the roles and personal needs of people involved in change. The book provides strategies for the thorough management of change, including utilization of: innovation configuration and change component checklists that help to determine the range of activities involved in the change process; a list of seven stages of concern about change model (CBAM), with interventions responding to each stage of change; and tools for assessing the degree of use of innovations and for evaluating progress.

**Mundry, S. E., & Hergert, L. F. (1988).** *Making Change for School Improvement.* **Andover, MA: The NETWORK.**

This simulation game provides a team-building activity for your group while they learn how to effectively plan and manage a change effort. Based on the Concerns Based Adoption Model (CBAM), a district equity team works to achieve student benefits by planning activities and engaging stakeholders in the team's work. An excellent resource for a planning retreat and to forge a new group or provide reflection on their working style for one that has been ongoing.

**3. Examine stories and models from other school districts.**

Your efforts to develop new leadership roles for all stakeholders can benefit from the experience in other locales. Some suggested resources that describe these efforts follow:

**Wagner, T. (1994).** *How Schools Change: Lessons from Three Communities.* **Boston, MA: Beacon Press.**

Tony Wagner, the president of the Institute for Responsive Education, recounts the stories and lessons learned in three communities who engaged citizens in town meetings and focus groups to "reinvent" schools. Methods are included to foster safety for real dialogue, to create "disagreement without being disagreeable," and to break down suspicions between teachers, parents, and school officials. The community meetings described centered around three questions: 1. What important things should all graduates know and be able to do? 2. What values should the schools reinforce? and 3. What are the immediate priorities for school improvement?

**Lewis, A. (1996)** *Believing in Ourselves: Progress and Struggle in Urban Middle School Reform, 1989-1995.* **New York: Edna McConnell Clark Foundation.**

Stories from five districts engaged in middle school reform over a period of five years. The topics include: teacher empowerment, staff development, principal development, assessment, unions, central office leadership, and policy implications.

**New American School Design Corporation. (1996).** *Working Towards Excellence: Early Indicators from Schools Implementing New American School Designs.* **Washington, DC: Author.**

This paper, excerpted from research by the RAND Corporation, describes the work of seven of the New American Schools design teams. Short summaries of the design, its locations, early indicators of progress in the areas of :recognition, student achievement, student and teacher engagement, changes in curriculum, instruction, and organization; and family and community involvement; and ongoing evaluation mechanisms are included. Contact numbers for each design team are included.

**4. Examining the role of central office staff and other groups in district leadership.**

**Cross City Campaign for Urban School Reform. (1995).** *Reinventing Central Office: A Primer for Successful Schools.* **Chicago, IL: Author.**

The functions of curriculum and instruction, personnel, budgets, accountability, governance, and facilities and services are examined from the standpoint of a new vision.

# 8. Resources

**SUPPORT STANDARD**

## 8. Resources

Provide financial and human resources necessary for the change process.

Please circle a number on the scale below that best represents the status on this standard

1 .................... 2 ........................... 3 ..................... 4 ..................... 5

**Not Present**          **Somewhat Present**          **Clearly Visible**

### EXAMPLES

| | | |
|---|---|---|
| Bureaucratic dissemination of resources | → | Resources allocated by school needs and plans |
| School budgets determined centrally | → | Schools control their budgets |
| Personnel assigned arbitrarily – Staff at middle school may not want or be prepared for this level | → | School input/control over personnel configuration/hiring |
| Little time or resources available for professional discussion/development | → | Resources allocated for professional exchange |
| Inequity of resources/ facilities across district | → | Resources focused where needed |

## QUESTIONS FOR GATHERING DATA ON YOUR DISTRICT

Sharing budgets and information on resource allocation are some of the most sensitive areas in middle-grades reform. However, district and school budgets are important indicators of the real priorities in the system. Equity of resource allocation is an important question in large districts. Involvement of stakeholders in the development and maintenance of the budget at the school and district levels provides understanding of the real resources available and enables staff to make informed decisions about allocating resources to the top priorities and mobilizing for increased resources.

1. How are district and school budgets developed? Do schools have input into their own and district budgets? What part of the school budget do local sites control? Do the budget allocations relate to the priorities and needs in the district and school plans?

2. Conduct a facilities, technology, equipment, and materials audit in each school and across the system. How do they compare among schools? Are plans in place to bring each school up to a base level of resources?

3. What funds are available at schools from their own fund-raising efforts? Is assistance provided to school staff on conducting fund-raising events, if fund-raising is a big part of the school's budget?

4. How are school personnel hired and assigned? How many of the teachers at each school are certified in the middle grades and in the content area in which they teach? How many years of experience do teachers possess? Can you track district-wide patterns in teacher and staff assignment by school?

5. How is time organized in the school and district? Does the calendar provide for regular non-teaching time for professional development? If not, how do schools find time for planning and training?

6. How does the district compare with others in the state for funding? Is equity in funding an issue in the state? What is the prognosis for remedies to funding inequities?

## 8. RESOURCES

**SUGGESTED ACTIVITY:**

*Time for Reform*

School improvement is fundamentally people improvement. The vast majority of school budgets are devoted to personnel. However, few resources are included in the budget for the time and consultation that school reform requires when teachers and other adults take on new and expanded roles. Teachers particularly feel torn between conflicting demands on their time. A cornerstone of the middle school concept is time for team planning. In an era of shrinking budgets, time for reform is hard to find.

This activity can be conducted with a district team or a school group. It is a brainstorming activity for how to use time and scheduling more creatively. It should accompany or follow the development of a strategic plan and school improvement plans.

1. Distribute articles that are to be read and shared with the group in the following manner:
   - "Finding time for collaboration" — two people
   - "Teacher professional development: It's about time" — two readers
   - the monograph *Time for Reform* – six people each read one of the six time creation devices, three people each summarize two or three of the seven ways to eliminate barriers to time.

2. After about 10 minutes of individual reading, each person will share the summaries in small groups taking about two minutes each. Then spend about 30 minutes in the group discussing the following questions:

   - Which of the barriers to time and reform are present in our system? Have we employed any of the strategies to lower the barriers? If so, what was the result? If not, which strategy would be a high priority? Are there barriers here that the monograph did not mention? (List these on a chart).
   - Which of the time creation devices mentioned in the monograph or articles are used in the district? Which ones seem most feasible? Which ones would require greater change in current practices? Which ones would yield the most value for the least cost?
   - Based on your discussion, what action to make time for reform does your small group recommend? What are the costs/benefits associated with this choice?

3. Share each group's top priority action, as well as its perceived barriers and feasibility summary of recommended actions.

4. Compile the recommendations and bring to the appropriate decision-making bodies. Report back within one or two months on the outcomes of these decisions.

# RESOURCES

**Berne, R., & Stiefel, L. Measuring Equity at the School Level: The Finance Perspective.** *Educational Evaluation and Policy Analysis 16* (4), 405-421.

This article describes the conceptual and empirical issues that are related to funding equity at the school level. Most analyses of equity have previously been applied to the district as a whole. Funding formulas are described and then examples provided on New York City. The article presents some initial questions and raises many others. One important finding is that subdistricts serving poorer children received more funds per pupil in district office, non-allocated, and indirect categories, and less in specific classroom allocations. In addition, poorer students are taught by less well-educated and less experienced teachers.

*Educational Leadership, 53* **(3) (1995). Special Issue: Productive Use of Time and Space. Alexandria, VA: Association of Supervision and Curriculum Development.**

This issue is filled with examples of scheduling and space use to improve student learning. In addition, the Contemporary Issues section offers three articles on "Does Money Matter?"

**A Special Report on Finance and Equity: Funding for Justice (1995). Milwaukee, WI:** *Rethinking Schools,* **9 (4). An Urban Educational Journal.**

*Rethinking Schools* is a provocative journal advocating the reform of urban schools and emphasizing equity and social justice. Their articles link classroom issues to broader policy concerns and include the perspectives of teachers, parents, and students. This special issue looks at: state equity suits and litigation history, revisits Kozol's book, *Savage Inequalities*, addresses computer equity, how money is spent in U.S. education, and making money make a difference. A glossary of funding terms is also included.

## Articles related to time for reform:

**Purnell, S., & Hill, P. (1992).** *Time for Reform.* **R-4234-EMC. Santa Monica, CA: the RAND Corporation.**

This monograph presents the rationale for increased time for reform, outlines seven strategies to eliminate the barriers to increased time, and six time creation strategies. The practical strategies are garnered from actual schools and districts working on reform. The explanations are clear and realistic about the context of public schools.

**Price, H. B. (1993, May 12). Teacher Professional Development: It's About Time.** *Education Week* (pp. 32 and 24).

This article provides the premise that time for teacher professional development will come from less teacher time with students. The author provides suggestions on academically productive time away from regular teachers for the equivalent of one day a week. The suggestions include community service, instructional television, occasional large classes, higher order assignments and projects, and extracurricular activities.

**Raywid, Mary Anne. (1993). Finding Time for Collaboration.** *Educational Leadership, 51* (1), 30-34.

Raywid surveyed schools around the country to determine how they were making time for collaboration among school personnel, especially teachers. From this research, she offers fifteen good examples of schools that have built in time for teacher collaboration. She also discusses a number of other approaches which have potential to free up teacher time for collaboration: service learning (older students teaching younger ones); hobby day (all adults in the school teach a variety of exploratory lessons to students); larger class sizes; partnership frameworks (university partners handle some instructional activities), and grants providing start-up money for collaborative time.

**SUPPORT STANDARD**

# 9. Coordination/ communication

Provide mechanisms for coordination and communication among schools, grade levels, departments, and external constituencies.

Please circle a number on the scale below that best represents the status on this standard

1 .............................. 2 .............................. 3 .............................. 4 .............................. 5

**Not Present**  **Somewhat Present**  **Clearly Visible**

### EXAMPLES

| | | |
|---|---|---|
| Administrative meetings with one-way communication | ············→ | Networks for dialogue/ professional discussion in place at district and schools |
| Strategic plans/departments isolated | ············→ | Mechanisms to involve departments/schools across grade level/area for coordination |
| Staff isolated by job title | ············→ | Multi-role teams involved in planning |

## 9. COORDINATION/COMMUNICATION

**QUESTIONS FOR GATHERING DATA ON YOUR DISTRICT**

1. What mechanisms exist for communication/coordination between schools, teachers, principals, families, businesses, community groups, and students?

2. In current meetings, what part of the agenda is devoted to exchange of ideas related to curriculum and instruction? What part of the agenda is devoted to interaction among participants?

3. Survey the perceptions of different constituencies relating to the vision, plan, and implementation of middle-grades education in the district. How do they compare to the stated vision? Is there unity or confusion about what is going on beyond their individual department or school?

4. What vehicles exist for multi-role decision making? How well are they working? Who gets the most air time in the meetings? Who makes the decisions in the group?

5. What mechanisms exist for articulation of the transition between elementary, middle, and high school, including subject area and content meetings, service collaboratives, and mechanisms to follow students' progress?

6. Review district and school vehicles for public relations/communication with various audiences. How do they communicate about middle-grades education? Is there a consistent voice/message sent in all vehicles? Are all constituencies and stakeholders being reached?

## SUGGESTED ACTIVITY:

*The Town Meeting*

**Time required: 2-3 hours**

**Who attends:** A large (up to 300) multi-role group of all middle-grades principals, selected elementary and high school principals, teachers from each subject and grade, central office departments, school board, superintendent, students, families, community agencies, business, and advocacy groups.

**Resources needed:** A large meeting room equipped with overheads, portable mike, large chart paper on walls, markers, and small tables for meetings of each constituency group.

**Facilitors:** A small core planning group that represents all constituencies and has planned and shares in facilitating the agenda.

**Goals of the meeting:** To share the perceptions, priorities, current status, and hopes for middle-grades education in the district across constituencies. To get all the constituencies face to face to open up dialogue and communication. To set common goals and vision for the future.

### Agenda

| | |
|---|---|
| 15 min. | Member of Planning Group—Welcome to Town Meeting<br>Purpose/Ground Rules<br>Agenda |
| 30 min. | Visioning of future outcomes for middle-grades—Guided Image<br>Small groups multi-role—share input |
| 60 min. | Current State<br>Pose three questions—What is the best thing, the worst thing, and what needs further study in middle grades education in this district?<br>Consensus groups answer questions |
| 40 min. | Meet as a constituency: answer questions, select reporter<br>— What is your current role in the district in middle-grades education?<br>— What is your relationship to other constituency groups?<br>— What are your perceptions related to the consensus items?<br>— What would you like your role to be? |
| 40 min. | Report back from constituency groups<br>Questions from the audience |
| 30 min. | Fishbowl on next steps |

**Follow-up:** Create a task force to improve communication/coordination, and to establish a consistent and clear plan and vision for middle grades education in the district.

# RESOURCES

## Communication

**Education Commission of the States. (1991).** *Communicating About Restructuring.* **Denver, CO: Author.**

This kit presents practical information on how to develop and implement a state or district communications plan about restructuring. Chapters include: Building Support, Describing Restructuring, Getting the Message Out, Working with the Media, Showing Progress, and Anticipating and Responding to Criticism.

See Standard 6, Parent and Community Involvement, and Standard 7, New Leadership Roles for additional ideas on outreach and communication.

## Forming Networks

**Miller, L. (1988). Unlikely Beginnings: The District Office as a Starting Point for Developing a Professional Culture for Teaching. In A. Lieberman (Ed.),** *Building a Professional Culture in Schools* **(pp. 167-185). New York, New York: Teachers College Press**.

This article states that district networks to develop curriculum, implement new programs, conduct evaluation, and present staff development provide opportunities to build a professional culture for teachers. Specific examples are provided and results assessed.

**Smith, H. & Wigginton, E. (1991). Foxfire Teacher Networks. In A. Lieberman & L. Miller (Eds.),** *Staff Development for Education in the '90s* **(pp.193-221). New York: Teachers College Press.**

This article describes the support and collegiality provided by the networks established for Foxfire teachers. The authors trace the development of the network and the lessons they have learned in one of the most successful teacher networks in the country.

**Lieberman, A. & Grolnick, M. (1997). Networks, Reform, and the Professional Development of Teachers. In A. Hargreaves (Ed.),** *ASCD Yearbook 1997: Rethinking Educational Change with Heart and Mind.* **Alexandria, VA: Association of Supervision and Curriculum Development.**

This chapter presents a theoretical background on networks, presents information on contemporary reform networks, and examines 5 organizational themes of networks. The themes are creating purpose and direction; building collaboration, consensus and commitment; creating activities and relationships as building blocks; providing leadership through cross-cultural brokering, facilitating and keeping the values visible; and dealing with the funding problem.

## SUPPORT STANDARD

## 10. Information/research

Provide schools with current research on academic and performance standards, teaching strategies, and practices that contribute to the academic and social development of young adolescents.

Please circle a number on the scale below that best represents the status on this standard

1 .................... 2 ...................... 3 ..................... 4 ...................... 5

**Not Present**  **Somewhat Present**  **Clearly Visible**

### EXAMPLES

| | | |
|---|---|---|
| Research kept at central office | → | Research used at schools to guide decisions |
| External research focus: questions developed centrally | → | Faculty engaged in action/research |
| Isolated from best national practices | → | Knowledge base and networks based on national practices |

## 10. INFORMATION/RESEARCH

**QUESTIONS FOR GATHERING DATA ON YOUR DISTRICT**

1. How do research and information on best practice inform policies, programs, staff development, and other key practices and beliefs in middle level education in the district? In schools?

2. How are new initiatives adopted? How are they investigated and data on their effects examined?

3. How are faculty and staff involved in study and research? How do they get access to current information and research in teaching, learning, and school climate and organization?

4. What vehicles exist for collection, dissemination, and discussion of current research and best practices?

5. How do the district and school staffs' implicit beliefs reflect or clash with current research on best practice? How are beliefs and research explored in key policy areas such as student retention and suspension?

6. How many faculty and central office staff belong to professional organizations and take part in ongoing professional growth networks and conferences? How does information from state and national meetings come back to the district and schools? How is it shared?

7. What resources are available at the district level to assist school faculty in conducting background research and a literature review?

8. Do partnerships with universities provide access to information and research? How does local university research relate to the school district's research questions and needs?

**SUGGESTED ACTIVITY:**

*Establish a District Action/Research Group*

Teachers are often isolated from each other and have few opportunities to share information and research related to key problem areas. Often the same "solutions" to persistent problems recycle because decisions are made without access to information or research on how these solutions actually worked to improve student performance. A district action/research group to study, explore, and try out solutions to a persistent need area can result in plans with powerful strategies to address need areas. With a task force to explore the current literature and to share experiences, the best thinking of classroom teachers, central office specialists, and university researchers can be tapped. It does not result in an "instant solution" but a more sound long term improvement plan.

Identify a key and persistent problem area in middle grades education across the district. Search collectively for the "root" of the problem. (Often the most apparent causes may not be the root cause). Once the key problem is identified:

1. Gather an action/research group to address the problem. Provide the group with its charge which should include: the product they will develop, the parameters of decision making, the resources they have available, and a time line for work. Make sure the group membership includes various points of view and expertise, but that each member understands that the purpose of the group is inquiry and research leading to development and implementation of a long-term solution.

2. Using multiple sources of current data such as student performance and school plans, set goals for how the organization, teachers, and students will "be" when the problem is solved. What are the desired outcomes? Be as specific as possible here – the outcomes need to be measurable.

3. Assign members of the group to investigate solutions to take the problem from the current state to the desired outcomes. Sources of information can be websites, ERIC, university research, program descriptions from conferences, other districts, universities, and journals and books, among others. Summaries of research in various areas are also available.

4. All group members should read the research and information reviewed and then prioritize the solutions in terms of potential cost, ease of implementation, and expected effects, especially for students.

5. Select two or three top solutions and concentrate on deeper analysis of these solutions. What will be required to implement each? Will training need to be provided? Will policies and organizational arrangements need to change? What resources will be required? Make recommendations based on the answers to these questions and the cost/benefit analysis.

6. When beginning implementation of the solution, involve action research groups in the ongoing assessment of its implementation and its results.

**For more information on action/research and study groups see:**

**Sagor, R. (1997)** "Collaborative Action Research for Educational Change" (pp. 169-191). in the *1997 Association for Supervision and Curriculum Development Yearbook.*

Discusses the research base, practical application, and professional benefits of conducting action research. Three main categories of action research are discussed: teacher development, school development, and organizational development. Case studies and factors contributing to success of the action research group are presented.

**Murphy, C. and others (1995, Summer). Study Groups.** *Journal of Staff Development, 16* **(3), 37-55.**

This section on study groups discusses whole faculty study groups to integrate initiatives and focus school improvement efforts on increased student and teacher learning. Educators from several districts share their experiences.

## RESOURCES

Review of individual research articles taxes the limited study time available to teachers and principals. Staff developers, curriculum specialists, and research and evaluation staff members can work together to provide planning groups and school improvement teams with a synthesis and summaries of research in a given area. Most resources are quickly dated; however, the sources that follow provide an overview of other resources available.

**Lipsitz, J., Jackson, A. W., and Austin, L.M. (March 1997). What Works in Middle-Grades Reform.** *Phi Delta Kappan,* **517-556. (insert copies available for $3 each or 100 copies for $15 from** *Kappan***).**

This insert summarizes 25 years of work to improve schooling for young adolescents. Sections summarize research results from a longitudinal Middle Grades Self Study, and from the reform initiatives of the Carnegie, Kellogg, Lilly, and Edna McConnell Clark Foundations; outline a Manifesto for Middle-Grades Reform, and provide several pages of essential readings on middle level education and reform.

**Maryland State Department of Education (1991).** *Syntheses of Research on Effective Instructional Practices.* **Baltimore, MD: Author.**

Eight-booklet series summarizes current research in these areas: Thinking and Learning; English/Language Arts; Mathematics; Science; Social Studies; and Early, Middle, and High School Learning Years. Each synthesis offers research finding, rationale, and annotated references.

**Wittrock, M. (Ed.).** *Handbook of research on teaching.* **(4th ed.) Washington, DC: American Educational Research Association.**

### Research Digests On-line

The ERIC Digests are two-page research syntheses, complete with bibliography. Over 1600 syntheses are available, and subjects can be found specific to middle-grades education. They are available at http://www.ed.gov/databases/ERIC_Digests/index/

In addition, various government reports related to Goals 2000 and other federal programs are available on-line at http://www.ed.gov/pubs

Sites maintained by the research laboratories for education can be found at http://www.nwrel.org/national/regional-labs.html

AERA: The American Educational Research Association publishes papers presented at their annual conference on a web page. Special interest groups for middle level, school reform, action research, and a host of other topics are included in these postings.

## 11. Culture | SUPPORT STANDARD

# 11. Culture
**Model and sustain a culture of continuous improvement.**

**Please circle a number on the scale below that best represents the status on this standard**

1 .............................. 2 ................................. 3 .................................. 4 .................................. 5

**Not Present**                  **Somewhat Present**                  **Clearly Visible**

### EXAMPLES

| | | |
|---|---|---|
| Reward compliance | → | Reward responsible risk taking |
| Competition between schools | → | Encourage collegial structures/sharing |
| Encourage development for others | → | Model lifelong learning |
| Hierarchical separation | → | Encourage cross-role sharing |

## QUESTIONS FOR GATHERING DATA ON YOUR DISTRICT

Culture is often invisible to those immersed in a setting. Team members from outside the school district can help you to identify the "way we do things here" that embody the culture of the district. In addition, team visits to other school systems can provide you with contrasting cultures that will help you to see the elements of your own district's culture. Compiling data on culture requires going beyond a reliance on what is stated to observe what is enacted.

1. What artifacts and examples can you gather that illustrate the culture of the school district and middle-grades education?

2. Does the district have a slogan or motto that embodies its stated philosophy? If so, how do the elements of culture, such as its rituals, rules, beliefs, roles, and relationships support or contradict this slogan?

3. What metaphors do stakeholders use to describe the system and the reform effort?

4. How conscious are leaders about establishing a culture or environment that supports the system's change efforts? What efforts at reculturing have been initiated? What are their results?

5. What things are not discussed in the district? What does this tell you about the culture of the district?

6. What things does the district do that support the development of a culture of continuous improvement and a community of learners? What things detract from that culture?

## SUGGESTED ACTIVITIES/RESOURCES

Education reform and strategic planning are often described very rationally, with specific outcomes, action plans, and time lines. The literature of change has often focused on the technical aspects of education reform. Lessons from failed reforms and the intractability of large bureaucracies to change, have turned attention to the culture and non-rational side of the change process. Many articles and studies now look at the emotional and cultural aspect of school reform. In reculturing the district, anthropologists and artists can play a particularly helpful role. Reculturing comes about from experiences that connect the heart, mind, and hands together and provide enrollment in a common vision and mission. Here are some suggestions to begin that work.

1. **Use metaphors, models, and role plays to explore and redefine the district's culture in middle-grades.**

Ask multiple stakeholders to work together in small groups to draw a picture illustrating the middle-grades reform effort. They can use a metaphor to do this, describing the effort as if it were an animal, machine, plant, organization, business, or sport. Make sure they explain the parts to your team members. Compare the drawings or metaphors, using the following questions. What are the common themes? Are certain elements always absent? What lessons can metaphors teach us?

For more details on using metaphors to spark real dialogue in a group see:

**Champion, C. (1993). Tools for Change Workshops. Oxford, OH: National Staff Development Council (pp. 95-104). Workshop #6 includes step-by-step procedures and handouts to engage a group in using metaphors as described above.**

Von Oech, R. (1990). *A Whack on the Side of the Head: How to Unlock Creativity*. New York: Warner Books.

2. **Hold a planning and team-building retreat and pay attention to setting the cultural norms and creating time for meaningful dialogue.**

Senge, P.M. (1994). *The Fifth Discipline Fieldbook*. New York: Doubleday.

Senge presents a view of team learning, which he believes goes beyond conventional "team building" skills, to more fundamental changes in the organization. Team learning is founded on dialogue to engender shared meaning. Skillful discussion is then used to reach a decision. In skillful discussion team members follow five basic protocols: 1. Pay attention to your intentions; 2. Balance advocacy with inquiry; 3. Build shared meaning; 4. Use self-awareness as a resource; and 5. Explore impasses. Guidelines for practicing dialogue and skillful discussion are presented along with cases from groups that have used these principles.

**Champion, R. H. (1992). Learning and Using Facilitation Strategies to Maximize Retreats.** *Journal of Staff Development, 13* **(3). Oxford, OH: National Staff Development Council.**

**3. Choose an important aspect of the culture of continuous improvement you want to reinforce in the district. Model this cultural value in all parts of the school system.**

Depending on the cultural value you want to emphasize, different resources may be helpful. For example, a value of caring would lead to resources by Nel Noddings and others. General resources on culture building include:

**Sergiovanni, T. J. (1995)** *The Principalship: A Reflective Practice Perspective* **(3rd ed.). Needham Heights, MA : Allyn and Bacon; and** *Value-Added Leadership: How to Get Extraordinary Results in Schools.* **New York: Harcourt Brace Jovanovich.**

In the first book, Sergiovanni explores metaphors for schooling and leadership in schools, provides examples on building community, and looks at teacher development and supervision from the lens of community building. Appendix 4-1 contains tools to assess organizational and community values in the schools. Many of the suggestions here could apply to the school district level as well. The second book uses examples from successful corporations and schools to establish a new and compelling view of leadership as infused by moral vision and commitment to improvement.

**Deal, T. E., & Peterson, K. D. (1994).** *The Leadership Paradox: Balancing Logic and Artistry in Schools.* **San Francisco, CA: Jossey-Bass Inc.**

Deal and Peterson examine the technical and culture-building roles of the principal and how to balance them. They use metaphors to explore the roles of the principal and utilize case studies to illustrate these roles. The cases show how principals build culture and go beyond charismatic leadership.

**Hargreaves, A. (Ed.). (1997).** *Rethinking Educational Change with Heart and Mind.* **Alexandria, VA: Association for Supervision and Curriculum Development.**

In this ASCD yearbook, chapters by Hargreaves, Fullan, Elkin, Oakes and others explore the depth of cultural change that must take place to transform schools.

4. **Learn from masters at building a community culture.** Business and schools are filled with case examples of successful and failed examples of reculturing an organization. Read the cases and identify the common strategies. Choose several to initiate in your district. Some sources of cases:

*Educational Leadership.* (1996). Creating a Climate for Learning. (54:1). and (1992). Building a Community for Learning. (50:1). Alexandria, VA: Association for Supervision and Curriculum Development.

Both issues include stories of establishing positive cultures in schools and districts. They also examine some of the key conceptual and research background to these efforts.

**Tools for Change Workshops: see Champion above. Workshop #4 "Learning Lessons from Successful Culture Builders"** includes a step-by-step procedure and handouts to read about and discuss two principals who have been successful culture builders.

**SUPPORT STANDARD**

# 12. Staff development

**Provide staff development based on the district plan, school plans, and proven models for individual and organizational change.**

**Please circle a number on the scale below that best represents the status on this standard**

1 ................... 2 ........................... 3 ..................... 4 ..................... 5

**Not Present**          **Somewhat Present**          **Clearly Visible**

### EXAMPLES

| | | |
|---|---|---|
| Staff development consists of centrally planned in-service programs provided by outside expert | → | Most staff development planned at school site based on school improvement plans. District provides support and guidance |
| Staff development given lip service, but few resources | → | Time and resources devoted to staff development |
| Single workshops main vehicle | → | Job embedded staff development: various models used including study, action research |
| Workshops with no follow-up | → | Most resources go for follow-up implementation |
| Limited models for coaching | → | Coaching/peer interaction, one-on-one help in place |

## 12. STAFF DEVELOPMENT

**QUESTIONS FOR GATHERING DATA ON YOUR DISTRICT**

1. What are the top priorities for staff development in the district? How do these relate to improved teaching and learning in the middle-grades? Do these priorities relate to school priorities and to identified need areas? Has staff development been focused on individual or organizational development and/or both?

2. How is staff development content and process selected? Who is involved with the decision? How is staff development planned? On a long-range plan, a yearly plan, or as need arises?

3. Who provides the majority of staff development? What models are mostly used to provide staff development?

4. How effective has staff development been? Has it resulted in new attitudes, beliefs, behaviors, and/or policies and structures? How has it impacted classroom practice and student learning?

5. How has staff development been evaluated and monitored in terms of its outcomes?

**SUGGESTED ACTIVITIES:**

*Mapping the Cycle of Staff Development*

The following activity will assist your group in answering the previous questions. In addition, the single visual will allow you to look at all the staff development initiatives in the district at once. Conduct this activity with the district staff development committee, which should include a representative from each middle school's staff development group, curriculum specialists, and any special program personnel.

# Mapping the Cycle of Staff Development

Materials needed: Large tree of staff development visual, enough small ones for each individual, post-it notes for each participant.

1. Collect school improvement plans, the district strategic plan, the middle-grades education plan, Chapter 1 plans, the district staff development plan, and any other plans that involve staff development at the middle grades. Ask participants to prepare by reviewing and bringing information about staff development at their school or in their program or department.
2. Convene the group at tables with an individual tree and post-its for each participant. The large visual should be displayed on the wall where all can see it.
3. Explain the purpose of the meeting: to get a complete picture of all the staff development in the district related to middle-grades. If it is not specifically for middle-grades, but middle-grades staff is involved, include it on the list.
4. Using the post-its and writing one idea on each post-it, ask participants to review the tree with you. Each part of the tree will represent a staff development initiative which is blossoming, in full fruit, fading out, or beginning to be a bud. Work through a familiar example for each category on the large chart. Then give each person about 15 minutes to fill in each initiative on a post-it and place it on the tree where he/she thinks it belongs. Each school should complete one chart for the things being done at their school site. Each program and department should fill out one chart, and the staff development office should fill out one chart.
5. Post each of the small charts around the big chart. Spend about 15 minutes completing a tour of the wall, asking participants to search for the common threads of staff development across the district. Also ask them to record their impressions when viewing the charts.
6. Ask for impressions first. Allow time for a variety of constituencies to respond. Ask for those with different impressions to respond.
7. Then move to the common threads of staff development across the district. Using markers, write them on pieces of paper that will then be stuck on the chart with post-it glue. When the big chart is complete, take a break and ask each person to review the large chart and see if he/she thinks anything should be moved, or is missing from the chart.
8. Conduct a final round of input after the break. Then ask participants to meet with someone at their table from a different location and discuss for five minutes the implications of the chart.
9. Record these implications on an overhead or a wall chart. These should be turned over to the group planning overall staff development. Each participant should get a copy of the chart, as well as each principal and school improvement council member.

This activity adapted from the Bailey Alliance's Visual Templates

## 12. STAFF DEVELOPMENT

135

### *Using the NSDC Standards for Staff Development*

This book has set forth standards for staff development in middle schools. The National Staff Development Council "views high quality staff development programs as essential to creating schools in which all students and staff members are learners who continually improve their performance." The standards offered by the Council are grouped into three categories. Context standards refer to the culture, system or organization in which new learnings will be integrated. Process standards attend to the "how" of staff development; these describe the method and means by which new knowledge and skills will be acquired. Content standards address the actual knowledge and skills effective middle grades educators need to know or gain through staff development activities. The description of each standard offered by the Council contains the following sections: the standard, the rationale, the example, the outcomes, discussion questions, and references. Overall, the Council suggests five context standards, eleven process standards, and eleven content standards.

Pages 3-4 present ways to use the standards for individuals, schools, district, and state departments.

Pages 60-64 are a self-assessment tool that can be used to set priorities for improvement.

### ADDITIONAL RESOURCES

**Arbuckle, M. A., & Murray, L. B. (1989).** *Building Systems for Professional Growth: An Action Guide.* **Andover, MA: The Regional Laboratory for Educational Improvement of the Northeast and Islands. Now available from The NETWORK.**

This resource provides a step-by-step plan to develop a comprehensive long-range staff development plan for the district. It includes chapters on Educating the Decision Makers, Designing Collaborative Structures, Team Building, Determining Priorities for Professional Growth, Effective Designs for Learning, Evaluation of Staff Development, and Maintenance and Continuity. Chapter 2, Activity 5 on the Critical Attributes of Effective Staff Development is a wonderful introduction to the research on staff development. Handouts for all activities are included in the guide.

**Caldwell, S. D. (1996)** *Professional Development in Learning-Centered Schools.* **Oxford, OH: National Staff Development Council.**

A new book addressing the context of staff development, new roles in the school as a learning organization, process and content of learning, and building capacity within the system. This book provides chapters from a variety of well-known leaders of staff development and presents some of their most current thinking.

**Epstein, Joyce, Lockard, Bryan L., and Dauber, Susan. (1989, June)** *Staff Development in the Middle Grades.* **Baltimore, MD: Center for Research on Elementary and Middle Schools.**

The authors describe forms and purposes of staff development for middle grades educators. They claim staff development is a continuous process which begins with pre-service education and provides the base on which the next level, in-service programs, can be built. In-service activities extend educational opportunities as well as attend to the conditions and needs of staff in particular schools. Finally, advanced education and career development are also included in this continuum. They further argue that staff development activities serve several important purposes: awareness, information transmission, attitude change, skill acquisition, behavior, and student improvement. In the remainder of the manuscript, they detail: teachers' reactions to staff development, research on staff development and middle-grades educators, implications of research on staff development for the middle-grades, state policy recommendations on staff development, and a five-point guide for staff development in the middle- grades.

**National Staff Development Council, P. O. Box 240, Oxford, OH 45056. 1-800-727-7288.**

This organization's mission is "to ensure success for all students by serving as the international network for those who improve schools and by advancing individual and organization development." The journal, the annual conference in December, and other publications are designed specifically for leaders of change. For those new to individual and organizational development, they offer a two-year staff development academy connected to their conferences. Their annual conference guide provides names and addresses of presenters for those seeking consultation in specific staff development areas.

**Joyce, B. (Ed.) (1990).** *Changing School Culture Through Staff Development.* **Alexandria, VA: Association for Curriculum and Supervision Development, 1990.**

Joyce opens this yearbook by claiming that "the future culture of the school will be fashioned by how staff development systems evolve. How good schools will be as educational institutions – how humane and vital they will be as places to work – will be functions of the energy and quality of the investment in their personnel." The rest of this edited volume is dedicated to the structure, process, and delivery of staff development.

**Lieberman, A., & Miller, L. (1991)** *Staff Development for Education in the '90s.* **(2nd ed.). New York: Teachers College Press.**

This book "highlights the contemporary work on professionalizing teaching, restructuring schools, and rethinking teacher education." Part I provides Perspectives on Staff Development from the perspective of researchers active in the field. Part II: Staff Development at Work, uses cases of specific teacher roles and networks to illustrate the role of teachers. An Afterword by Gary Griffin integrates the various themes in a piece titled "Using What We Know."

13. SCHOOL IMPROVEMENT PLANNING 137

**SUPPORT STANDARD**

# 13. School improvement planning

Provide schools with data and assistance to assess their current state, and develop and implement improvement plans.

Please circle a number on the scale below that best represents the status on this standard

1 .................... 2 ......................... 3 ........................ 4 ........................ 5

**Not Present**  **Somewhat Present**  **Clearly Visible**

### EXAMPLES

| | | |
|---|---|---|
| Voluntary involvement | → | Low-performing schools targeted for assistance |
| Plans are the product of a few leaders | → | Facilitators work with all the stakeholders to develop a plan |
| Student performance not linked to plan | → | Plan based on student performance goals |
| Data collected centrally | → | Data collected at all levels |
| No work with schools to interpret data | → | Data analyzed with school staff |
| Focus on standardized test scores | → | Focus on rich multiple data sources |

## QUESTIONS FOR GATHERING DATA ON YOUR DISTRICT

Most districts now require schools to develop improvement plans. Fewer, however, align schools' improvement goals to district strategic plans, staff development, and to services provided to schools. In addition, school staff are provided with little guidance on how to collect and analyze data for the purpose of the school improvement plan.

Gather copies of the school improvement plans for each district middle-grades schools for the past three years. Review the plans with the steering committee.

1. Do the plans build on each other and target specific and measurable goals? How do the strategies chosen by the school mesh with student performance goals and the other need areas outlined in the plan? What data were used to inform the plan?

2. Are there common patterns and goals in the plans? How has the district used these common patterns to guide district priorities?

3. How are plans reviewed and updated? How are they evaluated and monitored? What happens when schools do not meet their target goals over time? How has this changed the process and outcome of the school improvement planning process?

4. How many people helped to develop and are aware of the plan? Were the school's target performance goals set by the school alone? By the district or state alone? or with input from all stakeholders?

## SUGGESTED ACTIVITY:

*Peer Site Visits*

Developing a plan that will be used in the school is the key to effective school improvement planning. A way to accomplish this is to engage peers or "critical friends" in a site visit to provide feedback on the plan's implementation. One method for this is the Protocol, developed by the Coalition of Essential Schools, and the California State Restructuring Initiative. After framing essential questions about teaching and learning tied to that school's improvement goals, a visiting team of teachers works together with the site's teachers to reflect on the questions. The visiting team should review the school's plan and then spend a day on-site to reflect with the improvement team on the critical questions. One aspect of the day should be small group reflection on student work, related to the questions. For more information on the protocol process, contact the Coalition of Essential Schools, Brown University.

## ADDITIONAL RESOURCES

**NEA National Center for Innovation. (1994).** *Decisionpoints: A Process for Rethinking Schools.* **Washington, DC: National Education Association.**

*Decisionpoints* is a game-like approach to school improvement planning. An excellent beginning process for a school planning retreat, the activity utilizes four decks of cards related to Curriculum, Teaching, Learning, and Culture/Organization. The faculty first discuss the purpose of schooling, and how students learn best. Each deck of cards involves various options related to various decisionpoints. The small group reviews the options on the decisionpoints card and chooses one that best describes the school's current reality or desired future. Each group chooses one option per decisionpoints cards and mounts them on a poster board. They then discuss their choices and how they relate to the initial discussion of the purpose of schools and how students learn best. They then bring their poster board for discussion in the large group. The discrepancies between the ideal and actual state for each decisionpoint can be the basis of the school's plan.

**Hirsh, S., & Murphy, M. (1991).** *School Improvement Planning Manual.* **Oxford, OH: National Staff Development Council.**

This complete manual provides an overview of long-range planning and complete sessions on how to develop a plan from readiness, to data gathering, to writing the long-range plan, to developing action plans. A recent update provides materials on maintaining the momentum for the plan.

**Hergert, L. F., Phlegar, J. M., & Perez-Selles, M. E. (1991).** *Kindle the Spark: An Action Guide for Schools Committed to the Success of Every Child.* **Andover, MA: The Regional Laboratory, now The NETWORK.**

This practical book provides guidance through five stages of school improvement. Each stage provides cases, activities and resources to illustrate how a planning team evolves. Appendices A, B, and C list excellent references, an annotated bibliography, and resource organizations. They give specific information on family/community involvement strategies, classroom practice, student support programs, and policies and structures.

**Hopfenberg, W. S., Levin H. M., & Associates. (1993).** *The Accelerated Schools Resource Guide.* **San Francisco, CA: Jossey-Bass Inc.**

This clear and detailed resource guide is intended to be used in conjunction with training and ongoing coaching with a certified accelerated schools coach in order to establish and support an Accelerated School. The philosophy and process for change to improve the schooling for children in at-risk situations outlined here is useful reading for any school improvement group. The Accelerated Schools governance and inquiry process involves all stakeholders in taking stock of the school, envisioning the future, and making change in the school.

14. CORE CURRICULUM & INSTRUCTION

**SUPPORT STANDARD**

# 14. Core curriculum & instruction

Establish core middle-grades curriculum that enables students to meet the content standards for eighth grade.

Please circle a number on the scale below that best represents the status on this standard

1 .................... 2 ..................... 3 ..................... 4 ..................... 5

**Not Present**  **Somewhat Present**  **Clearly Visible**

### EXAMPLES

| | | |
|---|---|---|
| Little curriculum guidance | → | Curriculum support provided by content specialists/school study |
| Fragmented curriculum | → | Integrated curriculum |
| Little attention given to characteristics and interests of young adolescents | → | Developmentally appropriate materials. Young adolescents give curriculum input |
| Textbook centered curriculum | → | Diversity of curriculum resources available |
| Broad shallow coverage | → | Goes in depth in fewer areas, based on key content standards |
| Rigid scope and sequence Tracking by ability group | → | Flexible, based on high standards for all and academic standards |
| One perspective/culture studied | → | Reflects diverse cultures |

## QUESTIONS FOR GATHERING DATA ON YOUR DISTRICT

Effectively understanding the curriculum and instruction in your district requires analysis of curriculum materials, classroom practice, and student work. These all should be examined in order to answer the question " How will this enable students to achieve the academic standard goals? If not, what do we need to do next?" While this is the overarching question for curriculum and instruction, some other information will help as well:

1. Who determines the district and schools' curriculum in the key content areas? Are teachers involved in planning the curriculum as well as its delivery? How are other key stakeholders involved? Does the district take part in any national or state curriculum and teaching initiatives? If so, how does this impact on the overall curriculum?

2. What kinds of training and follow-up supports are available to teachers in curriculum and instruction in the content area and how to teach to the high standards?

3. How well does the curriculum align with the academic standards? What mechanisms are in place for teachers to explore this alignment, and to adapt their curriculum to reflect the standards?

4. What curriculum resources are available at the schools – in the classroom and the library media center, and at the district level? What resources in the community, at the state level, and at the national level are available to teachers and students? How is technology used in the content areas?

5. What do students feel about the curriculum and teaching in the school? Are they engaged in their school work? Do they have a chance to provide input into learning experiences and the curriculum? Do they provide regular feedback on teaching and their learning? Does the curriculum reflect the needs, interests, and skills of young adolescents? Does it relate to real world tasks and inquiry in that content area? Does it result in important products?

6. Do students understand what they must know and be able to do by the end of the 8th grade? Can students communicate about their own progress and do they understand each teacher's expectations of them? Are these expectations communicated clearly and consistently? Are students provided with options that allow them to meet these expectations in different ways and over varied time? Do the expectations reflect a belief that all students can perform at high levels of achievement?

7. How are these expectations communicated to families? Are families provided with information and support to understand the standards and curriculum and to effectively support their child academically?

8. When students do not understand a lesson, or do not keep up with the curriculum, what supports are in place to assist the student? How is differentiation in the curriculum provided to meet individual student needs and prior knowledge? Do teachers regularly examine their lessons and student work to analyze how to improve?

9. Trace access to classes and kinds of grouping present in the middle school. What are the patterns of assignment and achievement in higher level classes such as Advanced Language Arts and Algebra I? How are students assigned to these classes? Can they enroll on their own? Does this pattern of assignment allow all students to be involved in learning experiences that enable them to meet the standards?

10. How are curriculum, textbooks, and other resources decided upon? How often are materials reviewed? How is training and/or support provided for teachers to use the materials?

11. What teaching strategies are used most in the schools? Do teachers choose from a repertoire of research-based teaching strategies? How well does the class process fit the content presented?

12. Trace the percentage of teachers in each middle-grades school who have certification and/or significant expertise in the content area they are teaching. What do these patterns say about curriculum and instruction in the district?

13. Do interdisciplinary teaching teams exist at the school? How do teams work together to enable students to meet high standards? How do teams and subject area departments interact? How is curriculum aligned over the grade levels and integrated within grade levels? Are curriculum maps, syllabi, and/or guides available at each school?

## SUGGESTED ACTIVITIES/RESOURCES

1. **Conduct an analysis of student work, and how the curriculum and instructional practices used in the lesson allow students to meet a particular content standard.**

   The Protocol, a process developed by the California State Restructuring Initiative and the Coalition of Essential Schools, engages teachers with peers in an examination of specific student work. For more information on the Protocol, see Standard #13, School Improvement Planning.

   California Program Quality Review Process. (for more information see the Program Assessment Standard #17).

2. **At the system level, analyze district assessments, curriculum, and instructional methods used to see how they enable students to reach specific content standards at the level of performance indicated in the standards.**

Newmann, F. M. & Wehlage, G. G. (1995). *Successful School Restructuring: A Report to the Public and Educators by the Center on Organization and Restructuring of Schools.* Madison, WI: CORS, University of Wisconsin Center for Education Research. (1-13).

This report summarizes research in over 1500 actively restructuring schools. The authors began with a "focus on student learning." They define "circles of support" from external support, to school organizational capacity to authentic pedagogy and student learning. The criteria they developed for student learning and authentic pedagogy are useful for review by those engaged in standards-based reform. They describe the unifying principles of high quality teaching and learning across disciplines, and complement the academic standards development.

Walker, R. (1996). Map Skills: Chattanooga School Uses Curriculum Mapping to Travel to a Higher Level of Learning. *High Strides*, 9 (1), 1, 4-5. The bimonthly report on urban middle grades. Columbus, OH: National Middle School Association.

Describes the process of curriculum mapping for alignment of subjects across grade level and of units within grade level in order to meet academic standards.

ASCD, (1996). *Integrating the Curriculum.* Alexandria, VA: Author.

A two videotape packet that includes a discussion of curriculum mapping and examples of middle schools using interdisciplinary instruction. Also includes a copy of Heidi Hayes Jacobs' book, described below.

**Glatthorn, A. (1994).** *Developing a Quality Curriculum.* **Alexandria, VA: ASCD.**

Chapters 4, 5, and 9 in this monograph discuss how to develop the district curriculum, align the curriculum with objectives and standards, and conduct a curriculum audit.

3. **Review grouping, class offerings, and assignment patterns across middle schools. Analyze results and plan for changes.**

**Lynn, L., & Wheelock, A. (1997). Making Detracking Work.** *The Harvard Educational Letter, XIII* **(1).**

This entire issue deals with how to pay attention to the process as well as the content and instruction of eliminating tracking.

**The Education Trust, 1725 K Street, N. W. Suite 200, Washington, DC 20006. (202) 293-1217.**

The Education Trust was created to "promote high academic achievement for all students at all levels – kindergarten through college." Their work focuses on the schools and colleges most often left behind in education improvement efforts: those serving low-income, Latino, and African American students. They work with communities to undertake standards-based reform and accountability. They engage in six community compacts for student success, work with local and state K-16 Councils implementing lessons learned in compact sites, sponsor a Title I reform network, convene a national guidance and counseling reform initiative, sponsor a national conference on the progress of standards-based reform, and sponsor an advocacy group for equity in education, The Education Trust Action Network.

4. **Based on data, enable teachers to select and receive training in standards-based curriculum and instruction. Invest the most resources in follow-up support and methods for teachers to engage in ongoing reflection to improve teaching and learning.**

**Mitchell, R., Willis M., & the Chicago Teachers Quest Center. (1995).** *Learning in Overdrive: Designing Curriculum, Instruction, and Assessment from Standards. A Manual for Teachers.* **Washington, DC: Education Trust.**

This manual derives from teachers' experience in bringing standards into their classrooms. It shows step-by-step detail how to work backwards from standards to rich units of instruction. Blank planning forms and a sample standards-driven unit are included in the manual.

National Alliance for Restructuring Education, National Center on Education and the Economy. 700 11th St. N. W. Suite 750, Washinton, DC 20001. (202) 783-3668.

This organization is working on the development of standards and performance tasks and aligning instruction with standards. A recent article in *Educational Leadership* (May 1996) discusses HELPS (High Expectations Learning Process for Standards-Driven Units of Study), their process for planning curriculum and instruction linked to standards.

5. **Review curriculum materials using the national and district standards and national reviews of effective materials as guides.**

**Epstein, Joyce, & Salinas, Karen Clark. (1992).** *Promising Programs in the Middle Grades.* **Reston, VA: National Association of Secondary School Principals.**

Epstein and Salinas provide information about middle grades programs which show promise in improving education for all students, particularly students identified as educationally disadvantaged. In addition to providing information about specific programs, the goal of this monograph is to help educators decide upon goals, gather information, review evidence, and implement visions.

**Jacobs, Heidi Hayes. (Ed.) (1989).** *Interdisciplinary Curriculum: Design and Implementation.* **Alexandria, VA: Association for Supervision and Curriculum Development.**

The volume presents a collection of articles dealing with curriculum integration. The authors detail a range of different curriculum integration options, including concurrent teaching of related subjects, two week long units, residential study revolving around daily living, and year-long courses. They also offer criteria for making integrated curriculum choices and step by step approaches to integration. Themes addressed in the chapters include: the need for interdisciplinary curriculum content, options for integrated curriculums, intellectual and practical criteria for successful integration, descriptions of existing interdisciplinary programs, the selection of fertile themes for integrated learning, and integrating thinking and learning skills across the curriculum.

**Lounsbury, John H. (Ed.) (1992).** *Connecting the Curriculum Through Interdisciplinary Instruction.* **Columbus, OH: National Middle School Association.**

The guiding premise of this book is that "connecting the curriculum via interdisciplinary instruction is not an optional activity for middle level educators – it's mandatory." This edited volume is organized into four parts: what interdisciplinary instruction can do for you, planning for interdisciplinary instruction, interdisciplinary instruction in action, and nurturing and guiding growth. The goal of the book is both to offer specific methods and strategies for creating interdisciplinary experiences and to expand the vision and implementation of interdisciplinary education as an effective way to develop meaningful, relevant, and integrated curriculum based upon the characteristics and needs of young adolescent learners. The concluding chapter provides an annotated guide to select resources on interdisciplinary instruction and sources for interdisciplinary units.

**Maurer, Richard E. (1994).** *Designing Interdisciplinary Curriculum in Middle, Junior High, and High Schools.* **Boston: Allyn and Bacon.**

In this comprehensive sourcebook, the concept of the interdisciplinary curriculum and the research base that supports its use are examined and strategies for designing interdisciplinary curriculums are offered. In addition, the bulk of the book is dedicated to providing a variety of examples of varied length and complexity of successful interdisciplinary curricula, including 23 examples used in middle and junior high schools and 19 examples from the high school level. Maurer concludes by briefly discussing issues of implementation, assessment, and the future of interdisciplinary curriculums.

**Stevenson, Chris, & Carr, Judy F. (Eds.) (1993).** *Integrated Studies in the Middle Grades: 'Dancing Through Walls.'* **New York: Teachers College Press.**

The subtitle of this book, *'Dancing Through Walls,'* was selected deliberately by the editors to highlight the importance of removing the "walls" in middle grades education that keep adolescents from reaching their full potential. By walls, the editors refer to "the mental barriers that derive from a textbook-workbook-recitation-test orientation to instruction; the submission to vague pressures to 'cover' one curriculum or another; the isolation of colleagues in different disciplines; and incongruities between child development theory and prevalent instructional practices." They go on to discuss the benefits of integrated studies, involving the integration of traditional subject matter with student's individual interests. Throughout this volume, the editors present detailed examples of integrated curriculum units designed around topics inherently of interest to students. These units are grouped under studies of self, community studies, nature studies, and interest studies.

**SUPPORT STANDARD**

## 15. Student services

**Develop plans to address individual student needs that recognize student diversity and are based on current research and practices.**

**Please circle a number on the scale below that best represents the status on this standard**

1 ................................ 2 ................................ 3 ................................ 4 ................................ 5

**Not Present**           **Somewhat Present**           **Clearly Visible**

### EXAMPLES

| | | |
|---|---|---|
| Knowledge of diverse student needs reside in specialized departments | → | Staff development and teacher leaders at each campus help all staff meet students' needs |
| Exceptional education services/ plans isolated from school reform or regular education | → | Inclusion of special needs at all points and in plans |
| Little support except for ESL for bilingual students | → | Bilingual/bicultural programs for LEP and English students |
| Gifted and talented services and other student services separate | → | Gifted and talented services/ practices district-wide |

15. STUDENT SERVICES

**QUESTIONS FOR GATHERING DATA ON YOUR DISTRICT**

This standard includes many areas related to providing for the needs of students from a diversity of backgrounds. Supports for students who may need assistance to perform at the standard, guidance services, and programs for bilingual and special education students are addressed here. In addition mechanisms for student involvement in school and community service and for their roles in school discipline and climate are provided.

1. How do the district and schools assess student progress and needs and provide additional supports for students who are unable to meet the academic standards? What opportunities for acceleration and remediation exist at the schools?

2. How do schools provide student guidance? What are the goals of the guidance program? What are the roles and responsibilities of school counselors?

3. Do teacher-based advisory programs or other forms of student guidance exist in the schools? Have the programs' goals and results been assessed? If so, do they provide effective support for students' academic and socio-emotional needs, as well as provide guidance for students' academic and career decisions? What kind of training is provided teachers for their role in teacher-based guidance?

4. How are services for special education students planned and provided? Do general reform plans include provision for special education students? Does the district have an inclusion plan? If so, how are teachers provided with training and support to work with special education students?

5. How is student grouping decided upon in the schools? Do all students have access to a rigorous core curriculum that will allow them to meet the academic standards? If groupings are mainly heterogeneous, what training and planning is provided so teachers can effectively differentiate instruction needs within the regular classroom?

6. How are services for English language learners planned and provided? Do general reform plans include provision for English language learners and their families? How are teachers outside of the English as a second language program provided with training related to language acquisition in the subject areas?

7. Does the district provide a bilingual program as well as English as a second language? Are any two-way bilingual or other programs that build on the language abilities of English language learners provided? How is maintenance of native language and culture provided for?

8. How are students' health needs planned and provided for in the school? If not at the school, how are referrals to appropriate services maintained? Are case management systems provided that help coordinate the services to students and families?

9. How are students' diverse cultural, racial, and ethnic backgrounds recognized and affirmed in the schools? How are relations among different groups addressed? What provisions are made to look at data for students based on their race and ethnicity and to identify and rectify situations of differential treatment? Do families of diverse ethnicity and economic status participate with the schools? What outreach mechanisms exist to include underrepresented groups?

10. How are needs of students based on gender identified and provided for in the schools? Have participation of males and females in courses, activities, and organizations been assessed? Is training provided for faculty on gender equity and sexual harassment?

11. How are students involved in the schools and community as active decision-makers and contributors? Do students have a voice in school decisions and discipline? Do these programs include all segments of the student population?

12. What positive alternatives are provided for students who consistently cannot function in the regular school environment? What are the overall disciplinary and safety policies at the district and schools? Are mechanisms in place to ensure the safety of all students in schools as well as meeting the needs of disruptive students? How is suspension and attendance tracked and assessed?

13. If alternative schools or placements are available, how is the impact of such programs assessed in the short and long term? Have placement decisions been reviewed for patterns of unequal assignment? Are students in alternative schools provided with a curriculum that enables them to meet the academic standards?

## ACTIVITIES/RESOURCES

1. **Review data on suspension, attendance, and disciplinary placement. Review positive discipline alternatives at schools, across the system, and in other sites for the most effective practices.**

**Erb, T. (Ed.). (1996). The Future of Safe Schools. Special theme issue.** *Middle School Journal, 27* **(3). Columbus, OH: NMSA.**

This issue looks at safe schools through a variety of lenses: total school reform; conflict resolution; gay, lesbian, and bisexual issues, sexual harassment of students, and keeping juvenile offenders in school and at home. The "What research says" column looks at middle school discipline. A center section presents students' views on safety issues in the schools.

**Holland, H. (Ed.). (1996).** *High Strides, 8* **(3). Columbus, OH: NMSA.**

This issue looks at safe schools and student misbehavior through highlighting specific programs, alternative middle schools, a review of research, looking at health-promoting schools, and providing resources to other sites.

**Educational Resources for Violence Prevention: a list of curricula, videos, and other materials from the CSN Adolescent Violence Prevention Resource Center, Education Development Center, Inc., 55 Chapel St. Newton, MA 02158.**

2. **Provide training and support related to diversity of race, ethnicity, class, and gender for all staff.**

**Olsen, L. et al. (1994).** *The Unfinished Journey: Restructuring Schools in a Diverse Society.* **San Francisco, CA: California Tomorrow.**

This book, based on a study of restructuring schools in California, provides a wealth of resources on school restructuring to meet the needs of a diverse population. Various chapters relate to school-linked services, multicultural curriculum, flexible student groupings, bilingual education, and inclusive roles for diverse families. Section 4 Appendices includes resources for restructuring schools, a bibliography, a case study school contact list, the research methodology of the study, including questions and the phone interview protocol used.

**Nieto, S. (1992).** *Affirming Diversity: The Sociopolitical Context of Multicultural Education.* **White Plains, NY: Longman.**

This book uses student case studies and theoretical detail to help educators understand the profound impact on students of how their schools relate to diversity. Chapters in Part I use young people's interviews to illuminate the following Issues: racism, discrimination and expectations of students' achievement; structural factors in schools; cultural issues and their impact on learning; and linguistic diversity in multicultural classrooms. Part II of the book relates the implications of diversity for teaching and learning,.

**Gay, G. (1994). Coming of Age Ethnically: Teaching Young Adolescents of Color.** *Theory into Practice, 33* **(3), 149-155. Columbus, OH: College of Education, The Ohio State University.**

This scholar in the field of multicultural education discusses cultural diversity and its status in middle level education theory and how to modify middle level education to be more responsive to the ethnic and cultural diversity of early adolescents.

**Anti-Defamation League of the B'nai Brith. (1992).** *Names Can Really Hurt Us.* **New York: Author.**

This video documents a prejudice awareness and reduction program for middle school students in the New York City public schools conducted with Educators for Social Responsibility and the ADL (both of whom provide excellent resources related to diversity). Issues of prejudice and discrimination based on race, ethnicity, disability, and gender are addressed in this powerful video.

**Erb, T. (Ed.) (1996). Special Section on Gender Equity.** *Middle School Journal, 27* **(5). Columbus, OH: NMSA.**

A special section on gender equity presents varying views and strategies. NMSA has other resources available including a book on multicultural education, and videos related to diversity and sexual harassment.

**Coven, J. (1995)** *Girls in the Middle: Working to Succeed in School.* **Washington, DC: American Association of University Women Educational Foundation.**

Explores gender issues for young adolescent girls in a diverse range of settings. Includes general strategies that middle level girls use to successfully negotiate their environments and young adolescence.

3. **With school staff, review disaggregated student data to seek patterns based on race ethnicity, socioeconomic status, and gender in class assignment, program assignment, grades, and other performance criteria.**

See the resources in curriculum and instruction standard #14 and those above in diversity. Also review San Francisco's experience in a *High Strides* article, January 1977.

**For inclusion of special education students, see:**

**Johnston, W. F. (1994).** How to Educate All the Students Together (pp. 9-14), and Hines, R. Collaborative Teaching for Effective Instruction (pp. 3-6) in *Schools in the Middle, 3* (4). Reston, VA: National Association of Secondary School Principals.

**Mancini, G. H. (1995).** *Special Like Everyone: Including Special Needs Students in Indiana School Communities.* Indianapolis, IN: Middle Grades Improvement Program NETWORK.

This publication utilizes case studies from schools and districts in the MGIP network to illustrate how to: 1. Provide greater access to all students to courses that have heretofore been limited to a small percentage of the population, and 2. Re-examine and modify special education classification, identification, and treatment policies that segregate unnecessary numbers of students from the mainstream.

4. **Explore methods of coordinating or providing comprehensive services for students linked to the schools.**

**Dryfoos, Joy G. (1994).** *Full-Service Schools: A Revolution in Health and Social Services for Children, Youth, and Families.* San Francisco: Jossey-Bass,

In this book, Dryfoos gives specific examples of service programs currently provided in schools; presents a variety of different examples and models of collaborative arrangements between schools, social services agencies, mental health and health departments; and details evidence on how young people have been helped through full-service arrangements.

**Tanaka, G. (Winter 1996).** What's Health Got to Do With it? A Case for Health Programs in Middle Level Schools. *Midpoints, 6* (1). Columbus, OH: National Middle School Association.

This article addresses desired outcomes from school health programs, provides information on community linkages and access to services on or near the school site, and family and parent involvement in health services.

**Hechinger, F.(1992).** *Fateful Choices: Healthy Youth for the 21st Century.* New York: Carnegie Corporation.

5. **Review guidance programs in the schools, including the goals, roles, activities and outcomes of school counselors, teacher advisory, and career counseling.**

Galassi, J., Gulledge, S. and Cox, N. (1997). **Planning and Maintaining Sound Advisory Programs.** *Middle School Journal,* 28 (5), 35-42.

**Cole, C. G. (1992).** *Nurturing a Teacher Advisory Program.* **Columbus, OH: NMSA.**

Provides detailed guidelines for a teacher advisory program.

**6. Review the philosophy, policies and programs related to remediation, retention, and supports for failing students.**

**Cole, R. W. (Ed.). (1995).** *Educating Everybody's Children. Diverse Teaching Strategies for Diverse Learners. What Research and Practice Say About Improving Achievement.* **Alexandria, VA: ASCD.**

The ASCD Advisory Panel on Improving Student Achievement led to this publication, based on the 3-high achievement model developed in the Urban Middle Grades Network. This program provides overall instructional strategies for diverse learners, as well as specific strategies in reading, writing, mathematics and oral communication.

**Holland, H. (1997). Reconsidering Retention – Educators Seek Ways to Reduce Student Failure.** *Middle Ground,* **Spring. Columbus, OH: NMSA.**

This issue of middle ground provides research and resources related to retention and its prevention.

**Center for Research on the Education of Students Placed at Risk (CRESPAR) Howard University, Holy Cross Hall, 427, 2900 Van Ness Street NW. Washington, DC 20008-1194.**

This center is a joint project of Howard University and the Center for Social Organization of Schools at Johns Hopkins University.

This center conducts research and collects information on effective programs for students at risk of failure. The Talent Development Program for middle school students is currently engaged in research along with schools in Baltimore, MD to improve student achievement. A review of Ten Promising Program for Educating Disadvantaged Students is available from the Johns Hopkins group.

16. STUDENT ASSESSMENT 155

**ACCOUNTABILITY STANDARD**

# 16. Student assessment

**Assess student performance using multiple sources and compare to benchmarks for what students should know and be able to do.**

Please circle a number on the scale below that best represents the status on this standard
1 ..................... 2 ..................... 3 ..................... 4 ..................... 5

**Not Present**        **Somewhat Present**        **Clearly Visible**

### EXAMPLES

| | | |
|---|---|---|
| Standardized tests<br>Carnegie Units<br>Assessment by external criteria | → | Multiple sources of assessment Qualitative narratives. Students involved in their own assessment. Mastery emphasized over time. |
| Limited goals for student performance | → | Standards for student performance articulated for middle-grades |
| No school benchmarks for student performance | → | District works with schools to set performance benchmarks/goals |
| Multiple choice/rote knowledge tested | → | Performance/based review of student work tests problem solving higher order skills |

**QUESTIONS FOR GATHERING DATA ON YOUR DISTRICT**

1. How do the district's academic standards, curriculum and instruction, and student assessment relate? Do students know what is expected of them to meet the standards?

2. Does the district specify performance standards for students in the middle grades? At what grades? Are there state-mandated performance standards?

3. How is student progress toward performance standards assessed at the district and school? Are there state level performance assessments? What are they? Are they in alignment with district and school based assessments?

4. How are faculty and school staff included in the development and assessment of student performance? How are students involved in assessing and communicating their learning?

5. How are performance expectations communicated to parents and the community? How are the assessments, their results, and the meaning of the results explained to the community? Has there been community input in decisions about student assessment?

## SUGGESTED ACTIVITY:

*Create a District Assessment Library*

While many teachers and schools exhibit a willingness to try new teaching and assessment methods and strategies, they often do not have access to enough information or successful experienced-based approaches. Further, not all teachers have time to carefully construct alternative assessments. By creating a district assessment library, teachers can have easy access to a wide variety of assessment materials, including design criteria, exemplary and model tasks, and assessment templates.

Several categories of materials related to the theory, methods, and outcomes of student assessments can comprise this assessment library. These can include:

- **Books, Journals, and Videos.** Many current books explore alternative forms of assessment – their philosophy, purpose, limitations, forms, and results. Several of these are included in the resource section of this chapter. Articles on assessment are also commonplace in many educational journals. *Educational Leadership, Phi Delta Kappan,* and *Educational Horizons* have additionally dedicated theme issues to exploring alternative forms of assessment. There are also quality video series dedicated to assessment issues, including the Northwest Regional Educational Laboratory's 14 videos, *In the Classroom Video Training Series.*

- **Assessment Tools, Approaches, and Exemplary Tasks.** These can be grouped by discipline or by thematic unit. Providing teachers with a variety of different options can help them to explore alternatives and to find approaches that will work best for them. These should be culled from teachers within the district, as well as from state and national sources. Staff development and the development of teacher work groups on use of exemplary tasks can support the use of this material.

- **Case Studies.** Case studies provide a way to view the process, problems, limitations, outcomes, and impact of different assessment approaches that have been tried. Case studies can help potential users of an approach to anticipate and avoid common pitfalls before attempting new methods. Case studies can be drawn from teacher comments within the district, from articles detailing what happened when different methods were tried, and from assessment evaluations at any level.

- **Information on Workshops, Study Groups, and Resource Teachers.** Obtaining information from colleagues on the creation, use, and results of alternative assessment is a valuable, cost-effective resource for district teachers. As part of the assessment library, information should be readily available to teachers on when staff development activities will occur, which other teachers are working with new forms of assessment, and which teachers they can contact who have had success with different approaches.

**SUGGESTED ACTIVITY:**

*Workshop on Developing Benchmark Criteria*

Benchmarks provide criteria for assessing expected student performance at different levels. These criteria are essential in driving curriculum and instruction, providing students with a clear idea of what is expected of them, what they need to do to achieve a certain grade, and to put more meaning behind given grades. With the move to more alternative forms of assessment, teachers need information on how to develop meaningful criteria by which to judge student work. In *A Practical Guide to Alternative Assessment*, Herman, Aschbacher, and Winters offer a useful and straightforward framework for developing criteria:

- Investigate how the assessed discipline defines quality performance.

- Gather sample rubrics for assessing writing, speech, the arts, and so on as models to adapt for your purposes.

- Gather samples of students' and experts' work that demonstrate the range of performance from ineffective to very effective.

- Discuss with others the characteristics of these models that distinguish effective ones from ineffective ones.

- Write descriptors for important characteristics.

- Gather another sample of students' work.

- Try out criteria to see if they help you make accurate judgments about students.

- Revise your criteria.

- Try it again until the rubric score captures the "quality" of the work.
— p. 75

In addition to this criteria development framework, Herman, Aschbacher, and Winters' guidebook offers much useful information which can be used in planning workshops on linking assessment and instruction, determining purpose, selecting assessment tasks, ensuring reliable scoring, and using alternative assessment for decision making.

## ADDITIONAL RESOURCES

Brandt, Ronald S. (Ed.).(1992). *Educational Leadership, 49* (8). Theme issue on using performance assessment. Alexandria, VA: Association for Supervision and Curriculum Development.

Cizek, Gregory J. (1993). Alternative Assessments: Yes, But Why? *Educational Horizons 72* (1), 36-40.

Diez, Mary E., & Moon, C. 1992). What Do We Want Students to Know?...and Other Important Questions. *Educational Leadership 49* (8), 38-41.

Henning-Stout, Mary. (1994). *Responsive Assessment: A New Way of Thinking About Learning.* San Francisco: Jossey-Bass, 1994.

Herman, J.L., Aschbacher, P.R., & Winters, L. (1992). *A Practical Guide to Alternative Assessment.* Alexandria, VA: Association for Supervision and Curriculum Development, 1992.

National Education Association. (1993). *Student Portfolios.* West Haven, CT: NEA Professional Library.

Schurr, S. (1992). *The ABC's of Evaluation: 26 Alternative Ways to Assess Student Progress.* Columbus, OH: National Middle School Association.

Wiggins, G.P. (1993). *Assessing Student Performance: Exploring the Purpose and Limits of Testing.* San Francisco: Jossey-Bass.

Wiggins, G.P. (1992). Creating Tests Worth Taking. *Educational Leadership, 49* (8), 826-33.

### Videos

Northwest Regional Educational Laboratory, *In the Classroom Video Training Series,* (503) 275-9576.

San Diego City Schools. *Portfolio Assessment.*

## ACCOUNTABILITY STANDARD

# 17. Program assessment

Gather and analyze data with input from central office staff and stakeholders for use in evaluating and planning school improvement programs.

Please circle a number on the scale below that best represents the status on this standard

1 ..................... 2 ...................... 3 ...................... 4 ...................... 5

**Not Present**  **Somewhat Present**  **Clearly Visible**

### EXAMPLES

| | | |
|---|---|---|
| Limited time for reflection/ evaluation | → | Faculty reflection time built in |
| Outsiders evaluate programs – give results | → | District works with school to establish assessments, gather and interpret data |
| Assessment based on inputs and program features | → | Assessment based on results for students and staff |
| Quantitative assessment emphasized | → | Both quantitative and qualitative measures used |
| Arbitrary criteria | → | Criteria for assessment based on best middle-grades practices/ results. |

## QUESTIONS FOR GATHERING DATA ON YOUR DISTRICT

1. What are the primary means the district uses to assess student and school performance?

2. How are school improvement plans developed, assessed, and adjusted by the district and schools?

3. How are school staff, families, and students involved in setting performance standards, deciding on criteria for quality, selecting assessment tools, and evaluating program progress and results?

4. How does the district monitor and hold schools accountable for their performance? What supports and/or sanctions exist for schools that do not improve?

5. Do teachers, students, and families understand the criteria for school and program assessment? How are the criteria and school and program progress communicated to the public?

6. How are research and evaluation staff engaged with school staff to interpret evaluation data and to answer specific questions for school improvement planning?

**SUGGESTED ACTIVITY:**

*Assist Schools in Conducting Self-Assessments*

A key component of quality accountability programs is school-based self-assessment. There are a number of school self-assessment protocols and evaluation programs that have been developed and marketed to assist schools in conducting needs assessments and developing action plans. Important components to look for when examining these programs are: that they involve all school constituencies, are based on results for students and staff, and are undergirded by research-identified best practices for middle grades. In examining a variety of these programs, Clark and Clark (1994) identified seven organizational components that are common to all approaches to evaluation. These can serve as a framework for developing district specific school assessment programs or for adapting existing protocols to district and school needs. The components include:

- **Establish the goals and objectives of evaluation.** The first step to any evaluation is to determine why it is being conducted, what it will focus on and not focus on, and its breadth and depth.

- **Identify and select appropriate evaluation models, designs, and procedures.** Determine how the evaluation or assessment will be conducted, either creating or selecting instruments and strategies to gather data and information. More encompassing programs often include both qualitative and quantitative assessment measures.

- **Identify and generate the resources to support the evaluation plan.** Evaluation can be a very time and labor intensive process. Decisions about funding, personnel, and timing need to be established before the process is initiated.

- **Collect data.** Depending on the scope of data desired, this can be among the most time consuming parts of the process. Time lines for data collection, training in the use of materials, and the identification of responsibility all need to precede the actual data collection.

- **Analyze information.** Once data are collected, a significant amount of time needs to be spent analyzing them. A process for analysis should be decided before data are collected so that schools are not overwhelmed with information that they cannot process.

- **Report information.** Reporting mechanisms should also be established early on, and developed so that appropriate reports are constructed for differing constituencies.

- **Administration of Information.** Finally, data generated in school evaluations should be used for reflecting, determining strengths and weaknesses, documenting effectiveness, and improving school and program efforts.

Clark and Clark (1994) also offer four examples of middle level evaluations which utilize these elements. These are useful for districts to look at programs such as these, since using an already developed procedure can save a significant amount of time and can be tailored to school needs. The four examples they discuss are the Middle Grades Assessment Program (MGAP), the Shadow Study technique, evaluation developed out of *Turning Points*: *Preparing American Youth for the 21st Century*, and the Comprehensive Assessment of School Environments – Instructional Management System (CASE-IMS). Additionally, Hatch and Rosinia (1992) have prepared a Summary of School Assessment Processes and Instruments which is a useful guide to quickly determining the elements of various school assessment programs. The following is a list of some of the available school assessment processes, with key features and contact references or addresses.

**Middle Grades Assessment Program** (MGAP). Assessment is based on seven developmental needs of young adolescents and research-based elements of academic effectiveness. The program is used to produce a report on the current status of the school and a school improvement action plan. Contact:
Search Institute
700 South Third Street, Suite 210
Minneapolis, Minnesota 55415
1-800-888-7828

**NEA Mastery in Learning Project**. Developing a School Profile and Producing a Faculty Inventory is part of the Mastery in Learning Project, designed to create the conditions and climate that enable students to master important knowledge and skills. Contact:
NEA Mastery in Learning Project
National Education Association
National Center for Innovation
1201 16th Street NW
Washington DC 20036

**Evaluative Criteria for Middle Level Schools.** Examines characteristics of middle schools in seven general areas and eleven subject specific program areas. Three phases involved in this process include: self assessment, visiting team evaluations, and follow up. Contact:
National Study of School Evaluation
5201 Leesburg Pike
Falls Church VA 22041

**Comprehensive Assessment of School Environment – Information Management System** (CASE-IMS). An eight-step process which involves the formation of a School Improvement Management Team and the collection of data on six outcome variables. Seven instruments are used and data is interpreted using computer software. Contact:
 National Association of Secondary School Principals
 1904 Association Drive
 Reston VA 22091

**Clark, Sally, & Clark, Donald (1994).** *Restructuring the Middle Level School: Implications for School Leaders.* **Albany, NY: State University of New York Press.**

**Clark, Sally, & Clark, Donald (1990).** *Restructuring Middle Level Schools: Strategies for Using Turning Points.* **Reston, VA: NASSP.** Clark and Clark have developed procedures for using *Turning Point's* eight recommendations to assess how well middle schools meet these recommendations.

**Middle Level Assessment Instruments**. Middle schools are examined using staff, parent and student surveys in each of nine different dimensions. They can be scored and analyzed with a Center for Middle Level Assessment profile. Contact:
 Center for Middle Level Assessment
 518 East Fillmore Avenue
 Eau Claire WI 54701

*Evaluating School Programs: An Educator's Guide.* This guidebook is intended to help teachers and school administrators evaluate their programs. It includes sections on focusing the evaluation, collecting data, organizing and evaluating information, reporting information and administering the evaluation. Reference:
 Sanders, James R. (1992). *Evaluating School Programs: An Educator's Guide.* Newbury Park, CA: Corwin Press, Inc.

**California Program Quality Review, Middle Level**. This curriculum review process is designed for middle school leadership teams to undertake a self-review to examine how curriculum and instruction can be enhanced so that all students are engaged in high quality thinking and meaningful curriculums. Contact:
 California Department of Education
 School Improvement Office
 P.O. Box 944272
 Sacramento, CA 94244-2720

**Center for the Study of Testing, Evaluation and Educational Policy, Boston College, Boston, MA**. Center staff engage in action research with teachers, school administrators, and districts related to using various forms of assessment in order to improve instruction and learning. They advocate the use of matrix sampling of grades, students, and forms of assessment across the country for the purposes of accountability, and different forms of assessment for the purposes of program and instructional improvement. They utilize a variety of creative techniques, such as student drawings of classrooms and teachers to provide data for the school's use in program planning.

**ACCOUNTABILITY STANDARD**

# 18. Systems assessment

Review and align district practices with the articulated vision, reform plans, accountability mechanisms, and school and community needs.

**Please circle a number on the scale below that best represents the status on this standard**

1 .................... 2 ........................ 3 .................... 4 .................... 5

**Not Present**   **Somewhat Present**   **Clearly Visible**

### EXAMPLES

| | | |
|---|---|---|
| District evaluates schools | → | Whole system assessed including district |
| Schools ranked/compared | → | Individual benchmarks and targets set with schools |
| Lack of accountability for student performance | → | Student performance is bottom line |
| Compliance to bureaucratic state and federal guidelines | → | Integrated standards used to guide compliance based on student outcomes and equity concerns |
| Arbitrary rewards/sanctions | → | Rewards/incentives for improvement and risk-taking Rewards for excellent teaching Rewards for service to schools |

## 17. SYSTEMS ASSESSMENT

**QUESTIONS FOR GATHERING DATA ON YOUR DISTRICT**

1. What system-wide accountability mechanisms are in place in the district? Is assessment of how well the whole district functions a priority?

2. How do various stakeholders provide feedback to the central office? Are structures in place to solicit this feedback regularly?

3. How are district practices reviewed for their alignment with district visions, plans, and accountability procedures? Do mechanisms exist to make changes based on mid-course evaluations and assessments?

4. How are key stakeholders and the public at large informed about district progress toward established goals?

## SUGGESTED ACTIVITIES:

*Conduct a District Audit*

See Chapter 3 for the process and the procedure used for the district middle-grades reform audit.

Also useful for analysis of the system is:

**Senge, P. M. (1994). *The Fifth Discipline Fieldbook*. New York: Doubleday**

In the Chapters "Getting Started" and "Systems Thinking" Senge provides models to assess the current systems (internal), the environments (external), and the character of the organization. Tools provided range from a systems computer model to telling stories to uncovering patterns of behavior in the system over time. Typical systems dilemmas are illustrated and a way to analyze how trends influence each other. pp. 149-50 show "The Archetype Family Tree" to help identify how situations relate to and reinforce one another in a system.

*Develop and Distribute an Annual, Bi-Annual, or Quarterly Report for All District Stakeholders*

One of the most important aspects of system-wide accountability is sharing information about the district as a whole, including individual school's performances with all district stakeholders. This allows for accountability to stated plans and goals, as well as to the expectations of teachers, administrators, parents, students, and community members. Jaeger, Gorney, and Johnson (1994) suggest that school report cards are important mechanisms for sharing information, as they provide "public statements of the condition of individual schools and the results of their education programs" (p. 42). Reporting information from the district would serve to support individual school report cards sent to parents. Types of information that may be reported include:

**District Vision:** The district vision for what students should learn, know, and be able to do is a key factor in guiding decisions about policies and practices. This vision should be regularly shared and discussed with all constituencies. Furthermore, visions for particular educational levels, i.e., the vision for middle grades, should be elaborated upon.

**Content and Performance Standards:** These standards establish academic expectations for students. The public should be informed about how they are decided upon, updated, and where they are available for review. Reporting how well students perform in schools and the district is integral.

**Strategic Planning:** District-wide and school-specific strategic plans are meaningless unless they are actualized in practice. All constituencies should be kept informed about progress toward decided-upon and envisioned goals.

**Parent-Community Involvement:** Reporting on how, where, and how many parents and community members are involved in district and school activities reflects a commitment to connecting home, school, and community.

**Resources:** Adequacy and equity in the provision of resources to schools and district offices are important to highly functioning and successful school districts. Providing detailed information on the genesis and allotment of district resources is key to holding the district accountable to the demands of both adequate resource provision and equitable distribution.

**Assessment:** Student, program, and systems assessments are all important in evaluating the status of the district and evaluating performance toward established goals. Results of the different assessments undertaken in the district should be made available to all stakeholders. This is central to any meaningful accountability system.

Samples of such reports can be obtained from San Diego City Schools, Minneapolis Public Schools, Corpus Christi Independent School District, Long Beach City Schools, and Jefferson County, Kentucky Public Schools.

## ADDITIONAL RESOURCES

Darling-Hammond, Linda.(1992). *Standards of Practice for Learner-Centered Schools.* New York: National Center for Restructuring Education, Schools, and Teaching.

Jaeger, Richard M., Gorney, Barbara E., & Johnson, Robert L. (1994). The Other Kind of Report Card: When Schools Are Graded. *Educational Leadership, 52* (2), 42-45.

Jenks, C. Lynn. (1994). Evaluating an Educational System Systemically. In Charles M. Reigeluth & Robert J. Garfinkel, (Eds.), *Systemic Change in Education* (pp. 35-41). Englewood Cliffs, NJ: Educational Technology Publications.

Mauriel, John J. (1989). *Strategic Leadership for Schools: Creating and Sustaining Productive Change.* San Francisco, CA: Jossey-Bass Publishers.

# III.
## The Case Studies

The case studies provide a picture of district-wide middle-grades reform in four diverse urban school systems across the country. The districts differ in size, demographics, organization, and their state context for education reform. However, they all share a common focus on improving student achievement in the middle-grades. Each district is developing (and in some cases implementing) content and performance standards and setting target performance goals for 8th grade students. They are engaged in a diverse array of reforms. Three of the four received funding from the Edna McConnell Clark Foundation to plan and implement a multi-year standards-based reform effort with the Clark Foundation's Program for Student Achievement. The fourth received funding for a Middle Level Initiative through a local foundation, The Whitehead Foundation.

### Criteria for selection

The districts selected for funding by the Clark Foundation shared some features that the Foundation believed were prerequisites to systemically improving student performance. These conditions were: (1) large proportions of low-performing students, (2) a coherent system of middle schools, (3) demonstrated commitment to increasing student achievement by reforming middle schools, and (4) stable central office leadership with the capacity to implement middle school reform. These preconditions were based on the Foundation's six years of experience working with school districts in the Program for Disadvantaged Youth. Two of the four case studies presented, however, include multiple grade configurations at the middle-grades.

These districts are not presented here as exemplary success stories. Rather, they are accounts of districts grappling with the same challenges that face all urban districts, including the pressure of funding cuts in an era of rising expectations for student performance. In addition, they each face unique circumstances. Their stories are portraits of systemic reform planning and implementation in progress. Some of the districts have improved student achievement, reduced dropout rates, and improved attendance over the past three years. However, at the time of the audits it was too early to see the outcomes in student performance that should come when the content and performance standards are implemented in the classrooms. Each case study and the common themes that run among them suggest some general lessons about the district context and infrastructure necessary to develop, implement, and be accountable for a system of successful schools where all students meet high academic standards.

Primary information for the case studies was gathered through interviews, observations, focus groups, and consensus group discussions during week-long site visits by a team of four or five experienced urban middle-grades educators conducting the Center for Educational Leadership's Middle-grades Reform Audit in January 1995 through January 1996. In one district two DMGRP staff trained and led a local assessment team in conducting the audit. In keeping with the audit protocol, the team conducted focus group interviews with various constituencies, visited a representative number of schools, and reviewed district and state documents, school improvement plans, progress reports, student performance data, foundation evaluation reports, and newspaper and magazine articles. Follow-up interviews and review of documents were also carried out. In one of the districts, the DMGRP staff had provided technical assistance for five years prior to the site visit.

Each case describes the school system's overall history and current priorities, the state and local middle-grades education context, and uses the framework of leadership, support, and accountability to describe the current infrastructure for middle-grades reform and provide recommendations for its improvement. Finally, initial results of the district reform initiative and the audit will be discussed. These cases represent a snapshot of the district at the time of the audits; many of the conditions described have since changed and in many cases progress has been made. In one of the districts, across-the-board improvement in student test scores is seen as a result of implementation of standards-based reform.

# 5.
# CORPUS CHRISTI: Small Town Culture and Urban Challenges

Corpus Christi Independent School District (CCISD) displays many characteristics of a small town school system. The Superintendent of Schools attended the district as a student and came up through the ranks of administration. Many of the principals, teachers, and administrators attended district schools. They refer regularly to cousins or siblings who also work in or attend the district's schools. Unlike some other urban districts, the district's personnel are from the community; they feel ownership for the schools and the students they serve. However, the density of population, the large numbers of students the district enrolls – and their growing poverty – demonstrate the urban nature of the district. Of the 42,000 students in the district, approximately half qualify for free or reduced lunch. 10,000 of these students attend 12 middle schools. 70% of the middle-school students are Hispanic, 25% are Anglo, 5% are African American, and 1% are other. The student enrollment in the district reflects the population of the city, which is 50.38% Hispanic, 43.8% Anglo, 4.5% African American, and 1.3% other (1994).

### High-stakes state testing program

Corpus Christi prides itself on being the "best-performing urban district in the state." The Texas Assessment of Academic Skills (TAAS), a state-wide yearly test in mathematics, reading, and writing, provides widely publicized data on student performance. The State Department of Education provides Texas Successful Schools Awards, monetary incentives for significant improvement in TAAS performance. A state-wide accountability system, introduced the 1993-94 school year, rates districts and campuses based on criteria such as test scores, dropout rates, and performance (1994). Corpus Christi's students outperformed all other urban districts on the test. They met or exceeded their target goals for all students in reading, for white students in writing, but did not meet the goals in mathematics.

A school report card, prepared by the state, is distributed to each family with children enrolled in the school. Schools rated as low-performing by the state receive additional assistance from the state and district. If performance does not improve, schools may be restructured or closed. In 1994 five of Corpus Christi's 57 campuses were rated "low-performing." Performance improved at four campuses; the remaining middle school rated as low-performing was restructured into a fine arts magnet academy. In 1996 no schools rate as low-performing and the TAAS scores continued to improve. Principals, teachers, and central office staff, as well as the whole community, focus on "improving TAAS scores" as a key goal of any education reform in CCISD.

### District strategic plan

The school board, superintendent, central office leaders and principals in CCISD share a common vision for the district that is rooted in the District Action Plan and strategic plan. The highest stated priority in the district is to improve student learning and achievement, with a particular focus on closing the achievement gap between educationally disadvantaged students and others. The district uses the TAAS reading, writing, and mathematics scores, along with attendance, dropout rates, and college admission rates to set objectives for improvement in the District Action Plan and school improvement plans. The four priority areas of the current district plan are academic standards, mathematics, middle school systemic reform, and discipline.

### Academic standards

The district completed the development of academic content and performance standards for K-12 schools in 1995. This participatory process brought together over 100 teachers, principals, business, and community leaders. The group outlined the skills that will be required for Corpus Christi's high school graduates in the 21st century. Teachers then developed specific content standards in each core subject area that would also lead to the needed skills. For the first time, middle-grades teachers had an opportunity to meet with teachers from other schools and grade levels to discuss what students should know and be able to do in core subject areas. The content and performance standards have been widely disseminated to the public and families. An Academic Excellence Task Force composed of community members helped suggest the skills to include in the standards and reviewed the standards in several drafts.

### Vertical teams

In February of 1995, the district restructured into vertical teams that report to an executive director. These teams include elementary, middle, and high schools that share students and feeder patterns. The motivation behind this restructuring was to provide fewer schools for each director to work with and to increase the directors' and principals' accountability for student results in their team. Under this new arrangement, former directors of high school and elementary education now lead teams of K-12 schools. A single assistant superintendent for instruction and operations encompasses the duties often lodged in two divisions. The assistant superintendent, (one of the few prominent staff originally from outside the district), with the superintendent and board's guidance, has initiated many of the new reforms. The assistant superintendent is actively involved with principals and provides hands-on leadership both to communicate overall district priorities and goals and to provide assistance in implementation. Significant attention to aligning policies, practices, and priorities with the overall strategic plan is evident in most district plans. This integrated vision of all initiatives is shared widely by the central office leadership and, in most cases, the principals.

## State and Local Middle-Grades Education Context

Texas is one of 20 states involved in the Carnegie Corporation's *Middle-Grades School State Policy Initiative* (MGSSPI). Since 1990, each of the participating states received funds to develop and implement state policies and practices to improve middle-grades education based on the seven recommendations of the Carnegie Council on Adolescent Development's *Turning Points* report (1989). In Texas, the State Department of Education has initiated many activities and policies that impact on individual schools and, to a certain extent, local school districts. These include: (1) state policies requiring an interdisciplinary team planning as well as an individual preparation period for teachers in middle-grades schools; (2) state middle-grades teacher certification; (3) a middle-grades staff person in the State Department of Education, who initiated and chairs the Texas School partnership network; and (4) staff development assistance and funding for individual schools in middle-grades education (1994). For the past two years, individual demonstration schools have been funded through the MGSSPI to improve middle-grades curriculum, instruction, and assessment, and to provide comprehensive health service plans. These two areas had been the least fully implemented of the Carnegie Council's seven recommendations in the previous four years of project funding.

Through this initiative, middle-grades education has received increased attention throughout the state. Policy makers such as the Chief State School Officers and local superintendents have received technical assistance and been part of national conferences and networking meetings of the MGSSPI. Individual schools, and to a lesser extent local school districts, have responded to and benefited from this focus on middle-grades education. Two middle schools in CCISD are part of the state-initiated School Partnership Network. One of the Corpus Christi schools in the partnership is a designated mentor school, and receives visitors and provides assistance to other schools throughout the state.

Despite this focus on the middle-grades, the middle schools in Corpus Christi are still viewed negatively by families and the public. Many feel they are not safe. In addition, the academic performance of the district's students in the middle-grades is not as positive as at elementary and high school. A community discipline committee that convened during 1994/95 made many recommendations specific to middle school. The district leadership prioritized middle school reform to address these community concerns, to reduce the number of families who take their students out of the system for middle school, to improve safety in middle schools, and to improve student performance at the middle-grades.

## Leadership: Alignment of Policy, Structures, and Culture

### Policy and strategic plan

In CCISD, the key policy elements of the middle-grades education plan are in place. Systemic middle school reform is one of the four stated priority areas in the district action plan. The assistant superintendent for instruction and operations is actively involved in the initiative. The director of academics is the overall leader of the reform effort in addition to many other duties. No single director is solely responsible for middle-grades education, however. Policies and staff development plans from the district align with the performance goals stated by the district, but the school staff development plans do not always align with the district plan. In addition, school staff development plans do not always closely relate to specific student performance goals.

### Beliefs

All twelve middle-grades schools are 6-8 schools with individual and team planning time provided for teachers. Sixth and seventh grade teachers on each campus are teamed. The district and the state are committed to providing the resources necessary to maintain the team planning time.

### Culture and new leadership roles

Corpus Christi's leadership challenge areas are not those of lack of policy or structures for middle-grades education; they are more subtle. They relate to the culture of expected roles for leaders and followers. The district appears to have a long-standing culture that does not challenge leadership decisions or encourage open dissent or even debate. Most interviewee comments were supportive of all the leadership decisions, yet some cracks in the unanimity appeared in the short time the team was on-site. One person who expressed mild dissent for the vertical team model of organization approached the audit team the next day to apologize. Parents at several schools stated that central office staff and principals do not want to hear negative comments. "They want to sweep it under the rug," stated one parent.

### New leadership roles

The district initiated a comprehensive principal leadership training and recruitment program with a local university. This program was rated positively with principals. The new principal at the middle school magnet of the arts is a recent graduate of that program, having come from the teaching ranks. In Corpus Christi, the middle school principals are a close-knit group, sharing ideas and strategies freely. Central office-facilitated principals' meetings, now in vertical cluster teams, occur regularly. They often include staff development related to district priorities, such as math or technology. Principals to date have not had great input into the agenda or content of their meetings. In addition, the principals have been switched from school-to-school over the past several years. Most principals have been at their buildings for three years or less.

Many teachers mentioned the academic standards planning as one of the first opportunities in the district in which they were involved in making decisions. An instructional advisory panel of teachers from across the district meets regularly with the assistant superintendent to provide input and direction into district policies.

Few opportunities exist for students to participate in school or district decision-making. At some middle schools, student councils are active, but they do not provide input into curriculum and instruction decisions.

**Content standards**

Academic content and performance standards now are in place. Performance targets related to TAAS improvement come from the state; they are specific and detailed for each school. Eighth grade is a benchmark year for the test.

The audit team found that most teachers were aware of the new standards; their school's representative had kept them informed. Six of the twelve middle school campuses are piloting the standards and providing detailed feedback to the Academic Excellence Task Force that finalized them. In addition, most of the staff and community members interviewed understand that the development of the standards is the beginning of a process to improve teaching and learning. Standards on paper will not lead to improved student performance, it is how the standards development and discussion lead to use of new teaching skills and engage all students in key content that will make the difference in student performance. For this reason, the leader of the task force wanted wide involvement in the development and review of the standards. Volunteer schools are piloting the standards to provide additional feedback on their usefulness to teachers. The District Action Plan for 1994-95 includes staff development to implement the standards, incorporate multiple forms of assessment and align the curriculum with the standards, and develop interdisciplinary units that reflect the standards.

**Coordination and communication**

Reviewing the documents of Corpus Christi, one gets a clear idea of the stated priorities, the strategies to reach the goals, and how the initiatives will be implemented and evaluated. The vertical team structure of the central office and schools is designed to increase individual executive director's accountability for student performance, to mirror the current level of accountability for performance felt by principals and teachers. It also attempts to provide K-12 planning and articulation for a specific group of students. Some of the middle school principals expressed concern because the vertical team configuration was decided without their input. They also felt that it would neglect the important need of middle school leaders to plan together.

A proposal review team for the Clark Foundation (1994) suggested that the CCISD plan, while comprehensive, appeared to have been decided in a top-down fashion. At this point, district leadership is working to develop a more inclusive culture in which all stakeholders have input into and responsibility for policies and decisions. New avenues for staff, parent, and community input are in place, such as action teams of the strategic plan, the advisory council, the discipline committee, and the school-based decision making groups. It may take time for these actions to result in an atmosphere more encouraging to open debate. Opportunities for anonymous feedback, such as were provided in the middle-grades reform audit, may surface some of the differences. Individuality and team work need to complement each other in successful change efforts. An environment that does not support debate and difference of opinion may become subject to "groupthink," stifling much-needed suggestions for improvement.

### Parent and community involvement

Parent involvement varies from school to school. Some schools work with large numbers of parents, providing parent-to-parent outreach for classes about supporting school success. Volunteers provide classroom support. In other schools, the only parents involved are in the PTSA or on the decision-making team. These parents are usually from the higher socioeconomic status families. One task force of the strategic planning group is working on improving parent and community involvement.

Community organizations and businesses are getting more involved with the schools. Each school has a business partner. Community agencies and business representatives participate in various task forces and committees of the district and at school.

## Support: Prioritizing Shrinking Resources

### Staff development

Teachers and principals could cite many instances of central office support. They praised the staff development training offered by the central office. They felt that the instructional specialists who work with a variety of schools related to specific content areas and instructional strategies are very helpful, if spread very thin. In addition, site-based decision-making teams receive their own resources for staff development and planning. Unlike some systems with decentralized decision making that provides central office assistance only by request, CCISD has concentrated its central office instructional and staff development assistance with the middle schools and the lowest-performing schools. This reflects the priorities in the strategic plan.

### Resources

Teachers and principals expressed some concern about this approach, however. They stated that some schools got the money and priority treatment in order to improve their performance, while others are left to "fend for themselves." Equity of resources and programming between campuses and programs was a major concern of parents, teachers, and principals. Some parents wanted to know why all schools could not enjoy similar resources as the gifted and talented magnet. The gifted and talented magnet requires an IQ test for entrance. Indeed, access within schools to high quality instruction and curriculum materials also varies, and tracking of students into levels is common. In addition the schools designated low-performing and the new arts magnet received additional support. The justification for this differential resource allocation has not been explained to the satisfaction of the school communities that are not receiving the top priority support.

**Staff development for curriculum and instruction**

Curriculum and instruction support for middle-grades has been tied to three outside initiatives: Dimensions of Learning, the Curriculum Project, and Total Quality School training. Each of these initiatives is tied to priorities in the District Action Plan. Teachers and principals generally spoke positively about the content of the staff development. Teachers' main staff development concern was about the lack of follow-up to assist in the classroom application of the training they received. As one teacher stated, "It's hard to keep focused on what you learned. Other people from your school or team may not have gone (to the training). Unless you observe teachers and provide support in the classroom, it doesn't get done." To address this concern, teachers on released time for the year are providing in-class support on effective teaching strategies.

The use of the daily team planning time is uneven, with most teams using the time to discuss discipline and to coordinate daily activities. To improve teaching and learning, teams of teachers should sometimes use their planning time to read research, discuss implementation of a new strategy, evaluate the success of a strategy with students, or conduct action research related to priority school goals. Using teachers in conducting staff development leads to greater implementation of initiatives and also provides professional opportunities for master teachers without their leaving classroom teaching.

Resources and teacher preparation for the new standards were a great concern. Due to budget cuts, the district increased class size, resulting in the layoff of many teachers. Teacher reassignment has resulted in middle-grades teachers, particularly in social studies, teaching outside their main certification or content expertise. In addition, at the time of the switch, the social studies specialist position was vacant, so those teachers new to social studies did not receive much support to teach the new content area. A system review of teacher certification and experience, especially in language arts and mathematics, could provide guidance about staff development needs of reassigned teachers related to their new subject area responsibilities.

Students express varied views on curriculum and instruction in the district. In some schools and classrooms, hands-on activities, field investigation, community service, and challenging content are provided regularly. However, students still spend a majority of their time in individual seatwork and listening to the teacher.

### Student services

Student services should be strengthened in the middle-grades. Individual programs, such as Cities-in-Schools, provide mentoring and support for students that are at risk of failure in the regular setting. However, the whole school guidance and advisory role needs to be reviewed and expanded. Many counselors are spending their time on paperwork and registering students rather than working with student groups and planning advisement activities with teachers. The state-recommended comprehensive guidance program could serve as a study document for this review.

Limited English proficient (LEP), special education, and gifted and talented programs do not seem to be integrated in the overall plans for middle-grades reform and student services. Currently CCISD does not offer bilingual programs, but offers English as a second language. Research data on native language and culture preservation and student performance in English should be examined to see if CCISD's LEP program provides the support these students need to become effective learners in English.

At the same time that the class size increase was implemented and some teachers were reassigned out of their area of expertise, the district implemented an inclusion program for special education. Teachers did not have sufficient preparation to handle these transitions at the same time.

Safety and discipline are priority concerns of teachers, parents, and community members. Despite a zero tolerance policy that allows for removal of disruptive students, many teachers feel that the district needs to provide more alternative settings for middle-grades students who do not function well in the regular school setting. Currently there is a single alternative program for students with disciplinary infractions. They attend that program for a short amount of time, then return to the regular classroom.

### School improvement planning

Resources from the district and outside organizations are assisting schools in developing self-assessments to inform their school improvement plans. The central office provides dissagregated student data to schools, and the new school report card from the state also includes student performance data. More guidance about how to use data to develop effective strategies for a school improvement plan is needed, as school improvement plans do not always align with the district plan or student performance goals.

## Accountability: Moving Beyond State Tests

### Student assessment

Student performance goals and benchmarks are currently based on the TAAS results. These results also form the core of school assessments. To align with the standards, teachers are developing rubrics for the assessment tasks and exploring multiple forms of assessment, including portfolios and performance tasks. In several middle schools, student-led teacher/parent conferences to discuss progress have shown great promise. In addition to involving students in assessing their own work and taking responsibility for analyzing their progress, student-led conferences show dramatic potential for increasing parent attendance at school open houses. When students lead the conferences, parents get a more complete picture of the students' work – what they know and are able to do, and the changes they have made over time.

## Program assessment

Led by an outside consultant, each middle school's leadership team reviewed its school's strengths and weaknesses and set priority improvement goals in spring of 1995. These assessments did not include an evaluation of each school's implementation of staff development strategies, the new academic standards, or the Discipline Committee's recommendations, however. Assessment of how team planning time is used and how it relates to school goals was also not included in the assessment. As more decision-making power goes to site-based teams, they will need guidance and assistance on how best to evaluate their school's initiatives and how the strategies outlined in their improvement plans will lead to their student performance goals.

## Systems assessment

The middle-grades reform audit was the first attempt by the district to evaluate the system in terms of the effectiveness of a grade level group of schools. Some task forces, such as the Discipline Committee, had evaluated and made recommendations regarding some aspects of the systems' functioning. The vertical teams will be expected to evaluate their students, the articulation of their curriculum, and to make joint plans for all schools represented in the team. Some of the vertical teams have begun this process. At one middle school the audit team observed a meeting of the vertical team's elementary, middle, and high school mathematics teachers to develop plans for improving math instruction and content. Mathematics improvement is also one of the core goals of the district.

The Instructional Advisory Council provides input into decisions at the district level, and makes recommendations based on informal assessment of district work. Formalizing the role of this group and the vertical teams in assessing the effectiveness of the central office functions could be a valuable addition to the assessments already in place. In addition, it would model the continuous improvement and participatory management the district seeks.

## Results of the Audit

The audit team visited all the middle schools in CCISD, talked with all executive directors, met with portions of the board, the superintendent, district staff, and then met with all executive directors for feedback. The Middle-Grades Reform audit in CCISD came at the beginning of a new structure of vertical teams and the implementation of academic standards. The opportunity for all stakeholders to provide anonymous feedback on the district's efficacy in developing a system that supports high-achieving middle schools was timely in the district planning cycle. The visit by external colleagues provided a new perspective on the district's current state and concrete suggestions for improvement. It signaled the importance of the middle-grades initiative and informed multiple stakeholders about the district's accomplishments and challenges. As one of the executive directors stated at the audit team's debriefing session, "We've had a lot of consultants and outsiders visit. This audit provided us with a common understanding of where we are, and some realistic suggestions for improvement." Following the audit recommendations, several changes were made in the district's practice. These are: implementation of study groups to provide follow-up to staff development and for teachers at the same school to support each other as they learn new skills; teacher mentors who will provide on-site support for staff development content; a review and reassessment of the use of team planning time; the development of an intensive demonstration school in which language acquisition strategies will be researched and demonstrated, and multiple methods to communicate the meaning and application of the standards to the community and the schools.

## Summary

Corpus Christi Independent School District has established many of the foundational policies and structures crucial to middle-grades reform to allow students to reach high academic standards. The state context, which includes strong support for middle-grades education, facilitates the district's goals and plans. Funded projects such as the Carnegie Middle School State Policy Initiative and the Clark Foundation's Program for Student Achievement provide technical assistance, networking, and outside impetus for improving and utilizing research-based innovations. Shared vision for structures to build a culture of continuous improvement bespeak a thoughtful and committed leadership in the district. The relative numbers of middle schools, the uniform 6-8 grade level configuration, and the feeder patterns all contribute to a manageable group of schools that can plan for implementing the middle school concept, as well as meeting the K-12 needs of students in the vertical teams. These substantial facilitators for middle grades reform may be offset by the lack of a single central office person or a steering committee whose sole responsibility it is to lead systemic middle-grades reform. However, the shared responsibility for middle-grades reform effort requires coordination and communication of work among the executive directors, the directors of academics, principals, and school staff.

Further targeted attention now must turn to sustained staff development and follow up to ensure implementation of policies and practices that allow all students to meet high standards. The expertise of language acquisition specialists and special educators will contribute greatly to this effort. With increased standards and expectations for student performance, the guidance and support mechanisms also should be strengthened, especially the teaching team's guidance and support role. Further development of participatory decision making, especially involving teachers, students, and traditionally under-represented groups of parents will enhance the ownership by all groups involved in the ambitious plans. These constituencies can contribute new perspectives on district challenges and suggestions on how they may be solved.

Accountability mechanisms currently are focused on improvement of TAAS scores. Support and staff development will assist teachers in utilizing multiple forms of assessment that reflect the depth of student learning and the quality of student work. Program and whole system assessment, such as the district audit, could be expanded and conducted by stakeholders in the district. In this way, high-stakes accountability for student performance will be shared among all the stakeholders, and will move beyond viewing the TAAS scores as the major indicator of school and student success. ❑

## Resources

Corpus Christi Independent School District. (1995). *District action plan: 1995-1996 Update.* Corpus Christi, TX: Author.

Corpus Christi Independent School District. (1995). *Implementation grant proposal to Edna McConnell Clark Foundation.* Corpus Christi, TX: Author.

Corpus Christi Independent School District. (1994). *Planning year proposal to Edna McConnell Clark Foundation.* Corpus Christi, TX: Author.

Corpus Christi Independent School District. (1994). *State of the district report.* Corpus Christi, TX: Author.

Corpus Christi Independent School District. (1994). *Strategic planning project implementation schedule & progress report.* Corpus Christi, TX: Author.

Corpus Christi Independent School District. (1995, February). *The curriculum quickletter.* Second Edition. Corpus Christi, TX: Author.

Division of Instruction and Operations, Corpus Christi Independent School District. (1995-1996). *Middle school course catalogue.*

Dalton, Herbert F., *Corpus Christi Independent School District excellent schools program.* (1995, March). Middlebury, VT: Foundation for Excellent Schools.

# 6.
# MINNEAPOLIS: Balancing School Choice and Systemic Accountability

Minneapolis Public Schools boast a national reputation for innovation. Minnesota was one of the first states to adopt legislation in the area of school choice. According to a May 1994 *Kappan* article, in 1992-93 more than 113,000 (14%) of Minnesota's K-12 students actively selected their schools. In Minneapolis, over 11,000 middle-grades students attend 19 different schools. Grade configurations vary from K-6, 6-8, to K-8. Magnet centers offer alternative programs with a thematic approach and specialized courses in pre-international baccalaureate, math/science/technology, urban environmental, or international fine arts.

## Decentralization of curriculum

Since 1989, Minneapolis schools have used site-based management for curriculum and program decisions. During 1989, budget cuts, all centralized curriculum planning, and central office curriculum coordinator positions were eliminated. Since that time, schools have designed their own curriculum without central guidance or coordination. An internal curriculum review in 1994 found that "students are not prepared for post-secondary education or employment, that students found the curriculum boring, irrelevant, or culturally biased, and that student achievement had declined since the lack of central coordination." Based on this review, in 1994 the district began to develop K-12 core content and performance standards to improve the consistency of expectations and outcomes for student performance throughout the system. Led by a part-time curriculum specialist in each subject area, teachers in math, language arts, science, and social studies are developing the content standards. The state guidelines for student performance have been in flux over the past several years. As of October 1995, the state required broad 12th grade graduation requirements, and had no curriculum frameworks for their implementation.

## Improving student achievement referendum

In 1990, a five-year public referendum provided funds to improve student learning. $160 million were allocated for reduced class size, staff development, and early childhood education. Middle school class sizes are limited to 26 students. Most of the staff development activities centered on instructional strategies, such as cooperative learning, separate from subject matter content. As part of the reemphasis on content standards, the staff development focus over the next several years will couple curriculum and instruction.

### Superintendent pay linked to performance

Since 1989, the district has had four superintendents. In December of 1993, Peter Hutchinson and his private firm, Public Strategies Incorporated, were contracted to run the district. Mr. Hutchinson's compensation is based on meeting target goals in the district's "Improvement Agenda." Minneapolis is one of three districts in the United States that directly ties compensation of the superintendent to performance targets. The target goals have been based on student test scores, attendance, behavior, and family support indicators. The district's primary goal for 1994-95 as expressed in the Superintendent's contract with the Board of Education is (1) "to raise the average achievement of our students to at least the national norm and (2) to eliminate the gaps that exist between racial and ethnic groups as well as between female and male students. Doing so means concentrating on and believing in all of our students — without exception."

### Central office service role

Since Mr. Hutchinson's employment as superintendent, district functions have been reexamined. The central office has been restructured to reflect a service orientation. "Meeting and exceeding the expectations of customers" is one of the major criteria for effectiveness of each division. A District Strategy Team convened and developed a "Strategic Direction" with accountability benchmarks for the district. In addition, several task forces representing Board of Education members, principals, teachers, administrators, parents, and community members have reviewed and made recommendations for site-based management, conducted a quality of education review (The Quality Schools Study), and made recommendations about grade configuration, student attendance areas, student assignments, and program identification in the District Options Project report. At the time of the middle-grades audit team's site visit to Minneapolis, these reports and service center restructuring efforts were so new that several of the reconfigured central office divisions had not yet met together.

## State and Local Middle-Grades Education Context

### Middle schools reconfiguration

In 1991-93, Minneapolis moved from a junior high to a middle school model. Six junior high schools were challenged to restructure their programs into fully implemented middle schools by the end of June 1995. The schools conducted the Center for Early Adolescence's Middle-Grades Assessment Program as part of the planning process for the middle school transition. Schools also submitted proposals to the district for funds to implement specific programs. K-8 and K-6 schools were not involved in the planning or transition to middle schools.

As the priorities of new superintendents changed and funding priorities shifted, the middle school principals perceived a lack of continuing commitment by the district to the middle school restructuring. "It's as though they got us all excited about this new idea, and then cut out the rug from under us. We were asked to go ahead and implement our plans without the funding and support for middle-grades staffing," commented one principal.

## Choice and focus

In addition, school choice with so many different grade configurations and closed enrollment for new students in many K-8 schools meant that middle schools competed with K-8 and K-6 schools for 6th grade students, and that many of the more transient and needy students enrolled in the middle schools. The middle schools have small numbers of 6th grade students, with the majority of their students entering in 7th grade. In a district where choice is a central value, the middle schools have not been perceived by many families as a positive choice, but as the place students go if they don't attend a K-8 program. According to the district Quality Report, families perceived the middle schools as less safe than K-8 schools. The district loses enrollment of students at the middle-grades, with some families reporting that they take students out of the schools for middle-grades and return them for high school.

The K-8, K-6, and 6-8 schools offer very different programs, elective offerings, and content throughout the district. During the parent focus group conducted by the audit team it became evident that the parents at the meeting were surprised by the very different offerings and programs among the schools their children attended. Parents at the meeting felt that while the choices were good, they were not sure that many families knew how to access the system to make the best program choices for their students.

Parent and community involvement in the district is quite active. Community members serve on site councils, on district evaluation committees, and in the schools. Many of the schools utilize community service as part of the curriculum. However, there is still greater participation and knowledge and access to the system for well-educated families, who are predominately white. Greater percentages of white students attend specialty and magnet programs than do children of color. The District Quality Report set a priority of improving equity of access to all programs. At several schools, parent outreach coordinators and committees are working to assist parents in selecting appropriate educational settings for their children and in helping parents to support their child's progress in school. In addition, parent committees are working to help teachers better understand the culture and neighborhoods of the schools. This knowledge is particularly important at the middle-grades with the different program offerings at the middle school and K-8 settings.

## Reasserting the vision

To reestablish the focus on middle school restructuring, in spring of 1994 the district's middle school principals began meeting to discuss common issues. Those meetings began to be convened by the district and were expanded to include teacher representatives from all schools, middle-grades students, and community organizations. This group is facilitated by a middle school coordinator (a curriculum specialist position) from the Teaching and Instructional Services Division, and a liaison from the School Services Division.

At the time of the audit, this advisory group was anxiously awaiting the results of the District Options Report that would recommend student assignment patterns and grade configurations. The middle school principals, particularly, were concerned whether the recommendations would signal a strengthening or a weakening of the district's commitment to middle schools.

### Results and recommendations of the audit

One immediate result of the audit was to provide a forum for teachers, principals, and central office staff to share their views on the strengths, challenges, and areas that need investigation in middle-grades in Minneapolis. It brought a national perspective on middle-grades reform to the School Board, Superintendent, district leadership, and school personnel that helped to provide direction for next steps. It signaled to the schools that the district was serious about modeling continuous improvement and self-assessment. The following sections will not cover all the findings or recommendations for the district, but will highlight the main themes that arose in the district related to leadership, support, and accountability.

### Leadership: Modeling System Evaluation and Accountability

Minneapolis Public School System has exhibited a willingness to reexamine and transform the district's leadership. One of three districts in the country with a public/private partnership running the district and with the superintendent's compensation tied to Improvement Agenda goals, the district leadership has been refocused on meeting service goals. The relationship between the local American Federation of Teachers officials and the district leadership is very supportive, and the division directors work cooperatively with little regard to turf. Participatory structures are being developed with students, families, teachers, principals, and other administrators working together.

The District Improvement Agenda provides overall goals, objectives, tasks, and success indicators for the Minneapolis Public Schools for 1994-95. The improvement agenda is not very explicit about district plans for middle-grades education, however the Board approved a resolution supporting systemic reform of middle-grades education in 1994. This will require a more detailed vision of the common elements of middle-grades education across all schools. The middle school program as a positive choice that meets the developmental and academic needs of young adolescents and that offers unique programs needs to be articulated and communicated to all constituencies, especially families.

The District Options Report recommended reducing the number of grade configurations offered in the city and providing more flexibility in middle school enrollment. This would reduce competition for 6th graders and ensure adequate numbers of 6th graders at the middle schools. With more options at the middle schools, parents could choose which middle school program for their students to attend, within broader boundaries.

The development of content standards and multiple sources of assessment will require central communication and staff development for its successful implementation in the classroom. In the schools already utilizing portfolios, non-graded options, and other new forms of assessment, some parents expressed confusion and frustration about how they would know about their students' progress in relation to benchmark achievement targets. One parent said, "Each team in this school works in different ways. How do I make sure that my child is achieving what she needs to, so she can make it in high school?" Family members and teachers will need to be informed about how to interpret and successfully utilize the new forms of assessment.

### Central coordination – individual school flexibility

The policies, plans, and leadership roles for the district are a work in progress. The restructuring plans and policy statements are so recent that it is difficult to judge how they will be implemented. The district leadership seems very open to review data, acknowledge weaknesses, and make improvements.

The biggest challenge facing the district leadership is how to reestablish central coordination in a district that has been so decentralized without hampering an individual school's flexibility to develop and offer unique program choices. The district has launched several initiatives to address this need. The first and most central of these is the development of curriculum and 8th grade performance benchmarks for all students. As one principal put it:

> *For the first two years after the central organization was dismantled, we did not feel the loss. Experienced teachers had internalized appropriate standards and current research. Now the research is stale...we need to keep going, develop consistent and challenging standards. There is no alignment between schools and between the high school and the middle school. What we call algebra varies widely in content across the district.*

The decentralization of curriculum and content planning had a particular impact at the middle-grades. Different facilities, certification, and numbers of students at K-8 and middle schools resulted in very different course offerings from program to program in the middle-grades.

### Participatory decisions at the school system level

A second effort towards systemic leadership for middle-grades education is the development of an advisory group that involves teachers, principals, parents, and students, as well as central office staff in district-wide planning for middle-grades education. One concern of this group and the principals, however, was the need for a voice in budgetary priorities for the middle-grades at the district level. The school site-based management teams and decision-making groups have latitude in making school decisions, but many district decisions heavily impact schools. There currently exists no structured mechanism for input from the school management teams and principals into this budgeting process. One outcome from the audit report recommendations was for the principals to meet with the Strategy Group (similar to the Superintendent's Cabinet) and provide input into the budget and decision process for middle-grades education. In addition, many school management teams seemed unaware of the 1994 district guidelines on site-based decision making. Broader dissemination and discussion of this policy document may clear up some of the confusion and frustration about parameters of authority between the district and schools.

**Focus on priorities**

A third effort of the district is the development of policies that improve articulation across schools. Some of these policies include consistent specialty choices at middle-grades and high school and consolidation to fewer grade configurations. An additional leadership need recognized by teachers, principals, parents, students and the district as a whole is for focus. As stated in the district's review of programs, the Quality Report of 1994:

> ...districts tend to generate many new initiatives simultaneously, but superficially. (Loucks-Horsley et al. 1987)...these many new initiatives (launched in the past 3 years) challenge the ability to focus....Most of our energy should be on direct approaches for increasing student learning and building collegial energy around student learning....when schools feel inundated with many weakly supported initiatives, everyone becomes frustrated and it is difficult to understand what should be a priority for staff, students, and community. The most important decision a school district makes is selecting which initiatives are priorities.

This re-establishment of a proactive vision and leadership with clear-cut priorities of initiatives will be essential to closing the achievement gap between students and to reducing the quality differential between middle-grades schools in Minneapolis.

## Support: Establishing Services to Schools

District support functions assist the schools and provide district-wide leadership roles for teachers, parents, and students in implementing the policies and plans for middle-grades education. Without sustained and ongoing support, the best policies will never translate into classroom changes and student learning. The Minneapolis school system is beginning to reassert the support functions of the central office, after a period of emphasis on decentralization and reduced support. The new service orientation of the district divisions and the re-establishment of content and curriculum leadership and support are paramount to this reorientation. This focus is very new and is not yet in evidence in most of the schools. Principals, teachers, and parent leaders were all puzzled when asked about support functions provided by the district to schools. Many teachers could cite former ways that the district provided support, but said that those had been discontinued.

### Resources for professional development

If not personnel assistance, the district has provided key resources to improve teaching and learning over the past five years. Central office reductions, reduced class sizes, and additional funds for staff development have demonstrated a commitment to directing resources towards students and classrooms. At the same time, the way district resources are allocated remains a source of concern for principals and site-based management teams. Middle school principals, particularly, felt that resources were not adequate to provide the staffing needed for their programs. A participatory district budgeting process could assist in prioritizing spending where schools feel it is most needed.

### Coordination and communication

Another important central office support function is to establish a culture of sharing best ideas and of continuous improvement. Minneapolis has some of the best and most innovative programs in the country, yet principals and teachers reported feeling isolated, unaware of the programs and activities at other schools. As one teacher expressed, "There is a great lack of cohesion between schools. We have no mechanisms for articulation between grade levels and high school."

The development of content standards is the first time that teachers from different schools and grade levels have gotten together to discuss common goals for what students should know and be able to do by the end of 4th, 8th, and 12th grades. Principals from both middle and K-8 schools are beginning to communicate and plan together through the district's middle school advisory group.

Coordination and collaborative planning in the central office is underway. The Teacher and Instructional Services Division is responsible for the support of teachers and instructional teams in the areas of curriculum, staff development, content standards, and assessment of curriculum and instruction. The School/Site Services Division is responsible to school site principals and management teams and evaluates principals. As in many districts, in Minneapolis these two divisions had a history of competitiveness and lack of communication so that curriculum and staff development efforts remained unaligned with school leadership. In the restructuring, the Division leaders for Teacher and Instructional Services and School/Site Services were so committed to working cooperatively that they recommended that their divisions be merged. Staff from the two divisions are co-chairing the middle-grades advisory group in an attempt to "...look together at the problems instead of looking just at our department....We cross all kinds of boundaries."

### Staff Development: Focus on Academic Content Standards

A third area of support for schools is in staff development to improve curriculum and instruction. Staff development is at the heart of middle-grades reform and is a high priority in Minneapolis. Since the referendum, each school has developed its own plan for staff development based on its school improvement plan. However, no overall staff development plan links district goals for middle-grades improvement to staff development offerings.

Many teachers are new to the system and to middle schools and have not had specific preparation related to the needs and characteristics of young adolescents. Staff development that ties curriculum and instruction to effective school environments for young urban adolescents was a frequently cited need from all constituency groups.

Curriculum support remains decentralized in Minneapolis with schools getting curriculum guidance from school curriculum chairs or by participating in national professional organizations or funded projects such as the Harvard Performance Assessment Collaborative in Education. Even within schools and teams, students and families report very different curriculum and levels of challenge. Mechanisms for sharing and improving access to challenging curriculum are beginning, such as a "best practices" city-wide conference, and teacher study groups on portfolio assessment. As the content and performance standards are developed and shared, the curriculum will need to be aligned to the new goals.

While racial equity and gender-fair curriculum are the goals in Minneapolis, there appears to be much work to be done to reach the goals of a curriculum that reflects, builds on, and celebrates the diversity of cultures of Minneapolis middle-grades students. This is particularly important at the middle-grades where students are defining their identity in relationship to peers, society, and ethnic and gender roles. Students and parents both recognized this need. Students expressed varied opinions of teachers from those who "know how to relate to us, and provide challenging, fun activities," to those who "yell at you, disrespect you and just make you do worksheets."

Staff development for principals has not been well developed. The changing role of principals as leaders of site-based management teams, and providing instructional leadership to improve student achievement in middle-grades schools was a stated need for staff development.

Many resources over the past five years have gone to improving instructional strategies. The district staff development document states the need for effective follow-up and coaching for staff development content to be implemented, but the follow-up provided from the central office is extremely limited. In addition, levels of implementation of innovations in the classroom have not been targeted or evaluated at most schools, leading to differences between teachers, teams, and subjects in the same school.

An overall staff development plan tied to a middle-grades vision, new leadership paradigms, the content and performance standards and the district improvement agenda could assist with the district's commitment to prioritize and focus initiatives.

## Accountability: Making It Count

The Minneapolis school district is one of a very few in the nation that connects monetary compensation of the superintendent to reaching student performance and customer satisfaction goals. This sets a strong district context for accountability for student performance. Newly developed and implemented customer satisfaction surveys of families will be given great weight in district planning.

The school improvement planning process and school progress reports provided by the Accountability Department provide student performance data to school communities. In addition, assistance is available for school improvement teams to analyze the data and apply it to their program plans. These provide vehicles for school communities to set goals and report progress on them. At this time, no specific mechanisms are in place to assist schools that do not meet improvement goals over time; nor rewards for those schools that excel. The district is currently reviewing methods of improving accountability and monitoring school results.

### Targeting support to low-performance schools

In order to effectively close the achievement gap, more targeted assistance and accountability for performance will need to be developed. One method of developing further district accountability prioritized in the District Quality Report will be evaluation of the outcomes of specialty programs for students. The district board, central office, and school staff hope that content and performance standards and benchmarks will provide impetus to further focus school performance planning so that assistance can be targeted where it is most needed.

### Matching assessments to goals

New academic standards and accountability mechanisms require new assessment tools. Norm-referenced standardized tests will not provide a useful measure of students' engagement in problem solving, or of their application of in-depth knowledge and skills. The assessment tools used to gauge school progress in district accountability reports will need to align with the content standards and new teaching and learning goals. In addition, teachers will need extensive support and guidance as they change their curriculum, instruction, and assessment processes to better meet the higher order skill and knowledge goals needed by students today. Quite a few schools are using portfolios and ungraded progress report models for student assessment. Mechanisms to review these assessments across schools could improve and spread the use of these assessments. Parents and families could also benefit from sessions to help them understand the content and performance standards and the assessments that will be used. They need to know how to understand their child's progress in relation to the academic standards.

## Summary

The central theme in Minneapolis Public Schools is choice. This is coupled with an equally strong commitment to high levels of achievement for all students. With a six-year history of decentralization and an emphasis on individual school innovation and autonomy, the district can claim many exemplary programs and schools. This autonomy without much central oversight has resulted in vastly different educational experiences (in content and quality) for students attending different schools. In a district with choice as a core value, middle schools have been seen as the stepchild, the place where students go if they don't attend a K-8 program. The multiple grade configurations locate 6th grades at K-8, K-6 and 6-8 buildings. K-8's closed enrollment after 1st grade along with the many K-6 schools results in larger numbers of newcomers and transitory students being assigned to middle schools. In addition, K-6 students begin middle school at 7th grade, meaning that small numbers of 6th graders attend most middle schools. The middle schools also serve larger numbers of students of color and impoverished students than do the K-8 schools.

The district is currently engaged in the challenging task of reestablishing central focus, goals, and standards for all of middle level education in Minneapolis. Central office staff will need to provide guidance and accountability for implementation, without stifling the innovation and continuous improvement of choice programs. While this effort is still very new, much can be learned from the district's frank appraisal and dissemination of its shortcomings, needs for improvement, and its beginning accomplishments. ❑

## Resources

Johnson, Carol. (1994, September). *A proposal to plan for systemic middle school reform with the Minneapolis schools.* Edna McConnell Clark Foundation. Minneapolis, MN: Minneapolis Public Schools.

Minneapolis Public Schools. (1994, November). *District options project report.* Minneapolis, MN: Author.

Minneapolis Public Schools. (1994, August). *Minneapolis Public Schools grade eight. 1993-94 school information report. Minneapolis Public School progress indicators.* Minneapolis, MN: Author.

Minneapolis Public Schools. (1994, September). *Organization of district service center.* Minneapolis, MN: Author.

Minneapolis Public Schools. (1993, September 14). *Quality schools study. Proposed directions.* Minneapolis, MN: Author.

Minneapolis Public Schools. (1994, June). *Site-based management in Minneapolis Public Schools.* Minneapolis, MN: Author.

Minnesota Department of Education. (1994, June 2). *Minnesota profile of learning: High school standards.* Draft.

Nathan, J., & Ysseldyke, J. (1994). What Minnesota has learned about school choice. *Phi Delta Kappan.*

Sha, A. (1994, June 30). Minneapolis curriculum scores poorly. *Minneapolis Star Tribune.*

# 7.
# SAN DIEGO: Middle Schools for a Changing America

San Diego, located in the southwestern corner of the United States, is a gateway to the Pacific Rim and Mexico. Large numbers of immigrants come to the city daily. Its rapidly changing economy and demographics foreshadow the United States of the 21st century: an increasingly diverse and impoverished population located in a competitive, globally-linked economy. Since the 1990s, San Diego's "boom town" economy of defense industries, construction, and tourism faded as part of the prolonged general recession in Southern California. This recession caused cutbacks in state and local education funds. Over the past three years, the district's budget remained at a level dollar amount per pupil, necessitating reductions to compensate for increasing costs. California ranks 46th in pupil support in relation to personal income, reflecting the results of California's pioneer tax bill, Proposition 13, which limited property tax levies for education (San Diego City Schools, 1994). Declining revenues and increasing costs have led to polarized teacher union/administration relations, despite an innovative "interests-based" bargaining approach to employee contracts. At the time of the audit team's visit, the rumor of a teacher strike was strong. (The strike did take place in the fall of 1996.) The district's teaching and administrative force consists of newcomers and long-time veterans. Many took advantage of the district's retirement incentive package in 1994, resulting in an influx of new principals and teachers.

San Diego City Schools (SDCS) is the 8th largest urban district in the nation, enrolling 127,000 students in grades K-12. Approximately 23,000 of these students are enrolled in 21 middle schools or junior highs. In the 1993-94 school year, district students were approximately 17% African American, 18% Asian (predominately Filipino and Indochinese), 31% Hispanic, 32% white, and 2% other. This reflects the overall city demographics. Since over 26% of the students are classified as English Language Learners (ELL) and come from homes speaking more than 60 different languages, improving literacy skills for all students is a high priority.

SDCS includes the city's most urban communities as well as many suburban areas. Many schools draw students from out of their neighborhood through a Voluntary Ethnic Enrollment Program. Rising numbers of special needs and bilingual students, along with identified gifted students, are now being served using an inclusion model, which provides support services for special needs within the regular classroom setting.

### A national leader in education reform

SDCS holds a national reputation as a leader in educational restructuring. Since 1987, multiple district initiatives have been implemented to improve student performance. Among these are: increased site-based decision making; institution of "interest-based" collective bargaining; reductions in class size at grades 1 and 2; implementing a core curriculum with rigorous graduation standards; implementing a district structure of overarching design tasks in five key areas; setting 16 benchmark expectations for student achievement and for schools; instituting a management evaluation that includes accountability for the benchmarks; and establishing K-12 content standards in language arts, math, science, and social studies. The school district is engaged in systemic reform efforts with multiple foundation partners, including the Panasonic Foundation, the New Standards Project, the Harvard Performance Assessment Collaborative in Education (PACE), Edna McConnell Clark's Program for Student Achievement, and the Rockefeller Foundation's Staff Development Initiative. In addition, state reform initiatives such as the Senate Bill 1274 Restructuring Demonstration Grants included schools in San Diego.

Central Office consolidation and restructuring since 1989 has resulted in a reduction in central office staff. Schools are administratively organized in five area clusters representing feeder patterns of elementary, middle, and high school. Each Assistant Superintendent is responsible for a cluster of schools, and a content area or specialty across all schools, such as bilingual or special education.

## State and Local Middle-Grades Education Context

California is part of the Carnegie Foundation's Middle-Grades School State Policy Initiative. The middle-grades philosophy and plan for the state was distributed in a 1987 monograph *Caught in the Middle,* developed by the State Department of Education. State Department-initiated partnership networks, a large and active state middle-grades association, and state-initiated curriculum initiatives focused at the middle-grades gave local districts a framework to guide school improvement. Across San Diego, middle-grades schools are perceived as the leaders in innovation and reform.

### Middle schools on the move

A constellation of forces converged to support an active middle-school initiative. In 1989 six grade configurations existed for young adolescents in SDCS. Since that time the district more than doubled its number of 6-8 middle schools; going from 6 to 14. This was facilitated by an intensive summer interdisciplinary institute for teachers, supported by both the Panasonic and Clark Foundations. The institute brought in experienced teacher teams to assist San Diego teachers in utilizing the team structures to provide student support, develop interdisciplinary curriculum, and use assessment modules based on essential questions. Interdisciplinary teams exist at all middle schools. The teachers' enthusiasm for the interdisciplinary institute prompted its expansion to high school and elementary teachers after the second year. Synergistically, the PACE and New Standards Projects engaged middle-grades teachers in developing new assessments based on content standards in the core disciplines. Performance tasks, projects, and portfolios are parts of the district's assessment process, including teacher and school portfolio assessments.

Through the Clark Foundation's support, a district middle school conference, regular middle school principal meetings, and a district steering committee for middle-grades reform have been initiated. Dropout rates have declined at the middle level; in 1992-93 they dropped by more than 30% in grades 7 and 8. Reconfiguration of junior highs to middle schools continues with support of an experienced consultant, who originally provided assistance to the pilot schools in the first Clark Foundation initiative.

### Leadership: New Leadership Paradigms Meet Classic Conflicts

#### Policy, strategic plan, beliefs

The San Diego City School District describes itself as standards-based. In a July 1994 "Plan to Improve Student Achievement and Organizational Effectiveness," sixteen expectations outline specific benchmarks related to student achievement, such as reduction in absences, suspensions, and dropouts, increase in students' meeting University of California entrance requirements, and in taking the SAT and Advanced Placement courses. For schools, benchmarks include:

- Use of portfolios and exhibitions to assess student progress along with tests and grades;
- Reduction in crime and increase in campus cleanliness and safety; parent satisfaction;
- Improved community and parent partnerships and involvement in decision making;
- The development of a school portfolio documenting the school program quality review, governance, use of staff development time, evidence of staff collaborative problem-solving; and
- The equity of participation regardless of ethnicity in co-curricular activities and in higher level courses.

Five design tasks developed with the National Alliance for Restructuring Schools guide the overall work of reform. These design tasks are: Curriculum and Instruction, Assessment and Technology; Standards and Accountability; Health and Human Services; and Public Support and Engagement. Specific actions by which schools will fulfill the sixteen expectations are now incorporated into each school's improvement plan. They provide the foundation for all initiatives. The superintendent, deputy superintendent, and assistant superintendents, school board members, central office staff, and small pockets of building level leaders – both teachers and principals – understand and buy-in to these policies and plans. However, scratching the surface uncovers skepticism about how these "lofty ideals can be implemented in their classroom and schools." Large numbers of teachers are still unfamiliar with the Carnegie *Turning Points* (1989) recommendations or California's statement on middle-grades, *Caught in the Middle*. Thus, a growing gulf in understanding of, and commitment to, the system's goals exists between the central office leaders and teachers. While interest-based and other new paradigms for collective bargaining are expressed, the relations between employees' unions and the district management exhibit the classic polarization of labor/management dynamics. These dynamics feed off the alienation and distance many teachers feel from the district's plans and goals. As one teacher stated:

> *I think they are all out of touch with the reality we have here. They are off reading and discussing abstract concepts. I think those are great ideas, but I need to know how to do it in a classroom with 38 kids, many of whom don't speak English, and others who are fully mainstreamed special education students. I don't think they understand us at all.*

### Leadership roles for parents, community, and teachers

Site-based management and opportunities for teachers and principals to participate in cluster and other district-wide meetings and interventions are in place. Nevertheless, many teachers and parents express a feeling of being cut off from district level decisions, and in some cases from school-based decisions.

While striving to develop new approaches to leadership, the central office-school relationship, and community/school participation, district leaders still need to do much work to convince the rank and file teachers, parents, and community members that these approaches go beyond surface rhetoric.

## Support: Coordinating Multiple Initiatives

### Resources

California and San Diego faced budget cuts for the past four years prior to the site visit. Reduction in district and state money has been offset by foundation grants. San Diego City Schools received $63,054,478 during 1994-95 in corporate, private, and federal and state grant funds. Each of these programs generates its own goals, objectives, activities, and evaluation logic. In addition, staff development, strategic planning retreats, networking opportunities with other schools and districts provide resources to those schools involved in various initiatives. Thus, the challenge becomes how to effectively maintain the overall focus and cohesion of the district vision and plan, given multiple priorities and initiatives. SDCS attempts to coordinate funded projects through joint meetings with all funders and by explicitly discussing the links in the superintendent's leadership meetings and in K-12 cluster meetings. In addition, district leadership works to assure that all programs mirror major district priorities such as portfolio and exhibitions assessment, reviewing student work to develop and implement content standards, and using the Program Quality Review process to guide each school's data-based decision making. At the time of the site visit, the district had applied for a Rockefeller Foundation Staff Development Initiative Grant to coordinate staff development and improve teaching and learning. This effort to coordinate and set central expectations and standards at times is at odds with the pre-existing culture of decentralization and school decision-making autonomy.

### Coordination and communications

Uneven understanding and implementation of the middle school philosophy and concept abound, and sharing between teachers, principals, and other school-based personnel is in the beginning stages. A district-wide middle school conference based on the standards and assessment, middle school principal retreats, teacher study groups on portfolios district-wide, content standards development, and the Program Quality Review Process, all help to share the best practices in the district between schools. Much of this staff development and networking is supported by external funds. This wealth of external resources connects the district and school personnel with the latest information and research in middle level education reform.

### Student services: bringing the needs of diverse learners to the reform agenda

The initial focus of restructuring in San Diego, as in the state of California, did not include a specific focus on the needs of second language learners and special education students. San Diego's demographics, which include 26% non-native English-speaking students, large numbers of special education students, and a two-tiered gifted and talented program, demanded specific attention to the diverse backgrounds and learning needs of its students in the reform process. Over the past three years, improving reading and writing skills has been a central focus of reform activities. Until the past year, however, the central office directors and specialists in bilingual education, special education, and gifted and talented services were not actively involved in the middle-level school restructuring discussions. Our site visit surfaced conflicting philosophies and practices from school-to-school regarding strategies to best meet these students' needs, and a disconnect between these departments and the school governance, curriculum, staff development, and assessment functions. This is typical of school reform across the country. In a study by California Tomorrow on restructuring schools in that state, only 15% reported that their English Language Learner programs were central to the restructuring (Olsen, 1994). Beginning conversations of how to coordinate efforts and use the expertise of special educators to inform the overall reform plan and practice were going on in the district, but had not been finalized into action plans.

## Accountability: Establishing Meaningful Standards and Assessment Tools

### Political winds and state assessments

Through its involvement in the New Standards Project and the Performance Assessment Collaborative in Education, San Diego City Schools' central office staff members, especially the Director of Assessment and Accountability, are national experts in standards-based assessment. Some of the pilot schools and teachers' teams, including several middle schools, experienced valuable training and practice in the development of content standards and designed benchmarks and assessments to measure students' progress towards the standards.

The state of California, from 1989-1995, developed and then implemented a state assessment (CLAS) that included writing samples, performance tasks, and other authentic assessments to align with the California curriculum frameworks. The state accreditation and school Program Quality Review (PQR) used the curriculum frameworks, and key areas of *Caught in the Middle* to assess schools. In the PQR, each school conducts a self-study in a major curriculum area, using class observation, examination of student work, and other performance-based assessments to plan school improvements. An external team of "critical friends" also conducts a study of the school, looking at curriculum implementation and student work as the core of the assessment. With these programs initiated, the state's curriculum frameworks aligned well with the student and school assessments used. San Diego School's personnel were active in the development and pilot implementation of the state assessment and the PQR protocol. However, public confusion and complaints about the new student assessment, coupled with a conservative political trend in the state, led to the shelving of the new CLAS test. Statewide, the Abbrreviated Stanford Achievement Test has been reinstituted. This test is not well aligned with San Diego's standards or 16 expectations; San Diego will use the performance tasks developed in the New Standards Project as its benchmark tests for student progress towards the academic standards.

### Pioneering new school and program assessments

SDCS continues to expand the number of schools using the PQR and the Coalition of Essential Schools' protocol, portfolios, and other authentic assessments to evaluate a school's progress and develop school goals. Through the Leadership in Accountability Demonstration Project in the district, the central office provides training and support for school teams conducting the PQR. They meet monthly and learn how to use student work to develop standards and performance goals and to gather and interpret data to inform the school's improvement plan. The leaders of this project recommend a single comprehensive site plan that would be used to integrate Chapter 1, special grants, and other specific grant funds with the school's core funds and improvement plans.

### System-level accountability: first steps

The sixteen expectations mark the first system-wide targets and accountability measures. Parent and student satisfaction surveys, review of school plans and student benchmarks, and assessing the central office and system's functioning compared to the high-performing system benchmarks is underway. The middle-grades reform audit was one of the first attempts to bring together a variety of stakeholders to assess the system's functioning in a given area. Through the New Standards Project, work with Panasonic and other initiatives, the central office staff, principals, and school board members engaged in strategic planning. They did not conduct a comprehensive evaluation prior to this planning, however. Mechanisms for regularly assessing and reporting on the system's progress in meeting the expectations are in the development stages.

While San Diego City Schools boast some schools and program areas with a sophisticated understanding and application of new assessment practices for students, programs, and the system as a whole, large groups of teachers and families still are not actively engaged in the process. As leaders in the system explain, "We have to figure out how to go to scale. We need to move beyond pilots." However, how to do this, and the pace with which it can be implemented seems to be contested ground in the district.

### Summary

San Diego City Schools is a national leader of standards-based reform. Some of the middle schools in the district are used as national exemplars, and staff from the central office and schools provide leadership to the standards movement across the nation. The district has established a strong foundation on which to build a system of high-performing middle-grades schools in which large numbers of students meet high standards. The middle level has been at the forefront of change and experimentation, utilizing California's *Caught in the Middle* recommendations, district-wide interdisciplinary team curriculum development institutes, a middle-level conference, and various other national initiatives to establish cutting-edge middle-grades practices at selected schools. Middle grades schools are viewed positively as leaders of reform to improve student performance. They piloted interdisciplinary teams, portfolio assessments, and the development of content standards. The current tasks facing the district relate to three main themes of (1) establishing better coordination, prioritization, and focus of reform efforts districtwide; (2) establishing clarity about the structures, channels, and parameters for input, decision making, and accountability between central office and the schools; and (3) providing intensive, focused, and sustained opportunities for staff development to help practitioners effectively translate the district's goals and expectations into district, school, and classroom practices. ❑

## Resources

Olsen, L. (1994). *The unfinished journey: Restructuring schools in a diverse society*. San Francisco, CA: California Tomorrow. A California Tomorrow Research and Policy Report from the Education for a Diverse Society Project.

California State Department of Education (1987). *Caught in the middle: Educational reform for young adolescents in California public schools.* Sacramento, CA: Author.

Pendleton, B. (1994, July). A plan to improve student achievement and organizational effectiveness. San Diego, CA: San Diego City Schools.

Callahan, Freda. (1994, January) Report and recommendations of the Comprehensive Planning Committee. San Diego, CA: San Diego City Schools, Planning, Assessment, and Accountability Division.

San Diego City Schools, Office of the Deputy Superintendent. (1994). *Clark 2001: High standards for all. A proposal to the Edna McConnell Clark Foundation.* San Diego, CA: Author.

San Diego City Schools, School Operations Division. (1984, December 10). *Specifications for middle schools.* San Diego, CA: Author.

Cisneros, E. (1985, January 29). *Summary. educational specifications for middle schools*. San Diego, CA: San Diego City Schools, School Operations Division. (J3)

San Diego City Schools, School Services Division, Area VI. (1993, March 23). *Report and recommendations of the student achievement accountability committee.* San Diego, CA: Author.

# 8. ATLANTA:

# Reaching for Student Achievement in a Center City School System

Atlanta Public Schools reflect a national pattern in urban public education – for 30 years citizens abandoned the center city for the surrounding suburban towns and school systems. Thus the center city population has dropped from over 625,000 residents to less than 400,000, while the student population of Atlanta Public Schools (APS) has declined from 115,000 to about 59,000 today. APS serves about 20,000 fewer African American students currently than in the early 1970s, while the white student enrollment has declined from 56,000 in the late 1950s to less than 4,000 today. During this period, the metropolitan Atlanta area enjoyed an economic boom. However, the center city and the Atlanta Public Schools faced a continuously eroding tax base and declining student population. The reduced enrollment put pressure on the system to close and consolidate schools. A heightened interest in the school system by the business leaders sparked a large community mobilization for the school board election of 1993. In this election six new board members out of nine seats were selected. In 1994 this new board appointed Dr. Benjamin Canada to the superintendency with a clear mandate to cut costs and bureaucracy in the system, while simultaneously improving student achievement and system accountability. The board's initial focus was to take stock of the district's current functioning and to develop a strategic plan for the schools.

### District strategic planning

The district launched a strategic planning process in November 1995. Over 150 individuals representing parents, principals, teachers, business partners and community leaders helped develop K-12 plans for the district. Action committees met to plan for student performance, cultural diversity, facilities, individual student needs, safe and disciplined school environments, staff development, and acquiring resources and maximizing community partnerships. The strategic planning group had just begun to meet in committees when the middle-grades district audit site visit was conducted in January. Several other audits also were conducted in the system shortly before the time of the middle-grades reform audit. These audits reviewed communications, facilities management, curriculum management, human resources, staff training and development, industrial technology, instructional technology, and operational technology. None of the audits were released by APS at the time of the visit, which caused some general skepticism and concern among participants about how the middle-grades audit recommendations would be disseminated and enacted. (The common findings from these audits were later included in the final district strategic plan).

Similar to many states across the country, Georgia administers the Iowa Test of Basic Skills to all sixth through eighth grade students. Students' scores are compared to others in the state and nation. School improvement plans are based on district-provided targets for growth in student test scores.

**Middle-grades education context at the state and district level**

In 1971, Atlanta Public Schools opened its first middle schools, created as part of a desegregation plan. According to a 1995 report by the Southern Regional Council:

> ...few Atlanta educators focused on a 'middle school concept' or a particular way of teaching early adolescents then. Creating middle schools was seen as a way to satisfy a court order – by creating new schools -- that would not overly disrupt the community.
>
> During the 21-year period between 1971 to 1992, some Atlanta children attended middle school, and some attended junior high, depending on where they lived. For the most part, middle school teachers and leaders operated without middle school policies or advocates at the central office. The middle-grades in Atlanta often fell through the cracks. However, schools did continue to reconfigure, and by 1992, all 10-15-year old students attended middle schools.

The State of Georgia adopted Middle School Program Criteria in 1990. These guidelines called for 6-8 or 7-8 grade middle schools, a four and one-half hour academic block in the core subject areas, interdisciplinary teams, common team planning time, and exploratory offerings. Half of the certificated staff serving as interdisciplinary team members needed to hold middle-grades certification or have received staff development on the middle grades learner. The state provided incentive grants for middle school programs to encourage reconfiguration of schools to meet the program criteria. APS adopted similar program criteria for middle schools in 1990.

Recently, Atlanta Public Schools demonstrated a renewed interest in middle school education. For the first time, an Executive Director of Middle Schools has been designated, Ms. Gloria Patterson, a well-respected former principal was selected for this post. APS launched a comprehensive middle-level initiative in the Fall of 1995, in collaboration with the Southern Regional Council (SRC). The Southern Regional Council promotes democracy and opportunity for all people in the South and beyond. SRC education programs connect community leadership with public schools to jointly implement reforms to bring about the success of traditionally low achievers. This initiative, supported by a grant from the Joseph B. Whitehead Foundation, organized a multirole Middle School Advisory Council to develop a long-range plan for middle-grades education. As described in the Southern Regional Council's report, *Middle School Reform: Next Steps for Atlanta*, "now that middle schools are universal throughout the city...and an Executive Director of Middle Schools is established, Atlanta is in an excellent position to mount a reform initiative with and for each of its 16 middle schools" (1995).

This audit and the resultant planning process, a principals' institute and monthly meetings, school assessments, and the Middle School Advisory Council are some of the components of the initiative.

### Results and recommendations of the district audit

Three District Middle-Grades Reform Project staff members trained and led an Atlanta-based team to conduct the audit. The Advisory Council decided to select a local audit team that did not include any district or school staff. The eight-member group included parents, university faculty with expertise in middle-grades education and equity issues, staff of a university-based math and science teaching improvement project, a community activist, and an education reporter and evaluator. All local members of the APS audit team volunteered their time. In a one-day training, the assessment team reviewed the criteria for the assessment (the 18 middle-grades reform standards), reviewed the various sources of data already available, and practiced interviewing techniques and the process for summarizing the data. Over the next five days, local team members, led by three DMGRP staff members, visited all 16 middle schools. They interviewed representatives of all departments in the central office and the superintendent's cabinet, and met with representatives from the school board and community, university, and business partners.

Team members individually summarized data and submitted it to the team leader to develop an initial draft of the findings and recommendations. An executive summary was disseminated, which included two pages of the major themes and recommendations drawn from the larger report.

District Middle-Grades Reform Project staff, local assessment team members, the Executive Director for Middle Schools in APS and SRC staff facilitated an initial meeting to present the audit team's findings. Attendees included principals, school-based instructional specialists, central office coordinators, and representative teachers. At the meeting the group prioritized the recommendations and generated ideas for how to use the report as a basis for the district's middle school plan. We wanted to model a process that could be used to gain input from a broad range of groups and to increase ownership of the data and the plans that would result.

"This is just a report with recommendations. We need to breathe life into it with your input. Whether or not it becomes meaningful depends on what you do next,"explained Charles Palmer, DMGRP consultant and President of the California League of Middle Schools.

The meeting included three stages. First, audit team members presented the major themes about the district's culture for middle-grades reform, and the team's recommended changes. Members reviewed the process used to conduct the audit, including the criteria used, the interview protocol, and the summarization process. The 46 detailed recommendations were displayed for all participants to view. Second, each participant individually identified the top eight priorities for improvement. The consensus of the group was high. Recommendations from this group echoed the four major recommendations from the audit team's report: (1) increasing hands-on learning opportunities for students; (2) providing more effective alternatives for disruptive students; (3) increasing opportunities for participatory decision making; and (4) reviewing school resource allocations for equity across the system.

Third, participants recorded their ideas for ways to involve all the stakeholder groups in reviewing the audit recommendations, stating their priorities, and preparing the action plan. The group decided to hold community meetings at each middle school co-facilitated by a member of the Middle School Advisory Council along with a teacher or other APS staff person. Additionally, the group brainstormed ways to gain additional input from students, parents, and board members, and disseminate findings to the public.

SRC staff led the training for community meeting facilitators. Each facilitator received a packet with all the materials needed, an agenda and script for the meeting, and a form to record the weight given to each of the recommendations. The community meetings began with a videotaped presentation from the Executive Director for Middle Schools. She shared the purpose of the audit and planning process and the importance of broad input to its success. Facilitators led the meeting as described above. They also solicited recommendations and recruited volunteers.

### Turning recommendations into a plan of action

The community meeting results were compiled by comparing each school's top six recommendations for action. As with all the previous meetings, consensus was high among the over 1,000 attendees. Four action teams, each with about 10 participants representing teachers, administrators, parents, and community partners convened to develop an action plan for the four top priority areas: (1) Hands-on learning and evaluation of curriculum and instruction; (2) Positive discipline and constructive support for disruptive students; (3) Reducing administrative paperwork and reviewing equity of resources across schools; and (4) Parent and community involvement. Each action team received the full audit report with detailed recommendations for their priority area, new recommendations that came from the community meetings and the Middle School Advisory Council, and additional resource material. Action teams took three weeks to develop a plan that included activities, timelines, and names of those who would accomplish each task.

The plans were then consolidated into a single timeline by the action team leaders. They presented their reports to the Advisory Council at the year's last meeting. Advisory Council members then provided feedback on the plans. A writing group representing all constituencies met for a day to consolidate the information into a three-year plan for the Middle School

Initiative. Additional council members were recruited for the action teams that began their work in the summer. Some of the work underway:
- Convening a teachers' council with elected representatives from each middle school. This group is charged with reviewing and recommending hands-on and rigorous learning programs in the schools.
- The initiation of the Performance Project to develop and pilot a multimedia culminating project in which each student will demonstrate the knowledge, skills, and talent acquired during middle school.
- Continuation of the Principals' Leadership Institute. This year principals are working on their roles as leaders of standards-based reform. They are visiting each other's schools and providing feedback.
- A conflict resolution course has been approved as part of the core elective offerings in each of the middle schools. In addition, the varied programs and practices of the opportunity teachers who work with at-risk students in each school will be reviewed and highlighted.
- A group of teachers and principals attended the National Middle School Association's conference and attended sessions to gather information related to the key action areas of the APS middle school plan.

## Overarching themes in the assessment team's findings

In Atlanta's audit, the team summarized the data using the project's 18 district middle-grades reform criteria. In addition, the audit team wanted to relate four overarching themes that stood out in all the data collected. The themes are: (1) vision and plan for middle-grades education; (2) communication and participation in decision making; (3) rigorous learning in safe schools; and (4) adequacy and equity of resources. The following sections summarize the main findings and present an overall recommendation for each of these themes. Following these broad summaries, the more specific findings are discussed, and further recommendations about how to improve the district culture to improve student achievement are provided.

## Vision and plan for middle-grades education

The comprehensive Middle Level Initiative launched in partnership with the Southern Regional Council includes: the middle-grades audit and three-year plan for middle schools; a principals' institute to provide support and professional development for principals; school assessments; a teachers' council with teacher representatives from each middle school; and utilizing the Middle School Advisory Council as an ongoing avenue for all stakeholder groups to provide guidance to the Initiative as well as to link the schools with the broader resources available in the community. Despite these steps, at the time of the audit the biggest concern expressed was a lack of clarity about the district's vision for middle schools. No clear plan for middle-grades reform existed and understanding of the middle school concept and its implementation were very uneven among schools.

*Recommendation: Create a middle school vision and plan with the participation of all stakeholders, especially teachers.*

## Communication and participation in decision making

Based on a history of top-down central office decisions, many principals, teachers, and community partners are skeptical of the superintendent's statements of a new openness and participatory structure. Teachers and principals expressed hopes for a new direction and cohesion for middle-grades education, one that will go beyond a push to improve standardized test scores. However, many of the teachers feel that curriculum and organization decisions are mandated to them by central office people who do not "understand what we face here every day." A large number of teachers feel that some of these innovations, such as whole language and an alternating block schedule "are not working for us."

Parents and community partners expressed readiness to support the schools but didn't know how to access the system to support the school goals. Breaking the legacy of mistrust between various constituencies in the system will depend on the consistency of actions taken by the administration to model this new participatory approach. Many of the constituencies, particularly administrators, expressed concern that the audit recommendations would not result in change. The superintendent and school board will send a stronger message through the implementation of specific recommendations than through any new policies.

*Recommendation: Increase real opportunities for participation in decisions by all constituencies.*

## Rigorous learning in safe schools

Students articulated their hopes for an active, rigorous, and safe learning environment where they are respected and where teachers can focus on teaching. Many excellent teachers and caring administrators work to provide these for students. An interdisciplinary team structure is in place to allow for teacher planning. Many teachers actively engage students in meaningful projects, but some rely on rote activities and are overwhelmed with discipline concerns. Many teachers do not feel they can implement the district's higher content curriculum with their students. The low reading level of many students was their major concern. All constituencies expressed concern about a group of "continuously disruptive students" for whom they have no effective disciplinary or programmatic alternatives.

*Recommendation: Increase knowledge and use of effective middle-grades practices to improve student engagement, literacy, and achievement.*

## Adequacy and equity of resources

While Atlanta has the highest per pupil expenditure in Georgia, the availability of up-to-date resources, and the way in which these are distributed were significant concerns of all stakeholders. Teachers, students, and parents alike noted the lack of resources available in some schools and the perceived inequity in resources among middle schools. All expressed concerns for improved materials, especially related to technology.

*Recommendation: Review current spending priorities. Reallocate to improve equity and increase classroom resources.*

## Leadership: Building a Collaborative Culture to Improve Student Achievement

### Vision, beliefs, strategic plans, and content standards

Leadership is a shared function that involves all stakeholders in providing the vision, beliefs, academic standards, policies, and plans for school improvement. The new commitment to middle-level education reflects a positive direction in leadership in the district. APS is also proactively and publicly integrating initiatives in a comprehensive strategic plan.

On the whole, students are clear about the teacher's stated objectives for each class and what they need to do to be successful in school. However, they seem less clear of the overall knowledge and skills they are expected to master by the end of 8th grade and how they will demonstrate this knowledge beyond improvement of standardized test scores.

While many teachers and principals refer to the middle school concept, actual understanding of middle school philosophy and practice is quite uneven. Some negative perceptions of the middle school philosophy and the needs and nature of young adolescents exist among teachers, principals, and families. Many teachers would prefer a junior high model.

*Recommendation: Provide forums to discuss the middle school philosophy and best practices with all constituencies. Reframe a middle-level vision with extensive input of all stakeholders, especially teachers.*

*Beliefs*: Demonstrate how specific district programs, curriculum, and teaching strategies align with the needs of the young urban adolescent and provide for high academic achievement. Provide support to assist educators in translating the vision of the early adolescent learner into practice.

*Content Standards:* Review district and state content and performance standards and set goals for student learning that go beyond improvement of standardized test scores. Involve more constituencies in this process. Explore district creation of content standards answering the question, "what should students know and be able to do at the end of 8th grade?"

### Policies

Policies, reforms, and activities at district and school levels focus on improved student performance. The management of middle schools is facilitated by the consistency in grade configurations and feeder patterns, and the manageable numbers of schools and students at each school. It is unclear, however, to what extent policies have been examined for their alignment with the Middle Level Initiative's goals. This is especially true of the diverse and often conflicting views about discipline policies, within schools and district-wide. This includes how best to provide effective alternatives for the students who repeatedly disrupt the regular class.

*Recommendations*
*Policies:* Ensure that all stakeholders are involved in the development of policies that affect them. Review the consistency of policies and their implementation across the district. Review policies for alignment with the middle school vision. Streamline paperwork and policies that prevent timely action on school needs. Continue to review personnel policies and assignments at the middle-grades, providing standards for teacher assignment and for school and community input into hiring and staff allocations.
*Strategic Plan:* Link school improvement plans with the district strategic plan and specific goals for middle-grades education. Utilize the Middle School Advisory Council to develop a middle-grades vision and plan and provide yearly external report on its implementation. Connect middle-grades schools to both elementary and high schools for articulation purposes.

## New leadership roles and parent-community involvement

Atlanta offers many able and willing university, community, and business partners for the public schools. Increasing participation in planning and openness about current challenges are being exhibited district-wide. However many school staff, parents, and community members believe that the district makes top-down decisions with little consultation with the principals and staff. This has resulted in a level of apathy about new initiatives and change as school staff feel that changes are being done "to them" rather than implemented with them. Principals have limited participation in developing their meeting agenda and in other decisions that affect their schools.

There is a limited amount of parental involvement and engagement in some of the middle schools and few perceived opportunities for parent input at the district level. There is a need to increase the level of communication and involvement of school staff, families, and the community in central office decisions, and to improve the effectiveness of some schools' involvement of families, students, and community members in site-based decisions. Students have very limited opportunities for input.

*Recommendations*
*New Leadership Roles:* Coordinate central office staff activities and decision making with building-level participation to reduce perception of top-down decision making and to provide buy-in and ownership from teachers and other school staff. Include principals in the district decision-making structure, in planning the agenda for their meetings, in their own professional development, and in policy and budget decisions that affect their schools. Provide avenues for meaningful student input and involvement in decisions that affect them at the district and school level.
*Parent-Community Involvement:* Continue to make parent outreach a priority, particularly targeting traditionally under-represented families. Hold

meetings at convenient times for parents, and provide multiple options for how parents can support their child's education. Provide clarity on how community and business partners can get involved with schools.

## Support: Staff Development and Classroom Resources

The best-articulated vision for middle-grades education will have little meaning unless it is implemented. Studies of successful school change emphasize the need for ongoing and sustained internal and external support and problem-solving mechanisms to assist in the implementation of innovations. Such support networks are still at the initial stages in Atlanta.

### Resources, information/research, and staff development

The district offers varied staff development specific to middle-grades, including the needs and nature of young adolescents, and subject and grade level specific approaches to pedagogy. Comprehensive follow-up to support implementation is not in place, however. Many of the organizational elements of the middle school such as academic teaming and a block schedule exist in most schools. Despite this, team planning time is not evenly utilized in all schools as a vehicle for whole school planning.

There is a perception of inequities in resources, attention from central office, and quality among schools and programs. Teachers state that supplies regularly take several months to arrive at their schools. Allocation of books and other materials appears to be made according to arbitrary formulas without regard for differing needs of schools. Some students and families described a lack of quality materials and activities in their classes, particularly in hands-on materials and choice of books in the libraries. The facilities that have been converted from elementary and high school to middle school are often not adequate for the middle school program. The 90 minute block schedule works unevenly from school to school and from class to class. Teachers do not appear to have been involved in its adoption or in preparation for teaching strategies appropriate to the large block of time.

*Recommendations*

*Resources:* Review current budget priorities so as to adequately and equitably share limited district resources across all schools, including targeting schools with the greatest needs. Evaluate current availability of curriculum materials, library books, and technology and make plans to improve the materials available in schools.

*Information/Research:* Create a central middle-level information clearinghouse or database at the district level and networks/study groups of school personnel for proactive idea and information dissemination.

*Staff Development:* Provide coordinated professional development. Provide several staff development models from which schools could choose. Each model should provide internal school structures to integrate, implement, sustain and evaluate content, instruction, and assessment innovations. All of the models would support and establish norms of continuous learning and collegiality. Evaluate and strengthen leadership development programs. Develop strategies to increase teachers' understanding of adolescent development, cultural diversity and urban learners. Increase their knowledge of how to effectively meet the needs of a growing diverse and impoverished student population. Diversify staff development by establishing study networks, utilizing "train the trainer" models and providing systematic follow-up at sites. Create an overall staff development plan that links staff development content to the strategic plan and the vision for middle-grades. Include time for follow-up and implementation of the plan.

## Culture, coordination/communication, and school improvement planning

Mechanisms for collegial sharing across middle schools are beginning to be implemented, including a Teachers' Council to improve instruction, a Principals' Institute and meetings and the Middle School Advisory Council. Many teachers and community members facilitated community meetings to prioritize the audit recommendations. Opportunities exist to work on targeted action areas, such as gathering promising practices from each school and reviewing the most successful teaching strategies in middle-grades education. The central office verbalizes its role as a service organization to the schools, but school staff feel there are limited examples of this in practice.

*Recommendations*

*Culture*: Continue to develop/strengthen cross-role groups for learning, monitoring progress, and making mid-course corrections. Award mini-grants for collegial study of priority areas.

*Coordination/Communication:* Continue to increase access to information about the district's reform initiatives across schools and to families and the community. Provide open access to the data and recommendations from the various program audits currently underway. Create a central office advocate or liaison to each school to avoid multiple foci or demands.

*School Improvement Planning:* Provide more intensive staff development on developing and implementing site-level improvement plans.

## Core curriculum/instruction and student services

Structures are in place at schools (two planning periods, teams, block schedules) to allow for academic team planning for smaller communities of learning. Curriculum and instruction decisions, such as the implementation of whole language instruction, appear to have been made without adequate preparation of teachers. Many misperceptions and negative perceptions about the goals and practice of teacher-based guidance and whole language exist. There are inconsistent co-curricular and curricular choices for students across schools, and exploratory teachers do not feel integral to the academic program. The school counselors spend much time in administrative paperwork, rather than in working with individual students or groups. Teacher-based guidance time exists in the schedule, but the program does not appear consistent. Some constituencies feel that the middle schools are not safe; safety concerns are particularly strong for travel to and from schools.

*Recommendations*

*Core Curriculum and Instruction:* Provide more intensive staff-development for teaching teams on the alignment of curriculum, instruction and assessment. Provide connections to standardized test goals and student learning goals. Increase hands-on learning opportunities for students, including project-based learning, service learning, and laboratory work. Seek opportunities for individual teacher development in content and instruction in key curriculum areas. Examine the schools for instructional leadership

*Student Services:* Assess current guidance and advisory programs across middle schools. Disseminate information on those found most successful. Free up school counselors to provide comprehensive leadership to guidance. Review philosophy, practice, and policies related to second language, special education, and gifted and talented education. Review and provide alternative programs for "habitual behavior problems" and other students that cannot function in the regular school setting. Review discipline policies for consistency with middle school philosophy.

## Accountability: If It's Good For Children, Make It So

Dr. Canada's overarching mission statement for Atlanta Public Schools indicates that all programs and activities must be assessed according to their benefits for students. Accountability requires that school communities take responsibility for instructional processes, school environment and climate, and student learning. It requires the collection and analysis of data to assess the implementation and results of specific programs and review the mechanisms by which the district supports middle school improvement and its principals, teachers, students, and families.

### Student and program assessment

Student achievement is the reference point for evaluation of program effectiveness in Atlanta. The central office provides assistance from the Office of Research to work with schools in interpreting their student data and develop campus action plans. Recognition and consequences based on target goals for student performance are being developed. However, no processes exist to support and monitor implementation of staff development content. Plans for closing and re-establishment of low-performing schools appear to have been adopted without participation of site staff. While principals and teachers feel very accountable for student performance on standardized tests, they are unclear about the procedures by which low-performing schools receive support and of the consequences for non-improvement. In addition, many seem to focus school goals narrowly on the improvement of test scores, without a close connection to achieving the broader goals of education.

*Recommendations*

*Student Assessment:* Develop multiple sources of student assessment beyond standardized tests. Align performance targets and achievement test goals with the curriculum and instruction provided. Conduct research on the reasons for the student performance dip at the 6th grade.

*Program Assessment:* Continue to provide schools with guidance on how to use data most effectively in improvement planning. Provide accountability mechanisms that clearly outline the rewards and sanctions related to improvement plan results, including the closing of schools. Assess the level of knowledge and implementation of priority strategies, including whole language instruction and teacher-based guidance. Provide effective follow-up mechanisms and assessment of results.

**Systems assessment**

The school system is currently engaged in a variety of efforts to examine how well it functions. However, no ongoing avenues now exist for school site staff and families to provide feedback on central office effectiveness.

*Recommendations*

*Systems Assessment:* Establish mechanisms for feedback on district performance from all constituencies, and establish accountability mechanisms. Set targeted goals for the Middle Level Initiative. Monitor with Middle School Advisory Council. Report progress to all stakeholders and the public.

## Summary

Atlanta Public Schools is in the early stages of implementing a variety of new initiatives in middle-grades education. In close partnership with the Southern Regional Council, the establishment of The Middle School Advisory Council, the principals' institute, and the teachers' council demonstrates new leadership, initiative, and willingness to implement improvement plans. Cross-school and cross-role opportunities for sharing and learning together, along with the broad dissemination of the key audit recommendations and the action priorities from the community meetings models a new openness and a growing participatory culture. The combination of internal and external support and pressure for change show great promise in sustaining the early momentum. As a new culture emerges, however, many old practices still persist. The growing involvement and engagement of the stakeholders must be nurtured. Continued opportunities for all stakeholder groups to provide leadership, along with visible changes that reach schools and classrooms and that reflect their concerns and recommendations, will provide the impetus to engage greater numbers of supporters and active participants in the movement to improve middle school education in Atlanta Public Schools. ❑

## Resources

Southern Regional Council. (1995). *Middle school reform: Next steps for Atlanta*. Atlanta, GA: Author.

Georgia State Department of Education, Office of Instructional Programs Division of General Instruction (September 13, 1990). Middle School Progam Criteria.160-4-2-.05. State Standards I12.1, I12.2. Authority O.C.G.A. 20-2-151 (b) (3); 20-2-290.

Middle schools: On the road to reform. (November 1995). *The Board Reporter. Vol. I,* No. 2. Atlanta GA: The Atlanta Board of Education, Atlanta Public Schools.

Professional development catalog FY '96. Atlanta, GA: Atlanta Public Schools. Dr. Chuck Fuller, Director, Professional Development

Good Government Atlanta. (1995, February). A Program of Financial Reform for the Atlanta Public Schools. Atlanta, GA: Author.

# About the Authors

**Holly Hatch** has worked for over 20 years as a teacher, program developer, curriculum specialist, and advocate to improve the social and academic success of urban youth. Her experience has ranged from science teacher at South Boston High School during the 1970s school desegregation to designing and directing middle-grades programs with metropolitan Boston Public Schools in hands-on science, race relations, leadership skills, and acceleration of academic engagement and achievement. For the past several years Hatch has directed the District Middle-Grades Reform Project located at the University of North Carolina, Chapel Hill. This project, funded by the Edna McConnell Clark Foundation, works with teams to conduct participatory self-assessments of the schools and district. Hatch also chairs the Urban Issues Committee of National Middle School Association.

**Kathy Hytten** is a professor of education at the University of Southern Illinois at Carbondale. A former project associate with the District Middle-Grades Reform Project, Hytten assisted in the development and field-testing of the middle-grades reform audit. An experienced qualitative researcher and evaluator, she teaches courses in social foundations and educational philosophy and has published on issues related to the philosophy of education, especially contemporary educational pragmatism.